ABRAHAM LINCOLN'S
WILDERNESS
YEARS

ABRAHAM LINCOLN'S
WILDERNESS
YEARS

Collected Works of J. Edward Murr

—⧈—

J. Edward Murr

EDITED BY
Joshua Claybourn

INDIANA UNIVERSITY PRESS

This book is a publication of

Indiana University Press
Office of Scholarly Publishing
Herman B Wells Library 350
1320 East 10th Street
Bloomington, Indiana 47405 USA

iupress.org

Manufactured in the United States of America

First printing 2023

Library of Congress Cataloging-in-Publication Data

Names: Murr, J. Edward (John Edward), 1898-1960, author. | Claybourn,
  Joshua A., editor. | Murr, J. Edward (John Edward), 1898-1960. Lincoln
  in Indiana.
Title: Abraham Lincoln's wilderness years : collected works of J. Edward
  Murr / J. Edward Murr ; edited by Joshua Claybourn.
Other titles: Collected works of J. Edward Murr
Description: Bloomington, Indiana : Indiana University Press, [2022] | Part 1
  contains portions of the unpublished manuscript titled "The wilderness
  years" by J. Edward Murr held in the archives of DePauw University. |
  Includes bibliographical references and index.
Identifiers: LCCN 2022003938 (print) | LCCN 2022003939 (ebook) | ISBN
  9780253062680 (paperback) | ISBN 9780253062673 (hardback) | ISBN
  9780253062697 (ebook)
Subjects: LCSH: Lincoln, Abraham, 1809-1865—Childhood and youth. |
  Presidents—United States—Biography—Sources. |
  Indiana—Biography—Sources. | Indiana—History—19th century—Sources.
  | DePauw University.
Classification: LCC E457.32 .M87 2022 (print) | LCC E457.32 (ebook) | DDC
  973.7092 [B]—dc23/eng/20220222
LC record available at https://lccn.loc.gov/2022003938
LC ebook record available at https://lccn.loc.gov/2022003939

CONTENTS

PART III: *Albert Beveridge Correspondence*

PREFACE

ABRAHAM LINCOLN'S WILDERNESS YEARS CONSTITUTES a new collection of J. Edward Murr's most significant scholarship and papers—a valuable source for Lincoln research. Part 1 features selected portions of Murr's book-length manuscript on Lincoln's youth, which he titled *The Wilderness Years*, published here for the first time. Part 2 offers a three-part series by Murr on Lincoln's life in Indiana, aptly titled "Lincoln in Indiana," which was published between 1917 and 1918 for the *Indiana Magazine of History*. Part 3 comprises letters between Murr and US senator Albert J. Beveridge, a prominent historian, about Murr's feedback on Beveridge's early manuscript for the posthumously published biography titled *Abraham Lincoln, 1809–1858*.

My first concern was to present Murr's unpublished work accurately. As a rule, I let Murr speak for himself when possible, often with spelling and grammar deviating from modern norms. Nevertheless, because syntax during Murr's era differs from ours today, faithful communication of Murr's meaning occasionally demands modification to punctuation, grammar, and sentence structure. I enclose any uncertainty about such changes in brackets. Also, for the sake of clarity or style, I sometimes substitute nouns for pronouns (including proper nouns) and vice versa.

Footnotes in this book need no explanation. Frequently, notes identify persons mentioned by Murr when their names first appear. In addition to noting corrections or clarifications to Murr's text, I try to identify sources for some of Murr's assertions and quotations. But I do not always include sources for annotated commentary derived from easily available published sources or from Murr's own research. Dates in notations follow military style—day, month, year without punctuation.

I wish to offer a hearty thanks to all those who assisted with reviewing and editing this book. Dr. Sherry Darrell spent many hours providing feedback and editorial advice on all aspects of the book. Bill Bartelt, widely considered the world's greatest scholar on Abraham Lincoln's youth, offered insight from a historian's perspective. James Hevron and Barbara Michel Hevron provided beneficial critiques. Michael Burlingame, who relies on Murr's work in his popular two-volume *Abraham Lincoln: A Life* (2008), encouraged me to pursue this project. Sheila Sullivan assisted in transcribing written documents into electronic versions. At DePauw University Archives and Special Collections in Greencastle, Indiana, Wesley W. Wilson, coordinator of archives and special collections, welcomed and assisted me.

I thank Indiana University Press for recognizing the value in Murr's work and for being patient in the midst of a pandemic. Finally, I wish to thank my friends and colleagues with the Abraham Lincoln Association and Abraham Lincoln Institute for their efforts to support and encourage scholarship. Indeed, I view this project as an extension of both organizations' missions.

ABRAHAM LINCOLN'S
WILDERNESS
YEARS

INTRODUCTION

ABRAHAM LINCOLN SPENT ONE-FOURTH OF his life—age seven to twenty-one—learning and growing in southwestern Indiana between 1816 and 1830. Despite the importance of these formative years, Lincoln rarely discussed this period; indeed, he said of his youth, "It is a great piece of folly to attempt to make anything out of my early life. It can all be condensed into a single sentence, and that sentence you will find in Gray's *Elegy*: 'The short and simple annals of the poor.' That's my life and that's all you or anyone else can make of it."[1]

In two separate autobiographical statements written for the 1860 campaign, Lincoln offered only a few details of his Indiana years.[2] He explained that the Lincolns left Kentucky in part to avoid slavery and in part to escape an antiquated system of land surveying and land recording. He noted the difficulty of clearing wilderness for a home, recounted his hunger for educational opportunities, expressed sadness about losing his mother and sister to illness, and referred to an eye-opening flatboat trip to New Orleans. These meager details nearly summarize the known history of Lincoln's youth.

Yet, with Lincoln's sudden, untimely death in 1865, historians sought to fill gaps in the record, and in his youth lay some of the greatest mystery. The first and most significant research came from Lincoln's law partner, William Herndon (1818–1891). Although Lincoln told Herndon some Indiana stories during their time practicing together in Illinois, Lincoln generally shared as little Hoosier background with Herndon as he did with the public. Later, Herndon sought to expand the story by speaking with those who knew Lincoln best. He interviewed several of the president's relatives, including Dennis Hanks, Lincoln's cousin and boyhood friend, and Sarah Bush Johnston, Lincoln's stepmother. By summer 1865, Herndon began reaching out to other residents in Spencer County, Indiana, and by September 1865, he visited the area to gather information and see the sites of Lincoln's youth.[3] Herndon's guide on the first trip was Nathaniel Grigsby, a boyhood friend just two years younger than Lincoln. Other Lincoln friends and neighbors also spoke with Herndon, and he kept in touch with them later, asking questions and seeking clarifications. With hundreds of letters and interviews, Herndon's work remains the most extensive and important source material (beyond Lincoln's own words) concerning Lincoln's youth.

Unfortunately, for Lincoln's associates in Indiana, Herndon came away unimpressed; he dubbed the area "a stagnant, putrid pool" and wrote that Lincoln grew up in "restricted and unromantic environments."[4] In fact, many historians and cultural commentators in the first couple of generations after Lincoln's death treated this frontier region as inconsequential to Lincoln's life and career, except perhaps as a detrimental influence.

Commencing research and writing nearly two decades after Herndon's visit to southern Indiana, Hoosier historians worked against the initial bias of skeptics and reasserted Indiana's importance to Lincoln's life and character. Hoping to boost Indiana's image and realizing many of Lincoln's boyhood acquaintances had already died before the turn of the twentieth century, these historians rushed to interview those survivors who knew Lincoln best.

For example, William Fortune (1863–1942), a newspaperman who grew up in Boonville, near Lincoln's boyhood home, interviewed Spencer County residents in October 1881 with the help of Civil War general James C. Veatch of Rockport, Indiana.[5] But Fortune's work yielded only a speech and some notes.

John G. Nicolay and John Hay, Lincoln's personal secretary and assistant secretary, respectively, set out to write his definitive biography. Their work appeared serially in *The Century Magazine* from 1886 to 1890 and then in book form as the ten-volume *Abraham Lincoln: A History* (1890). Although Nicolay and Hay did not focus on Lincoln's youth and did not interview his boyhood associates, they considered their massive work the definitive history.

When S. S. McClure began editing and publishing *McClure's Magazine* in 1893 and decided Lincoln's story remained ripe for new information, he asked Ida Tarbell (1857–1944) to compile a new history of the former president. When Tarbell sought Nicolay's help, he warned her there was "nothing of importance" left to publish about Lincoln's life. In Nicolay's view, the record was "complete," and Tarbell need not pursue a "hopeless . . . assignment."[6] In addition, as Anna O'Flynn, Tarbell's main source for Indiana research, began her research in 1894, General Veatch warned her:

> All these people or nearly all have passed away. . . . Beware of trusting to the stories of roving newspaper correspondents. Everyone of this class who passes Lincoln station on the Rockport Rail Road must send to his paper some thing about Lincoln. The train generally stops 15 or 20 minutes. The . . . Correspondent rushes out and finds in the nearest whiskey shop a crowd of old 'soakers' who are ready at a word to tell many things about Lincoln that no one else even knew.
>
> I have read many of these productions and corrected some of them but have not seen one single truthful account coming from such a source.[7]

Undeterred by Nicolay, Tarbell pressed on and consulted research from those such as Vincennes teacher Anna O'Flynn to investigate Lincoln's early years for a twenty-part series, *The Life of Abraham Lincoln*, which began appearing in *McClure's Magazine* in November 1895. In 1896, McClure published some of Tarbell's findings in *The Early Life of Abraham Lincoln*, and in 1900, the essays were compiled into a two-volume *Life of Abraham Lincoln*. Tarbell probably visited the area just once—indeed, O'Flynn, referred to only as "A. Hoosier," did the significant research in Spencer County in 1895 and 1896—but Tarbell's use of O'Flynn's research provided many previously unknown stories, albeit of varying degrees of truthfulness.[8]

Tarbell's biggest contribution involved portraying Indiana as a far more positive environment than did previous biographers. She suggested Lincoln succeeded, in part, not in spite of but *because* of his time in Indiana. The alleged "squalor and wretchedness" of Lincoln's youth was "overblown," Tarbell contended, for a frontier family with livestock, a featherbed, and all of the tools a family might need.[9] Moreover, the Hoosier frontier offered fertile ground for Lincoln's "imagination" and for "mystery."[10] Tarbell also sought to rehabilitate Lincoln's father, whom other historians often disparaged as overbearing, unsuccessful, and shiftless.

Just as Tarbell's work on Lincoln hit newsstands in the late 1800s, J. Edward Murr (1868–1960) began his own research. A Methodist minister who grew up with Lincoln cousins in southeastern Indiana, Murr later became acquainted with Spencer County residents while serving churches there between 1897 and 1902. Believing historians had overlooked Lincoln's youth, Murr gathered information from congregants and other locals who knew Abraham Lincoln first- or secondhand. Indeed, of all Abraham Lincoln's biographers, none knew his boyhood associates and Indiana environment as well as Murr. But Murr's most complete Lincoln research and scholarship has never been published—until now.

John Edward Murr was born on 20 December 1868 near Corydon in Harrison County, Indiana, close to where Abraham Lincoln's extended family settled in Indiana and where, Murr believed,

Abraham Lincoln's father first entered the state while scouting for new land.[11] Murr's interest in Lincoln grew in large part from this shared geography. "I chanced to have been born and reared," he wrote, "in the general community where Josiah Lincoln, a brother of the President's father lived and died. I thus personally knew the older Lincoln's [*sic*] who were cousins to the President."[12]

Like Lincoln, Murr initially wanted to practice law and even spent two years clerking for Judge (and later Congressman) Taylor Zenor. But throughout his flirtation with the practice of law, Murr remained "strangely impressed" that he belonged in the pulpit.[13] Consequently, he submitted himself for pastoral consideration before a committee of three who asked him just three questions: Can you read? Can you spell? Can you write? After Murr answered all three questions affirmatively, the committee laughed and assured him they would present him for ordination. Thus apparently qualified for the ministry, Murr received his official license as a local preacher in July 1897 at Rockport and was admitted to the Indiana Annual Conference of the Methodist Episcopal Church in fall 1898 at Princeton, Indiana.[14] Murr's circuit from 1898 to 1902 was based in Rome-Tobinsport and included Lincoln's boyhood home in Spencer County. Over his forty-two-year career in ministry, he also served churches in Grandview-Highland (1901), Charlestown (1903), Greenwood (1908), College Corner (1910), Sullivan and Greensburg (1914), Milroy (1916), Bayard Park in Evansville (1918), Capital Avenue in Indianapolis (1920), First Church in Princeton (1922), Paoli (1929), and First Methodist Church in Washington (1930), where he served as pastor for ten years before retiring in 1940.

In 1897, near the beginning of his ministry, Murr studied theology at DePauw University.[15] Interspersed with his later appointments throughout Indiana, Murr served a term of detached service in 1912 on behalf of Moores Hill College (a predecessor to the University of Evansville), where he earned a master of arts degree (also 1912), and in 1925 received an honorary doctor of divinity from Evansville College. Near the end of his pastoral career, from 1924 to 1930, Murr served as superintendent of the New Albany District of the Methodist Church.[16] Murr married Mabel Louise Connor (of Rome, Indiana) on 29 November 1899; the couple had three children together.[17]

Along with his work as a Methodist minister, Murr frequently turned to his love for Abraham Lincoln and what he saw as biographers' failures concerning Lincoln's important Indiana years. For instance, Murr criticized nationally known Lincoln historians for failing to spend more time researching in Indiana and dismissed early Lincoln biographers, such as Joseph H. Barrett, John Locke Scripps, Josiah G. Holland, William D. Howells, and Henry J. Raymond, because "none of these writers . . . visited either the Kentucky field or the Jonesboro, Indiana, community." Although Murr appreciated that Lincoln's former law partner, William Herndon, did interview Indiana locals, Murr criticized Herndon for relying too heavily on one erratic source, Dennis Hanks, and resented that Herndon arrived for his "hasty visit" with "pronounced preconceived convictions and notions."[18]

Also, Murr scorned Ida Tarbell, perhaps the most popular national expert on Abraham Lincoln at the time. He criticized her for spending only one day in Lincoln's old neighborhood and speaking to just one boyhood associate.[19] Tarbell visited Evansville, Indiana, in 1920 to deliver a presentation about Lincoln at a high school auditorium. Murr told a local reporter that Tarbell was "worsted" when former Lincoln neighbor James Gentry cussed out Tarbell during her encounter with Gentry.[20]

So which Lincoln biographers should we trust? For Lincoln's pre-Hoosier years in Kentucky, Murr favored Louis Warren and William Barton, the latter, perhaps not coincidentally, a fellow minister. He praised Warren's volume *Lincoln's Parentage and Childhood* as embodying "the whole of that which is reliable and dependable concerning the President's Kentucky childhood" because of Warren's time living in Elizabethtown and Hodgenville. Likewise, he complimented Barton for "his well-known comprehensive investigations" concerning Lucey Hanks, mother of Nancy Hanks Lincoln.[21]

Although admiring the Kentucky work of Warren and Barton, Murr implied—through omission—that no worthy history existed for Lincoln's Indiana years and that he might be best positioned to offer one. Murr wrote, "I do not propose to revolutionize the thinking of the Lincoln world, save that since Truth is perhaps always and ever more or less revolutionary and more especially so where error has long occupied the throne. In this discussion of the formative period of Lincoln's life, I have endeavored to introduce the much needed corrective in a number of instances and it would be strange indeed in view of my unusual opportunities, if I did not feel capable of doing this."[22]

Thus, Murr offered himself as a reasonable historian who could fill in some gaps in the historical record, but he also understood hurdles he would face. "The vast majority of the President's biographers have been well known to the public by reason of their labors in other realms," he wrote. "This is not true in my case, as I am quite unknown to the general public save throughout much of the southern half of my native state, Indiana."[23]

Despite his relative obscurity, Murr relied on years of research and decades spent ministering in and around Lincoln's boyhood home. As he noted some years later, "I became intimately acquainted with the many who had been neighbors and boyhood associates of the future President.... It was my rare fortune to thus know and frequently converse with those who had often been in the Lincoln cabin." Writing with a sense of duty to record his findings, Murr mused, "I must write it or it would not be told."[24] Murr's son J. Bruce Murr explained his father's approach to history:

> Let it be said at the outset, that my father was NOT a historian in the true sense of the word. Rather, he was a "source history" within himself. That is, he hunted down facts in the form of stories he gleaned from eye-witnesses or events in which he figured. These stories he related orally and also put to the written page. Hence, he was more of a raconteur than a strict historian,

although the things he could relate were the stuff from which history is obtained. For him, there was no buttressing of a story by exact dates, exact quotes from inscriptions, or signed notarized affidavits. There was no need of it, any more so than a reporter describing a hydrogen test blast would need to produce a college diploma showing evidence of having majored in physics. The account would still be credible nonetheless.[25]

Based on years of research and conversations with Lincoln's neighbors, Murr published a three-part series between 1917 and 1918 on Lincoln's life in Indiana for the *Indiana Magazine of History*. He received considerable attention, which spurred additional interest in his topic.[26] Murr later published an essay titled "He Knew Lincoln's Neighbors" in Bess Ehrmann's 1938 book *The Missing Chapter in the Life of Abraham Lincoln*. At some point, likely after World War II, Murr also wrote a book-length manuscript titled *The Wilderness Years*. He never formally published his comprehensive history, however, and instead quietly deposited *The Wilderness Years* in the archives of his alma mater, DePauw University. Murr's significant three-part series and his unpublished manuscript form the basis of this book, much of it published here for the first time.

—⚭—

Murr faced the challenge of chronicling a man who, in his words, "refuses to conform to the ordinary processes of generalization and analysis." Even as Murr asserted he would not "make Lincoln a saint or even have him, as a boy or man, appear saintly in the usual sense and meaning of those terms," he had "long since arrived at the conclusion that Lincoln was indeed a Providential character and as much so as was Moses and other ancient worthies."[27]

Murr's biography attempts to cover all of Lincoln's Indiana life, but at times it offers a unique focus. With his background as a minister, Murr relished exploring Lincoln's religious beliefs and his views on alcohol. Like Tarbell, Murr defended Abraham Lincoln's father, Thomas, who faced harsh criticism from some historians. Relying on interviews with countless local residents—identified and summarized in the appendix to this book—Murr also offered new insight into the Lincoln family's initial move to Indiana, their life in the wilderness, and Abraham Lincoln's characteristics.

Murr's continuing work and advocacy for greater attention on Lincoln's Indiana years helped influence the wider Lincoln historical field. In particular, during the 1920s, a small but determined group of amateur historians in southwestern Indiana shed additional light on Lincoln's formative years by filling gaps in the historical record and, like Murr, attempted to reverse negative Indiana stereotypes. Led initially by John E. Iglehart and led later by Bess V. Ehrmann, Southwestern Indiana Historical Society organized what came to be called the "Lincoln Inquiry." These writers assembled testimony about the Lincoln family and era, gave presentations, produced papers, and contextualized Lincoln within the broader framework of his neighborhood and southwestern Indiana. J. Edward Murr contributed to the Lincoln Inquiry through presentations and influenced some of the group's perspective.[28]

Albert J. Beveridge (1862–1927), a US senator from Indiana, achieved a widely acclaimed career outside elected office by writing popular history. He published a four-volume *Life of John Marshall* (1916–1919), which won a Pulitzer Prize, and then undertook a similar four-volume biography of Abraham Lincoln. Unfortunately, Beveridge died in 1927 with only two volumes completed, both published posthumously in 1928 as *Abraham Lincoln, 1809–1858*. Murr served as an important consultant with Beveridge on those two volumes, frequently offering ideas and suggesting changes that Beveridge often adopted. Some of their correspondence appears in part 3 of this volume.

More recently, other prominent Lincoln biographers noticed Murr's important efforts. Merrill Peterson cited Murr's work in *Lincoln in American Memory* (1994), and Michael Burlingame frequently consulted and referred to Murr's research to address

Lincoln's youth in his popular two-volume *Abraham Lincoln: A Life* (2008).[29]

—⟋⟍⟍—

At age ninety-one, J. Edward Murr died on 21 August 1960 at his home in New Albany, Indiana, where he had resided after retirement twenty years earlier.[30] Though Murr died in relative obscurity, his original research on Lincoln's youth continues to gain attention and appreciation.

Readers must, nevertheless, exercise some caution. Just as he criticized William Herndon for "preconceived convictions and notions," Murr himself approaches his subject with bias—he insists on portraying frontier Hoosiers positively. Moreover, he often passes along traditions and lore from local residents without challenge or skepticism. For example, in a few instances Murr refers to Lincoln's Indiana home as Jonesboro, even though that name never took hold until the Lincolns left Indiana.[31] Jonesboro was named for William Jones (1803–1864), who arrived in the area only about 1827, at least ten years after the Lincolns arrived.[32] Certainly the town and area would not have been called Jonesboro when the Lincolns came in 1816.

Occasionally Murr also offers the wrong dates or misrepresents paths the Lincolns took from one point to another. For example, he suggests the Lincolns arrived at their Indiana cabin in late summer 1816 rather than the more commonly accepted date of that autumn or winter.[33] In addition, Murr suggests the Lincolns reached Indiana by first crossing the Ohio River near Corydon in southeastern Indiana and then heading westward on the Buffalo Trail to what is now Spencer County—although this assertion rests on virtually no historical evidence, only on Murr's own views. Perhaps not coincidentally, this alleged path takes the Lincolns right near Murr's childhood home. My annotations correct and offer contexts for many of these deficiencies in Murr's work.

Despite these shortcomings, Murr's work provides important facts and source material that form rare, essential building blocks for any history of Abraham Lincoln's early life. As the first fully annotated edition of J. Edward Murr's Lincoln research, this volume can help preserve and promulgate important source material unique for studying Lincoln's years in Indiana.

NOTES

1. John L. Scripps to William H. Herndon, 24 June 1865, in *Herndon's Informants*, ed. Wilson and Davis, 57.

2. Abraham Lincoln, "To Jesse Fell, Enclosing Autobiography, 20 December 1859," in *Collected Works of Abraham Lincoln*, ed. Basler et al., 3:511–512; Abraham Lincoln, "Autobiography Written for John L. Scripps (June 1860)," in *Collected Works of Abraham Lincoln*, ed. Basler et al., 4:60–67. Lincoln also penned a forty-seven-word autobiography in 1858 for Charles Lanman in the Dictionary of Congress, but that terse entry's only allusion to Indiana reads, "Education defective."

3. Wilson and Davis, eds., *Herndon's Informants*, 29, 47, 78–80.

4. Herndon and Weik, *Herndon's Lincoln*, 4, 39.

5. Ehrmann, *Missing Chapter*, 69–70.

6. Rice, "Ida M. Tarbell," 59.

7. James Veatch to A. C. Flinn [Anna O'Flynn], 14 March 1894, Anna O'Flynn-Lincoln Research File, Regional History Collection # 324, Byron R. Lewis Historical Library, Vincennes University, IN.

8. Tarbell told the *Evansville Courier* that although she did not visit Lincoln City, she did stay for "several days" in Rockport for interviewing locals. Wick, "He Was a Friend of Us Poor Men," 273, citing Tarbell, memorandum: *In the Footsteps of Lincoln*, Tarbell Collection, Pelletier Library, Allegheny College, Meadville, PA.

9. Tarbell, *Early Life of Abraham Lincoln*, 42–43.

10. Tarbell, *Life of Abraham Lincoln*, 1:28.

11. J. Edward Murr was born on 20 December 1868 near Corydon, Indiana, adjacent to Thompson's Chapel. His parents were Jonathan C. Murr (1836–1917) and Sarah Catherine Murr, née Hislip (1841–1922), who married in March 1868. May, *Murr Family*, 9. Although his family remained loyal to the Union, Murr's father supported Stephen A. Douglas Democrats.

12. Murr, "Some Pertinent Observations," 1.

13. Murr officially joined the Methodist Church a day after his eighteenth birthday. Murr, *Glimpses of an Itinerant*, chronology.

14. Murr, *Glimpses of an Itinerant*, 5. Murr's autobiography gives his local-preacher-commencement date as 6 July 1897 (in a handwritten correction), but official Methodist records say 8 July 1897.

15. Murr entered the School of Theology in 1897 but did not graduate. The 1897–1898 university catalog lists him as a junior, but his name appears in no other catalog. From correspondence on 21 August 2019 with Wesley W. Wilson, coordinator of Archives & Special Collections at DePauw University Archives.

16. *Northwestern Christian Advocate* 60 (19 June 1912): 23, 795; Murr, *Glimpses of an Itinerant*, chronology. Murr noted that his admission to DePauw University likely occurred because of four years of prior schooling at Lebanon, Ohio. Murr, *Glimpses of an Itinerant*, 5; see also *Indianapolis Star*, 23 August 1960, p. 20.

17. Murr's three children with Mabel were Alleen (Stewart), J. Bruce Murr, and Roger W. Murr. After Mabel's death on 13 February 1951, Murr married Minnie Eitelgeorge of Canton, Ohio, on 22 October 1952. Minnie formerly lived in Perry County, Indiana. Indiana United Methodist Conference, 130th Session, 565.

18. Murr, *Wilderness Years*, 253, 255.

19. It is unclear how much time Tarbell spent in Lincoln's old neighborhood, but it likely occurred during just one trip. She relied primarily on other local researchers. Wick, "He Was a Friend of Us Poor," 272–273.

20. *Evansville Courier*, 30 and 31 January 1920. Murr's account to the *Courier* is disputable. Gentry's family rebutted Murr's assertion, and Tarbell later said she never visited the area, though she did apparently visit in 1922. Wick, "He Was a Friend of Us Poor," 272–273.

21. Murr, *Wilderness Years*, 7. In fact, Warren and Barton disagreed over Nancy Hanks Lincoln's ancestry, with Warren wrongly concluding Lucey Hanks descended from a Shipley family.

22. Murr, *Wilderness Years*, 15.

23. Murr, *Wilderness Years*, 10.

24. Murr, *Wilderness Years*, 13, 15.

25. May, *Murr Family*, foreword by J. Bruce Murr (1961).

26. The three-part series titled "Lincoln in Indiana" ran from December 1917 through June 1918 in the *Indiana Magazine of History* 13 (December 1917), 307–348; 14 (March 1918), 13–75; 14 (June 1918), 148–182.

27. Murr, *Wilderness Years*, 3–4.

28. For more on the Lincoln Inquiry and samples of their work, see Bartelt and Claybourn, *Abe's Youth*.

29. Peterson, *Lincoln in American Memory*, 266.

30. *Indianapolis Star*, 23 August 1960, p. 20. Funeral services occurred on Wednesday, 23 August 1960, at 10:30 a.m. at Trinity Methodist Church in New Albany.

31. According to the United States Postal Service, post office names and dates included Gentry's Store (1826/1835), Gentrysville (1835–1837), and Gentryville (c. 1844). The Jonesboro post office commenced in 1837 and ended in 1844.

32. *Lincoln State Park Interpretive Master Plan* (2005), Indiana Department of Natural Resources, accessed 13 October 2021, https://www.in.gov /dnr/parklake/files/sp-Lincoln_IMP2009.pdf.

33. Murr takes this position because he believes the Lincolns cultivated a garden that year, but most crops could not have been planted and harvested in such a short period. Most Lincoln scholars maintain the Lincolns arrived later in the year.

PART I

THE WILDERNESS YEARS

WHEN J. EDWARD MURR DIED in 1960, the bulk of his Lincoln research went to the archives of his alma mater, DePauw University. Among the unpublished material was Murr's comprehensive book-length history of Abraham Lincoln's youth written after World War II, which he titled *The Wilderness Years*. Although the manuscript's prose did not rise to the standard of Murr's published material, *The Wilderness Years* offers unique insight into Lincoln's Indiana years along with some historical assertions not found elsewhere.

The full manuscript of *The Wilderness Years* included twenty-three chapters, each detailing a different aspect of Lincoln's youth. Much of the substantive history presented in those chapters appeared earlier as a shorter, three-part series published between 1917 and 1918 in the *Indiana Magazine of History* and is included in part 2 of this book. As a result, part 1 includes only those portions of *The Wilderness Years* offering Murr's unique, noteworthy assessments not found elsewhere—those about Lincoln's parents, his birth, and his Kentucky childhood.

ONE

—·ɷ·—

THOMAS LINCOLN,
FATHER OF THE PRESIDENT

THE PIONEER HIGHLY ESTEEMED PHYSICAL prowess. The man who could lift the end of the biggest log at a rolling, outstrip the fleetest runner, and whip the crowing bully of his own or an adjoining community straightway became a local hero.

Tom Lincoln was never a bully, but he could have been one. He was physically an unusual man in certain respects. He was five feet and nearly ten inches in stature.[1] While in Indiana he weighed 195 pounds or more—usually a little short of two hundred pounds. He did not carry a single superfluous pound. To use the expressive phrase, his arms were like mill posts. His body was hard and compact, with the barrel or noticeably round shape, but was devoid of what is sometimes called "middle-aged spread." His shoulders were of the rounded sort—not sloping, nor yet of the square type—and they were, rather, much like the Dempsey or Joe Louis kind, thus capable of delivering a powerful blow. Most strong men have such shoulders.

"Old Tom" (he was forty when he reached Indiana) was the exact opposite in physical build from his illustrious son.[2] As is well known, the future president was not only tall—some seven inches taller than his father—but he was also exceedingly angular and all out of proper proportion. When he was younger, he looked as if he had been dressed with a pitchfork. Later in life, what might be called deformities—in the sense that Abe's limbs were not properly proportioned—were hidden or smoothed by his uniform custom of wearing the long coat. Old Tom's form, or frame, from top to toe suggested smoothness since he was perfectly proportioned, and there was not the slightest suggestion or even a small hint of angularity. His face was of the round variety, somewhat akin to the apple-dumpling sort. His eyes were brown, and they were far from the sleepy sort. His hair was unruly and his complexion dark. His cheeks, nose, mouth, and ears were of splendid chiseling, both sides of the face proportioned alike. His muscles were "as hard as nails." Wrestlers insisted that it was impossible to count his ribs. In his walk there was a noticeable hesitancy or what is sometimes spoken of as a halting movement. This was not due to injury—it bore a resemblance in certain ways to the fat man's rolling walk. Ordinarily Thomas moved slowly; his gait was slow and even lazy, but when aroused, he was surprisingly quick in his every movement.

Although he engaged in a number of fistfights, Thomas Lincoln was not a quarrelsome man, nor was he in the habit of looking for trouble. On the contrary, he was by nature peacefully inclined, with great good nature, and was proverbially kind and extremely generous. "Old Tom would part with his shirt."[3] Both in Kentucky and Indiana, he was more than once chosen as a peacemaker when neighborhood differences arose. The Little Mount Church at Knob Creek chose him to preside over the pronounced difference growing out of the question of slavery.[4] And at least once he was selected to preside over a matter of difference among Little Pigeon members at Jonesboro.[5] The elements of fairness, honesty, and truthfulness in him were responsible for his selection in both instances. His neighbors believed in him and trusted him. But if anyone presumed to encroach on his rights and liberties, there was straightway staged a fistfight or a footrace, but Tom Lincoln was never known to do any of the running. He was an exceedingly difficult man to handle in a rough-and-tumble fistfight. Some said that he was never bested in a fight. He was never disposed to pose as a bully, and while he might have gained such local notoriety as a local bully often enjoyed, the fact that he refrained from entering into this field at once becomes big with meaning.

The bully of our time has turned professional and capitalized on his physical powers and skill. Our present-day champion wrestler and prizefighter meets his opponent in a much publicized bout with prize money or a "stake" and wins a mythical belt as inducement or reward for his much-discussed knockout punch. His winnings have been known to go beyond a million dollars in a single contest. Unlike the foregoing, the frontier [fighter] received no "stake" and no belt; he fought for honor and glory. Physical prowess in those days was much regarded.

—⁂—

Thomas Lincoln was an official member of the Baptist Church, in both Kentucky and Indiana. He faithfully attended the preaching service and shared in the business sessions. At home, he said grace at meals. He was regarded as a good and loyal member of the local church. The fact that he united with Little Pigeon Church by letter rather than on confession of faith proves conclusively that he had been a member in good standing of Little Mount Baptist Church at Knob Creek.[6] Nancy Hanks was never a member of any church in Indiana for the very good reason that there was no church organization and no church building in and about [their Indiana community] in her day. It is true that the church was organized, or an agreement was entered into, to affect a local society having in view the erection of a place of worship in 1816. But this agreement or announced purpose did not culminate in the building of Little Pigeon Church until 1820—some two years after Nancy Hanks's death.[7] The presumption is, although no proof of this has ever been established, that Lincoln's mother was a member of Little Mount Baptist Church. Some writers assert that Nancy Hanks was a Methodist, but we have no proof of this. I am of the opinion that she was a Baptist, and I go a bit further by believing that she was a member of the Baptist Church before her marriage and thus before her husband became a member of Little Mount Church.

Although Thomas Lincoln and Nancy Hanks were married by Jesse Head, a Methodist preacher, that does not necessarily imply that Nancy Hanks was a communicant of that church.

Tom Lincoln was decidedly of the opinion that "edication" was not at all necessary in order to get on and up in the world. He was not opposed to readin', 'ritin', and 'rithmetic, and he joined Nancy Hanks in seeing to it that both Abe and his sister, Sarah, attended a school at Knob Creek. But anything beyond the rule of three was not deemed necessary in Tom's estimation.[8]

Eventually Tom Lincoln changed his attitude toward his son's ambition to obtain an education. Other than this reversal, the father of the president never experienced any other marked change in anything of character whatsoever. From his first appearance to the very last, he remained honest, truthful, and generous, even though exceedingly poor.

Thus, throughout the whole of Tom Lincoln's life, he appeared to be striving to maintain the standards of his Virginia forebears, who belonged to the undistinguished or middle class, citizens or families that were God-fearing, truthful, honest, and law abiding.

—◊—

The president's father was never a success in a material way. This fact does not justify the numerous slings hurled at him by his many defamers and detractors. He has been called a tramp, a poor rover, a typical representative of the poor "white trash," not only ignorant but also shiftless, lazy, thriftless, trifling, and hopeless; in fact, history may be searched in vain to find any other character who was connected with anyone—whether father or brother, or bearing any other kinship with a truly great man—who has been so repeatedly slandered and censured as has Thomas Lincoln.

Even John G. Nicolay and John Hay joined in this deep unkindness.[9] Certainly William Herndon and Ward Hill Lamon majored in this unwarranted and wholly unjust attempt to belabor and besmirch the character of the president's father.[10]

It is true that Tom Lincoln was far from a success if success is measured in terms of houses and lands, stocks and bonds, and all else that make for worldly plenty. Tom Lincoln, from first to last, did in fact own much land; but through no fault of his, this was lost to him.

Since when must a man be well to do or prove successful in business ventures in order to be regarded as a success in life? Was not Tom Lincoln's distinguished son, at a later day, a profound failure in a business way? Did he not, by his unbusinesslike management, pile up what he himself jokingly called "the National Debt"? Indeed, Lincoln proved a complete failure as a businessman.

American history reveals the fact that a number of quite worthy men—indeed, men who gained fame, honor, and place—were utter failures in money matters. What of Samuel Adams, the "father of independence"? Was he not ever and always but one day removed from poverty? But for his cousin John Adams, he could not have reached the seat of the Continental Congress. The making of money is a gift in the baby cradle.

Vice President John Tyler, when informed by Daniel Webster of the death of President Harrison, did not possess sufficient funds to travel to Washington to carry out his duties as the head of the nation. His business reputation was such (dishonesty was not alleged) that he struggled to secure the necessary loan! In his dilemma he appealed to the White House messenger, the secretary of state, Daniel Webster, but Webster, too, was in his usual state—penniless. Indeed, it was said of "Black Dan" [Webster] that while he never sent a "dun"—a statement to a client—he never met his own personal obligations except under pressure. Wasn't Ulysses S. Grant a business failure ever and always? The list is long of those otherwise truly worthwhile characters who, measured in terms of business success, remained failures.

Thomas Lincoln was poor throughout the fourteen years spent in Indiana, and for that matter, he remained poor for the remainder of his life in Illinois.[11] But the father of the president left no unpaid bills in Kentucky, and he met all of his obligations in Indiana. No one doubted his honesty.

—⚋—

The Spencer County court records make no mention of Thomas Lincoln as a lawbreaker.[12] If, indeed, he was ever at any time brought into the court of the local justice of the peace, it was due to some fistfight waged, and if he was fined for this, then it could be said that many others were subjected to the same treatment, since fist-fighting in those days was common. In Kentucky, Thomas Lincoln was brought into the courts, but in every instance, this was in defense of land titles. His character was never once involved.

The father of the president did frequently change his residence. He made some three changes in Kentucky and as many later in Illinois. Thus he resided in three states from first to last—Kentucky, Indiana, and Illinois. But Tom Lincoln never changed his residence except for good—very good—reasons. We have the statement of Abraham Lincoln that the family left Kentucky "partly on account of slavery but chiefly on account of land titles."[13] Thomas, like many others of that period, was dispossessed of his farm. He left Indiana for Illinois after the milk sickness plague had claimed Nancy Hanks, Thomas and Betsy Sparrow, as well as Levi Hall and his wife, and when the second plague began its ravages at [their Indiana community], this fact proved decisive in the matter of immigrating to Illinois.[14] He made his first change in Illinois by reason of illness, a statement by his son that the "entire family went down with chills and ague."[15] This [illness] resulted in moving elsewhere and, incidentally, was Abe's first affliction.

If Tom Lincoln is to be condemned for being a nomadic rover, then what shall be said of his kinsman and friend Daniel Boone? Was not Boone born in Pennsylvania, after which he reached Carolina, where he changed his residence a time or two? Then later still did he not reach Kentucky, and when he was dispossessed of his lands (as was Tom Lincoln), did not Boone seek a home in a foreign country? For that region west of the Mississippi was then owned—or at least claimed—by nations in the Old World. Here he lived and died and was buried. Are we to condemn Daniel Boone for his wanderings in order to justify criticism of the father of the president, or shall we prove sensible and condemn neither one? If we condemned both Boone and Lincoln, we would be obliged to condemn many others.

It is true that Tom Lincoln had certain weaknesses and shortcomings, but he was not at all the kind of man that William Herndon and Ward Hill Lamon and others would have the Lincoln world believe.

It is quite true that Thomas Lincoln never made much of a stir in the world, but he is entitled to fair treatment, [which] he has too often failed to receive at the hands of his defamers and detractors. Since Tom Lincoln could, in his crude way, defend a given position, I have wished it were possible for this unlettered wilderness man to be back here long enough to speak on his own behalf. It is just possible that his defense might take such form as the following: "You who write and speak harshly concerning me, denouncing me as a worthless and trifling man. Might it not be wise in you who do this, to maintain a respectful silence until it can be said of any single one of you, that which has been said of myself—'Thomas Lincoln was the father of the greatest man save Washington in the New World.'"

If you would have a truly great man, "you must begin with his grandfather."[16] Thus wittily spoke *The Autocrat of the Breakfast Table*, Oliver Wendell Holmes. The foregoing observation was not fully verified in the case of the president—at least there was nothing found in that Virginia grandfather who appeared prophetic of this remarkable grandson. The elder Abraham Lincoln belonged to an "undistinguished" or "second" family of Virginia. The Washingtons, Masons, Lees, Jeffersons, and the rest constituted what were spoken of as the First Families of the Old Dominion.

There was nothing especially noteworthy about Lincoln's grandfather from Rockingham County in the Shenandoah or, for that matter, any of his forebears in the remote past, nor yet in any single one of the elder Abraham Lincoln's descendants, save the president.

The Lincolns, wherever found, were, as a general rule, God-fearing, upright citizens—honest, truthful, and law abiding. This [uprightness] was true of them as a class in Massachusetts, Pennsylvania, Virginia, Kentucky, Indiana, and Illinois. I knew a number of the descendants of Josiah Lincoln [Thomas Lincoln's brother]; in every instance, they lived up to the standard of their forebears. Among them was George Washington Lincoln— widely called "Happy" Lincoln. He was quite poor, but I recall that others said vast wealth could be placed in his keeping, and every penny would be accounted for. As a class, this branch of the Lincoln family had good and upright citizens—honest, straightforward, truthful, and law abiding; moreover they were peaceful. But if you chanced to be hunting for trouble and wanted to find it, if you ventured to trespass on their honor or rights, you had no need to go any further, for they knew how to accommodate you.

An insistent family tradition among the Lincolns claims a Quaker connection. Perhaps the Massachusetts Lincoln who left that colony for Pennsylvania did so in order to dwell in the congenial atmosphere of the Friends, or Quakers, who were plentiful in Penn's Colony. The Virginia Abraham [the president's grandfather] had no Quaker affiliations while residing in the Shenandoah Valley, and certainly he had none during the brief remainder of his life after reaching the Green River country in Kentucky.

The elder Abraham's two daughters, Mary and Nancy, as well as his three sons, Mordecai, Josiah, and Thomas, were all born in Virginia, and none of them in later life became affiliated with the Quakers. As stated previously, Thomas became a Baptist, and Josiah's family—at least many of them—were members of the Disciples, or Christian Church. Some of them were Methodists. I am not advised as to the matter of church affiliation of Mordecai Lincoln's descendants.

The Quaker connection—if real in the remote past, which appears probable—was altogether too remote to produce a noteworthy or determining influence on the grandson Abraham, although the president appears to have had more or less pride in the fact that his forebears were, at least believed by him, to have been so connected. Certainly the president was always disposed to deal kindly and sympathetically with Quaker visitors at the White House. He extended a cordial welcome to the many Quakers who called on him and was considerate of them in their perplexity occasioned by war.

The Lincolns' emigration from Virginia to Kentucky in 1782 did not cause them to lose Virginia citizenship since Kentucky was at that time a Virginia county and thus under Virginia governmental rule. In fact, the president's grandfather Abraham died a citizen of Virginia, since Kentucky was not made a state of the Union until some years thereafter. Thomas Lincoln, the father of the president, was a mere boy in his tenth year in 1786 when his father was killed by an Indian.[17] We know comparatively little concerning the boyhood and even the young manhood of this youngest son of the Virginia Abraham and his wife, Bathsheba (or Bastab).

As might be expected in the case of a fatherless boy in the midst of an almost unbroken Kentucky wilderness, Thomas Lincoln grew up "literally without education."[18] In some manner, we know not how, where, or [by whom he was taught], he learned to spell his way laboriously through certain portions of the Bible and other books, and this aided his ability to write—to at least sign his name and perhaps something beyond that. He remained a poor reader his whole life and made sparing use of a pen after Sarah and Abe learned to read and write.

Certain biographers and Lincoln lecturers have from time to time made much of the fact that Nancy Hanks became Tom Lincoln's teacher after their marriage. But Kentucky public records show conclusively that Tom Lincoln put his name to legal documents some half dozen years before his marriage. Nancy Hanks was not Tom Lincoln's teacher. One marvels that these slanderers and detractors of Lincoln's father did not go even further by alleging that Lincoln's mother was hopelessly illiterate in view of the fact that on every public document on which her name appears, both in Kentucky and Indiana, she made her mark.[19] Doubtless these slanderers did not possess this knowledge, but since they are remarkable for what they did not know concerning the president's parents otherwise, it is just as well that they were not advised of the fact that Nancy Hanks invariably signed by making her mark.

From time to time, we hear of Thomas Lincoln as a young man being in a number of different places. He was in his brother Mord's home as well as in the homes of his married sisters and also with his brother Josiah. He likewise tarried briefly—perhaps one crop season—with his uncle Jacob Lincoln, who farmed near the Tennessee and Virginia boundary line. Then, too—as would be but natural—he visited his Uncle Tom for whom he had been named, whose farm site was near Lexington, Kentucky. Moreover, he made at least two flatboat trips down the Ohio and Mississippi Rivers—once as far as Memphis and at another time to the deeper South, and beyond doubt he journeyed as far as New Orleans. These flatboat journeys were made as a hired laborer.[20]

—∞—

In spite of the frontier privations and consequent discouragements, Thomas Lincoln managed to learn the rudiments of the carpenter's trade. Initially this meant little more than familiarizing himself with such tools as the jack plane, froe, adz, chisel, hammer, broadaxe, hatchet, and saw. Every pioneer in time became skilled using the chopping axe as well as the broadaxe and froe.

Thomas Lincoln possessed a natural bent as a worker in wood. And in time he developed more or less skill as a carpenter. His Indiana neighbors regarded "Old Tom" as a good workman.

Elizabethtown, Kentucky, was for some while a village of log cabins. That which was true of Elizabethtown was likewise true of many other frontier towns. Contracting and building in the more modern sense were quite unknown, but even so, Tom Lincoln's services as a carpenter were in demand.

Tom Lincoln was more of a farmer and less of a carpenter while a resident of the later portion of his Kentucky years and more of a carpenter and somewhat less of a farmer during his fourteen years' residence in Indiana. We hear comparatively little concerning his carpenter labors after he reached Illinois. He was then out of the wilderness.

The pioneer needed to be a man of all work, but natural aptitude and skill that the frontiersman denominated "ease," "a knack," or "a turn" stood Tom Lincoln in good stead. His Indiana neighbors recalled that "Tom Lincoln was a good carpenter" and that he "had the best kit of tools in Spencer County."

Soon after reaching [Indiana], Tom Lincoln constructed that necessary frontier institution called a sawpit, which served the general community. Sawmills did not appear in this wilderness until many years later.[21] He required some degree of skill to convert a wild cherry, poplar, oak, or black walnut log into serviceable lumber. Tom Lincoln excelled in this. Later, his son excelled as the "bottom" man, what was called the "pit man" in the operation of the up-and-down movement of the vertical saw.

When the president paid his one and only visit back to [Spencer County, Indiana] in 1844, he expressed a wish to see that sawpit. A number of his former chums accompanied him to the pit, and as he stood looking at it, he recalled how he had spent many a day "down in that hole pulling that saw" and spoke of how the sawdust rained down on him.[22]

In the Jonesboro "raisings," Tom Lincoln proved to be a handyman in constructing or superintending notching, fitting, and raising, or, to use the common phrase, Tom Lincoln was looked to as the "boss."

The "end men" who shouldered the notched logs and with brute strength climbed the corners, bearing the logs on their shoulders, had small need of skill, but it did require skill to cut or notch logs "with the eye" and thus make a good fit or smooth job of it. The Kentucky carpenter could do that. Tom Lincoln was also a good man to cut rafters as well as put the finishing touches on the completed walls, such as fitting windows and making batten doors.

We do not need to praise Tom Lincoln as a skilled carpenter in our modern sense, and I am not disposed to attempt that, but in such a community as was [Spencer County, Indiana], people greatly appreciated the president's father.

When the community decided to erect a log school building, this Kentucky carpenter was given the contract—at least he was chosen to superintend the construction, and no other man was so much as considered. Then, too, when the Little Pigeon Baptist story-and-a-half church building was decided on, the Kentucky carpenter was awarded the contract. These buildings were not pretentious affairs, but even so, the fact that he was awarded these contracts is big with meaning. The Kentucky carpenter's skill was greatly appreciated.

When many of the Jonesboro neighbors housed up for the winter, save for chores and occasional clearing, Tom Lincoln busied himself in converting his summer accumulation of whipsawed wild cherry and black walnut lumber into three-cornered cupboards, clothes chests, tables, chairs, and other household needs.

These designs were not at all ornate but proved serviceable. If something rather difficult to make was desired, Tom Lincoln knew how to lick it in shape. He was a handyman.

Shadrach Hall's nearby tanbark mill had to be supplied with bark.[23] This meant the free use of the chopping axe in felling trees as well as peeling or skinning of the trunks. Since Hall was a farmer, he often employed Tom Lincoln to perform that labor. He was also often employed by Hall otherwise. The tanner was—for that period—a rather large shipper to southern markets, chiefly to Memphis. His cargoes consisted of leather as well as farm products.

Nearly all of the farm wagons in and about Jonesboro at the first—and for that matter throughout the whole of the [Indiana] stay of the Lincolns—were homemade or handmade affairs. The first imported "honest-to-goodness" wagon that reached Spencer County made its appearance there in 1812. Its owner resided near the mouth of Anderson Creek (Troy), where Tom Lincoln landed his craft containing his household effects in 1816 and where Abe came years later and was employed as a ferryman for James Taylor.[24]

Ox yokes, wagon tongues, sled runners, wooden wagon wheels, handmade looms, chairs, winding blades, wooden pitchforks, spinning wheels, and suchlike farm tools and household conveniences were fashioned by this Kentucky carpenter. The father of the president did not make all of these cabin fixtures and barnyard conveniences for the entire community, but Tom Lincoln was easily the most skilled workman in that entire settlement, so his services were more or less in demand.

Tom Lincoln had a rather winning way with women. This merely means that he counted it all joy to please them in constructing many little household conveniences. To tell the whole truth, Tom Lincoln was more apt to devote his skill and time in fixing up and bettering other people's homes than he was that of his own. He could generously absorb praise for his labors.

I do not claim Tom Lincoln achieved any marked excellence, nor do I suggest he was "work brittle," but I aim to refute the oft-repeated and quite groundless charge of downright laziness [and charges] that he was shiftless, trifling and improvident. He was not lazy as such and far from what has been termed "improvident and no account," but like many other men he was often exceedingly busy about some more or less non-remunerative labor—at least he was not one of those gluttons for work. But he was usually busy with something.

In this rather hurried review of Tom Lincoln, I am not asserting that the greatness of his son was chiefly traceable to this unlettered and more or less narrow-minded man of the Kentucky and Indiana wilderness. On the contrary, I do not permit myself to lose sight of Tom Lincoln's well-known weaknesses and shortcomings; however, where well-established facts appear to warrant it, I wish to point out that Tom Lincoln was not as one sided as he has been painted by both writers and speakers.

The president's father was a product of the frontier, with all that may mean. He was approaching old age when he emerged from that big wilderness, so he continued to live the wilderness life in all of its essential aspects after he became an Illinois prairie dweller in 1830, and he continued to live there much after the fashion of his Kentucky and Indiana life until his death in 1851.

If it be true, as is sometimes asserted, that the entire world is only a few days removed from hunger and want, then it was especially true that Tom Lincoln felt this throughout much of his entire life. He was not only denied every possible luxury; he was also denied many of the present-day common conveniences and necessities.

The cultural things of life were always and ever somewhat removed from this son of the wilderness. Elevated moral standards and ennobling ideals usually require the bracing support of a number of other helpful agencies. These were not available in and about Elizabethtown, Kentucky, nor yet in [Spencer County], Indiana.

At best, the frontier was rough and rugged. Only the physically strong survived. Thomas Lincoln survived, and Nancy Hanks died early—she was in her thirty-fifth year.

NOTES

1. Thomas stood about two to four inches taller than the average man of his generation. Komlos, "On the Biological Standard of Living," 25. See also Associated Press, "American Men," 7.

2. The Lincolns arrived to make their new home in Indiana in December 1816 near present-day Gentryville. Thomas was thirty-eight years old at the time.

3. This quotation presumably originated with locals describing Thomas Lincoln to Murr.

4. Little Mount Church split in 1808 from South Fork Baptist Church in Hardin County, Kentucky, over slavery. Although the Lincolns were among about fifteen members who left South Fork, existing records do not document whether Thomas Lincoln presided over the split. Warren, *Lincoln's Youth*, 13, citing South Fork Baptist Church Record Book, 3 July 1808, and July 1810, photostats in Lincoln National Life Foundation, Fort Wayne.

5. Thomas Lincoln helped build Little Pigeon Baptist Church and later served as a trustee; the church was in a community called Little Pigeon Creek. Jonesboro did not yet exist by that name.

6. Joining "by letter" indicates that Thomas was already a member in good standing of an existing church. Although the Little Pigeon Church congregation formed in 1816, the Lincolns did not join that church until 1823, when it comprised forty-seven members. The Lincolns may have delayed joining Little Pigeon Church because their prior church in Kentucky had been part of a separatist Baptist sect.

7. Construction of Little Pigeon Church began in 1821, and the first meeting in the new church occurred in April 1822.

8. Traditionally, this "rule of three" refers to a way of solving proportions, what some today call "ratios," but Murr seems to use the phrase to instead refer to reading, writing, and arithmetic. See Lincoln, "To Jessie W. Fell," in *Collected Works of Abraham Lincoln*, ed. Basler et al., 3:511.

9. Murr refers to John G. Nicolay (1832–1901) and John Hay (1838–1905), Lincoln's personal secretary and assistant secretary, respectively, who authored a ten-volume biography titled *Abraham Lincoln: A History* (1890).

10. Lincoln's law partner, William Herndon (1818–1891), interviewed many of those who knew Lincoln best and published several biographies, including *Herndon's Lincoln* (1889). Ward Hill Lamon (1828–1893), frequently consulting Herndon's papers and research, published two books about Lincoln.

11. Although characterizing Thomas as "poor" is often accepted among historians, Thomas Lincoln's wealth has been a matter of debate. Historian Louis Warren notes that no family in the area of their Indiana home outranked the Lincolns socially, "and only the Gentrys excelled them economically" (Warren, *Lincoln's Youth*, 161). Thomas Lincoln held considerable land and livestock relative to his peers.

12. Because a fire at the Spencer County Courthouse in 1832 destroyed nearly all county records, even if Thomas Lincoln had broken the law, it is unlikely that government records documenting it survived.

13. This statement originates with Abraham Lincoln in his 1860 autobiography for John Scripps. (Lincoln, "Autobiography Written for John L. Scripps," 4:61–62).

14. "Milk sickness" is a name given to the illness resulting from poisoning of those who ingest milk or meat from a cow that fed on white snakeroot plant, which contains the poison tremetol. Thomas and Betsy Sparrow were aunt and uncle to Nancy, and Abe viewed them as surrogate grandparents. Levi Hall was a cousin to Nancy Hanks Lincoln.

15. The source of this quotation is unclear, although several historians refer to these illnesses, including Ida M. Tarbell. In a Decatur store in August 1830, the Lincolns purchased bark and whiskey tonic, a standard remedy for the ague involving fever and shivering (Tarbell, *In the Footsteps of the Lincolns*, 161). Dennis Hanks also noted they lost livestock to milk sickness shortly before the move from Indiana.

16. Abraham Lincoln's grandfather, Abraham Lincoln, was born in 1738 and died in May 1786 during a confrontation with Native Americans.

17. Thomas Lincoln witnessed the murder of his own father, also named Abraham. In spring 1786, while Abraham Lincoln the elder worked in his Kentucky field with his three sons, Native Americans attacked and shot him dead. Afterward, Native Americans were one of Thomas Lincoln's favorite subjects.

18. This quotation describing Thomas Lincoln comes from Abraham Lincoln, who also said Thomas "never did more in the way of writing than to bunglingly sign his own name" (Lincoln, "Autobiography Written for John L. Scripps," 4:65).

19. To put a "mark" typically means the person signing a document placed an "X" or some other symbol to indicate execution of an agreement or a contract. A person could, of course, sign his or her name.

20. Thomas Lincoln's flatboat trip to New Orleans occurred in early spring 1806. Lasting about sixty days, the trip involved transporting produce from West Point, Kentucky, to New Orleans. Any other flatboat trips by Thomas Lincoln lack firm historical evidence, although a distant relative named Augustus Chapman remembered Thomas making at least two flatboat trips. See "A. H. Chapman to William Herndon," in *Herndon's Informants*, ed. Wilson and Davis, 100.

21. In a sawpit, lumber is laid over a cross support and sawed with a long, two-handled saw by two men, one standing above the timber and the other below.

22. For more on Lincoln's 1844 return visit to Indiana, see Bartelt, "Aiding Mr. Clay."

23. The tanner referred to here is Shadrach Hall, whose son Wesley was a good friend of Abraham Lincoln's. The tannery was located near present-day Santa Claus, Indiana.

24. In 1816, Thomas Lincoln borrowed or rented a wagon from Francis Posey at Posey's Landing, located at Crooked Creek, about two and a half miles south of Troy, Indiana.

NANCY HANKS, MOTHER OF LINCOLN

THOMAS LINCOLN WAS THE LAST to marry of the five sons and daughters of Abraham and Bathsheba Lincoln. It appears that he never paid serious attention to the thought of marriage to any woman other than Sarah Bush and Nancy Hanks.

It is a matter of common knowledge that he originally wished very much to wed Sarah Bush, who subsequently did become his second wife. It is clear that Sarah Bush was Tom Lincoln's first choice.[1] This Elizabethtown lady was disposed to think "right well of Tommy Lincoln," but she preferred Daniel Johnston, Lincoln's rival for her hand. This marriage did not mar the friendship of Lincoln and Johnston, and certainly nothing subsequently occurred that lessened the neighborly regard and mutual esteem that Sarah Bush Johnston and Thomas Lincoln entertained each for the other.

A Kentucky tradition suggests that Tom Lincoln became interested in Nancy Hanks because of her deep religious devotion and regular attendance at various church services and, more particularly, her active interest in the camp meetings of that day.[2] It is probably true that the two did meet at some of these religious gatherings. The camp meeting as a religious institution—for such it became in time—had its rise in the general vicinity of where Thomas and Nancy resided.

The celebrated Cane Ridge Camp Meeting, which twenty thousand people allegedly attended, occurred during the summer of 1801.[3] Thomas Lincoln was at that time twenty-five years old and Nancy Hanks seventeen. Whether one or both of them attended this memorable assembly or whether neither was present—which is more probable—they at least heard a lot about this unusual event. Indeed, the words "Cane Ridge" and "Camp Meeting" were in the speech of Kentuckians in every nook and corner of the state and, for that matter, in other states as well.

The Presbyterians, Baptists, and Methodists were well represented in this new thing. After 1801, all of these religious denominations, for a time at least, held camp meetings. This new departure in religious worship remained in vogue during the remainder of the lives of both Thomas Lincoln and Nancy Hanks. It is therefore possible and even probable that Tom Lincoln and Nancy Hanks became interested in each other while attending these camp meetings. Both Thomas and Nancy were religiously inclined and were therefore regular attendees at various religious services. The frontier "hoedown" and church services were the main social activities during that period, unless rude sports such as horse racing, Saturday-afternoon wrestling, and fistfights were included. Women, however, were not in attendance at these gatherings.

There is no reliable account that either Tom Lincoln or Nancy Hanks frequented neighborhood dances. I know that one man in particular wrote later about Nancy Hanks being "the best dancer" and the "loudest shouter" in all that region. This man merely wished to capitalize on some of his made-to-order tales. It is possible that both Tom and Nancy attended some of these dances, but proof is wanting. This writer calls Nancy "the loudest shouter" and also "the best dancer," which suggests some sort of wild orgy, when in reality a camp meeting devotee in that was very different; if Nancy was indeed a camp meeting "shouter," she would not remain such for long if she became "the best dancer." The Methodist shout and amen heard around Kentucky were not pitched to the music of the fiddle in the hands of a whiskey-filled man of the world.

Since we know so little about Nancy Hanks during her early womanhood, there is no wonder that certain writers have relayed stories from time to time concerning her "shoutings and carryings on" at camp meetings. These irresponsible writers represent her as a typical frontier glamour girl, the observed of all observers, sought after by many. Yet these writers who defame the character of Tom Lincoln are obliged to agree that this "no account, lazy, improvident" lover won the hand of this backwoods beauty over all competitors!

Nancy Hanks was in her thirty-second year when she arrived in Indiana. It is quite true that marked changes can and often do occur in the lives of men and women in a very short while, but if Nancy Hanks was ever at any time during her girlhood and young womanhood the wild backwoods lady that she has been described as by these irresponsible writers, then she underwent marked and even revolutionary changes only a few years later. There were "hoedowns" in and about [Spencer County, Indiana], but this reputed "best dancer" in Kentucky never attended one of these.

Notwithstanding the fact that the cultural things were denied this dweller in the wilderness log cabin, Nancy Lincoln was possessed with a sweet disposition, quiet and reserved in her manner; she was exceedingly devout but was never loud spoken, and never once, so far as I could learn, did she disclose by word or deed the slightest kinship to the excesses so often found on the frontier.

—⚏—

But who and what manner of woman was Nancy Hanks who was destined to bring into the world a son whose fame gives him a place alongside that of Washington? All of the Lincoln students and inquirers are familiar with the long-continued discussion of the lineage of Lincoln's mother. Many conflicting claims from time to time have been made as to her forebears, some contending without the slightest reliable foundation that she was a Sparrow and not a Hanks;[4] others endeavoring to prove that she was a Hanks, but the daughter of Joseph Hanks Sr. and therefore a sister of William, Joseph Jr., Polly, and Betsy Hanks.[5] Still others insist that this woman was a Shipley.[6] This latter claim was made in spite of the president's own statement that his mother was of the Hanks family and, in addition to the president's statement, that the marriage license and the returns clearly show that her name was *Nancy Hanks*. The argument that Lincoln's mother was a Shipley is as far-fetched as could possibly be.

The Hitchcock contention—which was a Hanks effort—freely allowed that Nancy was a Hanks, but in attempting to establish her kinship claimed that the will of Joseph Hanks Sr.—a document discovered by Mrs. Hitchcock at Bardstown, Kentucky— settled the matter for all time to come as to Nancy's identity and kinship to the Hanks tribe. In his will Joseph Hanks bequeathed a cow or heifer to each of his daughters, Polly, Betsy, and Nancy. Specifically, Nancy Hanks was willed a certain speckled or pied heifer. The announcement of this discovery for a time created a near sensation, and since it specifically mentioned Joseph Hanks's daughter Nancy, there was, in consequence, a widespread belief that the legitimacy of the birth of the president's mother was definitely set at rest. Even Miss Ida Tarbell gave this discovery the stamp of her approval.

Joseph Hanks did indeed have a daughter named Nancy, but she was not the mother of Lincoln. She was the unwed mother of Dennis Hanks, or as he is sometimes spoken of, Dennis Friend. This Nancy Hanks subsequently married Levi Hall, the father of William Hall, who resided at a later day at Jonesboro and still later was a citizen of Illinois.

In 1818, the year in which Nancy Hanks Lincoln died, Levi Hall and his wife, Nancy Hanks Hall, reached Indiana. This Nancy Hanks, daughter of Joseph Hanks, who had been willed the "pied heifer" and later married Levi Hall, placed her son Dennis in the home of her sister Betsy Hanks Sparrow, who was then and ever afterward childless.

I deem it proper just here, in order to have the record clear, to state that Betsy Sparrow and her husband, Thomas Sparrow, together with this same Dennis Hanks or Dennis Friend, son of Nancy Hanks Hall, reached Indiana in 1817. The Lincolns, having vacated their half-faced camp and moved into their story-and-a-half cabin nearby, now turned the abandoned, half-faced camp over to the Sparrows, who lived there until their death in 1818, the year that Lincoln's mother died.

Visitors to the grave of Lincoln's mother must understand that both Betsy Sparrow and Thomas Sparrow were buried beside the grave of Nancy Hanks—Betsy placed immediately to the north of the president's mother and Thomas to the north of his wife. Additionally, Levi Hall and his wife, Nancy Hanks Hall, were buried at the foot of the grave of Lincoln's mother; thus there are five graves instead of one—but visitors see no evidence of other graves save that of Nancy Hanks, the mother of the president.[7]

There were those who insisted that Lucey Hanks, the mother of Nancy Hanks, was the wife of an unknown son of Joseph Hanks Sr., and therefore Lincoln's mother was in fact not a sister of William, Joseph Jr., Nancy, Polly, and Betsy, but a sister-in-law of the children of Joseph Hanks Sr.

It will be seen that every possible device was exhausted in order to get around the illegitimacy of Lincoln's mother. Every effort ended in failure.[8]

There appears to be confusion in the minds of many concerning the relationship or kinship of the Hanks family, not only in the case of Lincoln's mother but others as well. This is only natural and to be expected, due to the many intermarriages of the Hankses, Halls, Sparrows, Johnstons, and Lincolns. However, other than the identity of the unknown father of Nancy Hanks, the relationship or family tree appears to be reasonably clear.

As has been stated, Betsy Hanks married Thomas Sparrow. They remained childless, and, as is not infrequently true in such homes, Betsy became a real mother to her sister Nancy's son Dennis, who always addressed her as "mother." This was natural since Betsy reared him from infancy. Then, too, when Lucey Hanks left her father's roof tree and entered upon her questionable career, she thus left her daughter Nancy, the president's mother, in the care and keeping of Betsy and Betsy's mother, and when Betsy established a home of her own, she took Nancy Hanks with her and thus in a very large way reared the president's mother.[9] Later, Nancy did what many another girl or young woman in those days and since have done—namely, sought and found labor in other homes. And when her marriage day arrived, we find her in the Berry home and not in the Sparrow cabin.[10] Such things have frequently occurred.

Concerning the marriage of Nancy Hanks—she who had been willed the "pied heifer"—to Levi Hall, we thus perceive the confusion, since William Hall the son later married a daughter of Sarah Bush Lincoln, the second wife of Thomas Lincoln. Dennis Hanks, who was a half brother of William Hall, married the other daughter of Sarah Bush Lincoln. These half brothers also became brothers-in-law.

In order to clear the thinking somewhat in this tangle of intermarriages, note that when the Lincolns left Indiana in 1830 for the prairies of Illinois, there were thirteen persons in that emigrant train. There were the Lincolns (Thomas and Sarah Bush Lincoln, as well as Abe), Dennis Hanks and wife [Abraham Lincoln's stepsister Elizabeth] and their four children, and William [Squire] Hall and wife [Abraham Lincoln's stepsister Matilda] with their two children.

Joseph Hanks Sr. originally resided at no great distance from York-town, Virginia, where General Washington's army prosecuted the famous siege at that place, resulting in the surrender of Lord Corn-wallis's army, thus making for the close of the American Revolution.

Lucey Hanks, the oldest child of Joseph Hanks Sr., like many others of that region, frequented the dances staged in the rear of Washington's army. These dances, if not primarily for the enter-tainment of the patriot army, at least had many soldiers attend. In the absence of any definite information concerning Lucey Hanks's conduct and character during this period when she was eighteen, this much is established beyond dispute: a short while after her presence at these dances she became pregnant while unwed.

Whether this condition of Joseph Hanks's daughter was in part or wholly responsible for his departure from that section of Virginia, we must leave to conjecture. In any event, about this time Joseph Hanks did immigrate to a place in what is now West Virginia, where Lucey gave birth to a baby girl, whom she named Nancy. This daughter was destined to become the mother of the president.

While Nancy was yet a babe, the entire family immigrated to Kentucky. We have no knowledge whatsoever as to the rea-sons for this immigration. It is a matter of record that many other families in Virginia sought homes in Kentucky. Lucey's daughter Nancy was born in February 1784, and it is possible and even probable, as has been suggested by well-informed Lincoln biog-raphers, that the birth of Lucey's child was in part responsible for this change of residence.

Soon after the family reached Kentucky, Lucey's conduct was such that it gave her an unsavory reputation. She had left her father's home, leaving her child in the care of her mother and her sisters. After spending some time in towns, presumably as a servant in homes, she reached the old town of Harrodsburg. It was not long before her soiled character led to a legal charge of fornication.[11] This was and is still a matter of public record at that place. What might have been the result of these grand jury findings must be left to the realm of conjecture. The indictment was not acted on by the authorities, due to Lucey's marriage on 3 April 1791 to Henry Sparrow, a Yorktown soldier in Washington's army and a brother of Thomas Sparrow, who, it will be remembered, married Lucey's sister Betsy on 7 October 1796.

No one ever claimed that Henry Sparrow knew or met Lucey Hanks while the two were residents of Virginia. They did not become acquainted until they became citizens of Kentucky. And the claim made by certain writers, based on statements made by relatives of Lucey, that Nancy Hanks was a Sparrow becomes valueless if Henry Sparrow was the father of Nancy.

I never found a hint or intimation whatever on the part of the Lincoln or any of the Hanks families that Lucey ever saw her daughter Nancy after the mother's marriage to Henry Sparrow, which was when Nancy was seven years old. There was no mention of Lucey ever paying a visit to any of the homes of her sisters or brothers after her marriage. I am aware that William Barton's investigations revealed the tradition of Lucey visiting her father's home to mark the death and funeral of her father, and on her return to her own home, she took her daughter Nancy Hanks with her, where she spent some years.[12]

Barton's well-known reputation as a Lincoln historian, together with his advantages far beyond any like them in the Kentucky field, cause me to greatly hesitate to call in question the correctness of his findings in this instance, but I am obliged to express doubt that Nancy Hanks was ever at any time in the home of Henry Sparrow and his wife, Lucey. My doubt is based on my failure to find anything in Indiana so much as intimating any sort of interest by Lucey toward her daughter Nancy after her marriage to Henry Sparrow and for that matter somewhile prior to her marriage. I think it was highly improbable that Nancy Hanks ever saw her mother to know her as such. If indeed she possessed a memory of her mother at all, it was but a child's memory.

As is well known, Nancy Hanks was in her twenty-third year at the time of her marriage to Thomas Lincoln. No one knows when she came to understand who her mother really was. She was probably told of this together with other matters connected with her birth some time before her marriage to Thomas Lincoln. This much is unmistakably true—Nancy Hanks had been informed of the unsavory reputation of her mother as well as the fact that she herself was born out of wedlock.

Following Lucey's marriage, as Barton informs us, she became the mother of eight sons and daughters. Two of her sons became Christian ministers. It is altogether proper to here state that Lucey's reputation and character after her marriage were never called in question.

—∞—

Nancy Hanks might be eulogized beyond any other woman in American history—except Martha Washington—yet by far this marked partiality and consequent praise of her has in the main been confined to the realm of fancy and imagination and not based on historical facts.

We have paintings of Martha Washington and are therefore familiar with her form and features. Her blood and lineage, as well as the events of her everyday life, have been described and discussed by numerous writers. Her stature and speech, her likes and dislikes, her points of strength as well as certain little weaknesses have thus made her a familiar character to all. In short, the country's unusual interest in the life and remarkable career of our First Lady has been fully satisfied.

The exact opposite of all this is true for Nancy Hanks. The general public possesses exceedingly meager knowledge concerning the mother of Lincoln. No painting of the president's mother was ever made, nor was such a thing ever contemplated. Aside from a very brief statement made by her cousin John Hanks, as well as a characteristic statement or two by Dennis Hanks, we have nothing else. William Herndon could have interviewed those who possessed knowledge of the president's mother but did not do so.

It is true that her son did take occasion some two or three times to speak of his mother, but he did not attempt a description of her personal appearance.

John Hanks, who, it is claimed, was truthful and in every way reliable, stated, as revealed by Herndon, that his cousin "was tall; had brown hair, small grey eyes, dark face, and weighed about one hundred and thirty pounds."[13] It has always been supposed that John Hanks was describing Nancy Hanks as she appeared on her wedding day or about that time.

But John Hanks was certainly not present at Nancy's marriage on 12 June 1806, and if he had been present, he would not have been capable of giving us a satisfactory description of Lincoln's mother, since he was at that time only four years of age. Since John Hanks attempted a description of his cousin, it would be unjust to doubt his purported statement. But note that Herndon does not elect to quote John Hanks's exact wording. Certainly the language is not that of John Hanks but rather is the wording and language of William Herndon. The John Hanks statement is far more Herndon than it is John Hanks, but I do not doubt that Mr. Herndon's editing embodies the substance of Hanks's description of the personal appearance of his cousin. We do not know where or when John Hanks saw Nancy Hanks, nor do we know yet how often. Dr. Louis Warren doubted whether John Hanks ever had an occasion to see and remember Lincoln's mother, but the statement made to Herndon possesses all of the usual details that an eyewitness would be expected to notice. John Hanks must have known his cousin Nancy Hanks.

Herndon quotes Dennis Hanks rather freely in the matter. Dennis Hanks was undoubtedly in a position to give a satisfactory description of his cousin. Nancy did spend some while in the home of Thomas Sparrow and Betsy Hanks Sparrow, and since that was the only home that Dennis ever knew as a boy and young man until he was eighteen, he therefore remembered Nancy as a young lady in her later teens. He was daily in her presence in Indiana, from midsummer of 1817 to the death of Lincoln's mother in the fall of 1818. With certainty Dennis Hanks was in a position to describe the appearance of Nancy Hanks.

On one occasion Dennis states that Nancy had blue eyes, and on yet another occasion he speaks of her eyes as brown. However, he mentions the fact that Nancy was tall with a dark face and had brown hair. This latter statement is in keeping with the description given by John Hanks. The habit of Dennis to improvise on occasions comes to the fore when he exclaims: "Nancy wus as purty an' smart as you'd find 'em anywhere."

In Herndon's biography of the president, he says: "At the time of her marriage to Thomas Lincoln, Nancy was in her 23rd year. She was above the ordinary height in stature, weighed about 130 pounds, was slenderly built, and had much the appearance of one inclined to consumption [tuberculosis]. Her skin was dark; her hair brown; eyes gray and small; forehead prominent, face sharp and angular with a marked expression of melancholy which fixed itself in the memory of all who ever saw or knew her. Though her life was clouded by a spirit of sadness, she was in disposition amiable and generally cheerful."[14] This is well told, and the Lincoln world is indebted to Herndon.

In addition to the foregoing, Herndon quotes the president as saying: "She [his mother] was highly intellectual by nature and a strong memory; acute judgment and was cool and heroic."[15] The phrasing is Herndon's and not Lincoln's, but I do not doubt this voices the president's sentiments.

—⁂—

The fanciful dramatization by Ward Hill Lamon of Nancy Hanks is largely valueless. Lamon, it will be recalled, obtained the whole of his knowledge concerning the president's mother by way of

Herndon's manuscript.[16] Lamon's editing does not in any sense equal that of William Herndon's.

In Josiah Gilbert Holland's biography of the president, he appears to see Nancy Hanks from afar.[17] It is apparent that Holland merely appropriated some hearsay remarks without going to the trouble to verify them—a thing that he could have done. Holland's discussion of Nancy Hanks is quite brief. His unknown informant was in error on at least two counts. First, Nancy Hanks was tall and therefore much beyond Holland's statement of her stature—"five feet and five inches." Second, Holland speaks of her "pale face." The face of Lincoln's mother was not pale, nor yet white in the usual sense and meaning of that word. Her face was quite dark.[18]

Most of our Lincoln historians described the face and form of the president's mother, but in nearly every instance they used Herndon's findings by way of John and Dennis Hanks.

Reliable evidence concerning the personal appearance of Nancy Hanks may be reduced to a paragraph or two. I have been impressed with the belief that it is in my power, due to my long and extensive investigations, to make some worthwhile contribution in this matter.

Although possessing no ability as an artist, if I were capable of wielding the brush, I feel that I could, with my knowledge of the face, features, and form of this elect lady, place upon canvas a very good likeness of her. Although such an undertaking is not possible for me, it might be possible for others who possess this gift to undertake the enviable task, after a careful and painstaking perusal of Herndon's statements by John and Dennis Hanks, as well as a review of my own description of this woman.

My contribution in this matter embodies everything that was available from whatever source. I have made painstaking and selective drafts on history and personal testimony. I am firmly convinced that my description of Nancy Hanks is correct. The fact that I was in and out of the [Spencer County] community for a full quarter of a century, meeting those who frequented the Lincoln cabin and who thus personally knew Nancy Hanks, enabled me to reach a correct estimate of not only the president as a boy and man but at the same time many things of interest concerning both Thomas Lincoln and Nancy Hanks.

The hurried visitations made by Lincoln writers and lecturers usually proved more or less valueless and unsatisfactory. The old-time Hoosier, as a general rule, was not an easy subject for an interview. Often a scene was created when some down East Yankey breezed in and proceeded to obtain an interview. Some of these old-timers would shut up like a clam. If the visitor possessed preconceived notions concerning the president or his father and mother, this led to regrettable argument. I recall the visit of one Lincoln historian who later offered to the public one of the leading biographies of the president, and not only was there a regrettable scene, but this writer also went away in disgust, having interviewed just one Lincoln associate—and the investigator spent only one night in Spencer County! Unfortunately, some of the inquirers were led to think quite unfavorably of these old-timers. However, if, as was sometimes true of some of them, they proceeded on the theory that this old Hoosier was an ignoramus, they were rudely awakened. I remember one old-timer who naively remarked to me: "There is about as much difference in some folks as anybody and now and then a right smart more," and again, in characterizing some such a man as Dennis Hanks: "I wouldn't believe him on oath even if I knew he was telling the truth." The average old Hoosier was exceedingly resourceful in defending himself.

The fact that Nancy Hanks has long since been dead would ordinarily preclude the possibility of anyone at this late day making any reliable additional contribution concerning her personal appearance. But because my conviction is sufficiently grounded in certainty, I venture to assert that my description of her is measurably correct.

The Lincoln inquirers almost solely depend on the description of Nancy Hanks by John Hanks. Since he was only four when she was married at twenty-three, his memory of his cousin must have been of a somewhat later date than June 1806. If he saw her when the Lincolns left Kentucky for Indiana in 1816, then she was thirty-two and he was fourteen. Nevertheless, I think his description of her was circumstantial and exact. Since no affliction overtook her until a few hours preceding her death, she had not changed after reaching Indiana. Nancy Hanks died on 5 October 1818.

I can best describe the appearance of Nancy Hanks with a comparison to a beardless likeness of the president. Lincoln was in his fifty-second year when he began growing a beard. The general public quite naturally thinks of him as he appeared in the White House, but the citizens of Illinois and Indiana—at least large numbers of them—think of him as smooth shaven. That is my idea of Lincoln.

In most respects the mother's face and features were similar to those of her son; however, in certain things, which I shall point out, there were marked departures. While the president possessed certain distinguishing mental and physical traits characterizing the Lincolns, the contour or general outline of his face was a replica of the face of Nancy Hanks, but with certain highly important and even pronounced departures.

As is well known, the president's head was rather small in proportion to his other bodily measurements. The mother's head, on the contrary, was quite large—especially for a woman.

The son had the usual coarse black-brown hair of the Lincolns, wherever found back through the generations. I knew a member of the older Lincolns, and many of the younger generation as well, and every one of them had coarse black hair, usually unruly. When Lincoln was nominated for the presidency in the Wigwam at Chicago, the only available picture of him was that now-familiar likeness in which his hair was in wild confusion. Even the Chicago newsboys realized that the presidential nominee was not at his best—and accordingly went about crying their wares: "Read all about Abe Lincoln's nomination. He'll look better when he gets his hair combed."[19]

The mother's hair was a soft brown, and the word *dark* must be associated with the word *brown*. She had a heavy head of hair. This was parted centrally in the forehead after the fashion of that period, and in keeping with the prevailing custom, it was combed back on either side and then drawn into a knot and held in place by a large high-backed tuck or horn comb. The ears were not covered, and there were no curls and no bangs.

The forehead of the president disclosed so plainly in the Chicago photograph of 1860 was what we usually speak of as a retreating one, but in his case this sloping or retreating was not especially pronounced. There was no sort of resemblance between the mother's forehead and that of her son. Her forehead was quite broad and high and devoid of lines or wrinkles—it was quite smooth. (I am describing Nancy Hanks as she appeared from her thirty-second year to her thirty-fifth year.) The forehead of Lincoln's mother possessed no suggestion whatsoever of the retreating or sloping kind but, on the contrary, arose almost but not quite perpendicularly, a very slight suggestion of a slope.

The brows of Nancy Hanks were heavy and bony, with small gray-blue or blue-gray eyes—depending on the lighting. Her eyes were deep-seated or what may be called hidden eyes, but they were keen and bright.

Readers who are well informed know that the president's eyes were likewise small, with the gray color predominating, but at times there were traces of a blue.

The mother's cheekbones were high, with the lower portion of the face falling away into hollows on either side of the large but quite regularly formed nose. The mouth was large, but she had no pendent lower lip as did the son, and the chin was firm and strong.

The mother's ears were large and stood out from the head much like the ears of the president. The neck of Nancy Hanks was long

and small, and since her shoulders fell away rapidly, this served
to accentuate the length of the neck.

I have known Lincolns who were representative of four generations, but there was not a tall one among them; however, one
first cousin of the president greatly resembled the son of Nancy
Hanks, especially in face and build, although his stature did not
compare with that of the president. I have been told that some
sons of Mordecai, the uncle of the president, were quite tall. As
noted previously, the president's father, Thomas Lincoln, was a
tall man for a Lincoln—five feet and slightly over nine and a half
inches in stature, and his weight was in the neighborhood of two
hundred pounds, usually a bit less.

There was almost nothing in the president's face, features,
build, and stature that reminded one of his father, but he did
inherit certain Lincoln traits—the president's bodily structure
or build—with his angularity observed in his face, his long
limbs, and his build; otherwise he was a constant reminder of
his mother.

Nancy Hanks was a tall woman, somewhat above average. I did
not ascertain any measurements indicating her stature or measurements, but her height was not far from that of her husband's
stature—five feet and a little short of ten inches—perhaps she
was five feet and nine inches, or slightly more.

Lincoln's mother was exceedingly slender or what was known
or spoken of on the frontier as "spare made." Her limbs were long;
her chest sunken, giving the impression of possible speedy de-
cline, although she was never a victim of tuberculosis or what was
in that day called consumption.

It is well known that the president was inclined toward consumption. Herndon specifically alludes to this tendency, which
asserted itself all along, but Lincoln was never at any time the
victim of consumption. However, he perceived signs of this, and
that fact concerned him, both during his young manhood in Indiana and later in life.

Abraham Lincoln considered becoming a blacksmith in part due to his thought of combatting this consumptive tendency. He often assisted John Baldwin, the Jonesboro blacksmith, and did in fact find himself able to preside over the anvil, and thus he came perilously near becoming a frontier blacksmith. He considered this again after he reached New Salem, Illinois. His thought was that this trade would place him in the open and serve to maintain bodily strength.

As has been stated, both John and Dennis Hanks direct attention to the dark face of Lincoln's mother. If, as has been alleged, John Hanks in particular was describing the appearance of Nancy Hanks at about the time of her marriage, then the dark face was in evidence when she was but little beyond her girlhood. She certainly had a dark face while a resident of Indiana. She may have had a dark face all through her girlhood and perhaps during her childhood.[20] The president's face was also quite dark. Thus this "olive complexion," as some writers have it, characterized both mother and son.

Nancy Hanks was a quiet body, soft spoken, gentle, and kind. Her face in repose was exceedingly sad. Indeed, this was her usual appearance. However, her features would light up in conversation, and as is not infrequently true of the melancholy ones, she appreciated humor.

Lincoln had a sad face as a general rule, and it was his customary appearance right along. His deep sense of humor quickly changed all of this. His unusual gift in relating or acting certain parts—especially mimicking a given character—blotted out the usual sadness. Nancy Hanks was not a storyteller as such, and so she was prevented in overcoming her melancholy. The lion's share of the president's humor was a Lincoln contribution rather than a Hanks offering to him. Tom Lincoln not only had a generous assortment of stories; he also excelled in the fine art of telling these. The Lincolns throughout the generations have been more or less given to humor, and many of them could tell a story quite well.

The president, as reported by Herndon, spoke of his mother's coolness and her heroic spirit. Nancy Hanks possessed poise and met difficulties and problems cool and collected. There was never any argument or quarreling in that Lincoln cabin. When the husband expressed disapproval of Abe's constant reading, the mother had her way about it.

Tom Lincoln was almost the exact opposite of his wife in many ways. He was loud and boisterous. He was confident that something would turn up. He was a man of great expectations, but judged by his performance, his otherwise admirable optimism became in fact pessimism. Nancy Hanks, on the contrary, was a sane and sensible realist, but strangely she was a religious mystic. The two things are not antagonistic or incompatible. From Saint John the Divine to John Wesley, Loyola, Fletcher of Madley, the Venerable Bede, and many others, mystics wrestled with realities but grounded their faith in a Higher Law. This unlettered wilderness woman, with no sort of kinship with Oxford dons, nevertheless belonged to these notables by reason of her mysticism.

Tom Lincoln was a churchman, and his character gave him good standing. But if his son's training had been in his care and keeping instead of the mother of Lincoln, the world might have had only another blacksmith. Fortunately, this frontier woman who stamped her melancholy on his very being; who imprinted her own face and features indelibly on him; who managed in ways that only mothers can fully understand to impart her own faith to him and thus deeply imbedded in his soul the elemental things belonging to mysticism, Nancy Hanks bound her son as with hooks of steel to the teachings of the Decalogue and the Golden Rule and, having done her work so well, made possible not only one of the greatest men among the mightiest, but the mightiest man among the greatest in all time.

Curiously, Sarah Lincoln, the president's sister, had no dark face, and that face was a replica of the face of her father. Her eyes were brown, as were those of her father. She was lively, humorous, optimistic, with no melancholy whatsoever. She was her father's favorite.

Abe was a mother's boy. He and Sarah were greatly endeared to one another. She married Aaron Grigsby when nineteen and died in her twenty-first year, leaving only Abe, since Thomas, the third child of Thomas Lincoln and Nancy Hanks, died early and was buried in Kentucky. With home ties severed, since Abe and his father never got on well, he was destined to have the best of mothering by his stepmother, Sarah Bush Lincoln.

NOTES

1. Historian Louis Warren disputes this assertion and notes: "The tradition that Thomas Lincoln and [Sarah] Bush had been sweethearts before either was married seems most unlikely because of the difference in their ages" (Warren, *Lincoln's Youth*, 160).

2. A Kentucky woman who "was well acquainted with Nancy Hanks" alleged that Thomas and Nancy's courtship "became so ardent that Thomas and Nancy would make long trips together to camp meetings and such places." This Kentucky woman "informed Thomas that she disapproved of the long nocturnal absences of Nancy and him and considered such conduct as unbecoming to unmarried people" (Otis M. Mather, "Nancy Hanks Lincoln," talk given 13 July 1930 in Lincoln City, IN, pp. 5–6, Mather Papers, Filson Society, Louisville, KY).

3. The Cane Ridge Camp Meeting in northeastern Kentucky was one of the largest and most famous camp meetings of the Second Great Awakening.

4. Lucey Hanks, Nancy's mother, likely lived (unwed) for some period with Henry Sparrow, a Revolutionary War veteran. This controversial arrangement, or the second out-of-wedlock pregnancy, caused a Mercer County grand jury to indict Lucey on 24 November 1789 for "fornication." The couple formally married the following year on 3 April 1791. Lucey and Henry Sparrow resided together in Mercer County the rest of their lives and had eight children together from about 1790 through 1809.

5. Caroline Hanks Hitchcock, a member of the Hanks family herself, became the most prominent advocate of the notion that Nancy Hanks was born to legitimate parents. At the behest of Lincoln historian Ida Tarbell, Hitchcock published her findings in 1899 in a small book titled *Nancy Hanks*.

6. The Shipley theory's most prominent advocate was Louis A. Warren, a well-known scholar on Lincoln's youth and former director of the

Louis A. Warren Lincoln Library Museum in Fort Wayne, Indiana. Other historians endorsing this theory include Harold and Ernestine Briggs, Raymond Bell, and Christopher Child.

7. A woman named Nancy Rusher Brooner (1782–1818) also died about this time and is buried to the south of Nancy Hanks Lincoln.

8. Over the years, each of the various theories acquired support until a mitochondrial DNA study published in 2015 ended the century-old debate and proved that Lucey Hanks Sparrow was a daughter of Ann Lee Hanks and not, as Warren believed, a descendant of the Shipleys. Nearly all Lincoln historians now agree that Lucey Hanks was Nancy's mother and that Lucey was therefore Abe's grandmother (Shuda, "DNA Study"). Genealogist Suzanne Hallstrom started the Nancy Hanks Lincoln DNA study and created a website dedicated to her research and findings at GeneticLincoln. com. Because Nancy Hanks has no living descendants, to evaluate the Barton/Verduin theory, the DNA test examined matrilineal descendants of Elizabeth Hanks Sparrow (sister of Lucey Hanks Sparrow), Sarah Hanks (full sister of Nancy Hanks Lincoln), and two of Nancy and Sarah's half sisters, Margaret Sparrow Ingram and Lucinda Sparrow Richardson. To evaluate the Shipley theory, the DNA test examined matrilineal descendants of two of the Shipley sisters, Naomi and Rachel, the presumed sisters of Lucey.

9. After Nancy moved in with Thomas and Elizabeth Sparrow, the couple became Nancy's de facto parents. Elizabeth, known as "Betsy," acted as Nancy's mother, so Abraham referred to her as Granny; Thomas and Betsy were Abe's maternal relatives he knew best. History offers few additional clues about the Sparrows' appearance or character, but they reared Nancy Hanks as their own and provided shelter, love, and education.

10. Nancy may have lived briefly with Richard Berry and his wife, Polly Ewing Berry, friends of Thomas Lincoln and possible cousins to Nancy.

11. A Mercer County, Kentucky, grand jury indicted Lucey Hanks on 24 November 1789 for "fornication."

12. William Barton, a Congregational Church minister from Illinois, left the pulpit and moved to Massachusetts, where he grew enamored with all things Lincoln. After writing a book on Lincoln's paternity, Barton traveled to Kentucky, where he befriended a budding Lincoln historian named Louis Warren. Barton believed Lucey Hanks was Nancy Hanks's mother and had been disinherited because of bad behavior. Also, Barton found Lucey's certificate of age and consent to marry Henry Sparrow in 1790. He published his findings in the two-volume *Life of Abraham Lincoln* in 1925 and in *Lineage of Lincoln* in 1929.

13. This description used by Herndon appears to originate in a letter from John Hanks to Jesse W. Weik, 12 June 1887 (Wilson and Davis, eds., *Herndon's Informants*, 615). Murr likely had no access to these letters.

14. Herndon and Weik, eds., *Abraham Lincoln*, 10.

15. Herndon and Weik, eds., *Herndon's Lincoln*, 13.

16. Ward Hill Lamon (1828–1893), a friend and bodyguard of Abraham Lincoln, published two books about Lincoln. His more famous *Life of Abraham Lincoln* was ghostwritten by Chauncy Black and drew on Herndon's research. It received substantial criticism for questioning Lincoln's Christian faith and suggesting Lincoln was born illegitimate.

17. After Lincoln's assassination in April 1865, newspaper editor Josiah Gilbert Holland traveled to Illinois to interview those who knew Lincoln before his election. In 1866, Holland published the earliest full biography of Lincoln as *Holland's Life of Abraham Lincoln*.

18. Josiah Holland's full quotation on Nancy's height and complexion reads, "Lincoln, the mother, was evidently a woman out of place among those primitive surroundings. She was five feet, five inches high, a slender, pale, sad and sensitive woman, with much in her nature that was truly heroic, and much that shrank from the rude life around her." Holland, *Life of Abraham Lincoln*, 23. In fairness to Holland, other informants described Nancy Hanks Lincoln as pale as well; frankly, we do not know her complexion definitively.

19. In this quotation, Murr alludes to a story by Lincoln as recorded by Assistant Secretary of War Albert P. Chandler. A write-up in *Harper's Monthly* quoted Chandler recounting an incident he heard from Lincoln: "I departed and did not think of pictures again until that evening I was gratified and flattered at the cry of newsboys who had gone to vending the pictures: 'Ere's yer last picter of Old Abe! He'll look better when he gets his hair combed.'" Chandler in *Harper's Monthly* 32 (February 1866): 405. In a different version of the story Chandler himself wrote later, Lincoln stated the incident occurred prior to his nomination, rather than after, but contrary to Chandler's story, Lincoln was not in Chicago either time. Colonel Le Grand Cannon recounted a similar story he heard from Lincoln but stated it occurred in Springfield. The photograph Lincoln references was taken in 1857 and was used throughout the presidential campaign. In at least one letter Lincoln referred to the "disordered condition of the hair." Fehrenbacher, *Recollected Words of Abraham Lincoln*, 92.

20. Herndon spoke with several Indiana residents who described Nancy Hanks Lincoln as light skinned. Murr's description of her is in no way conclusive.

THREE

—ᴍ—

BIRTH OF ABRAHAM LINCOLN

HAD SOME NEW WORLD SEER possessing prophetic insight and power announced at high noon on Sunday, the twelfth day of February 1809, that a son named Abraham Lincoln had been born that morning to Thomas Lincoln and Nancy Hanks, it would have meant little more to many than the announcement of the birth of a slave child in that county of Hardin in Kentucky where whites and blacks were about numerically equal.[1]

But if that New World prophet with a seer's vision far into the future had proclaimed far and wide that the wilderness babe was destined to become the great Leader of the Nation, in a four-year bloody war that was to determine whether that nation was to long endure, that seer would not have been regarded as a visionary. But if this prophet with a strange certainty had announced in a voice sufficiently loud enough to be heard by all of the inhabitants of the land that this newly born wilderness son would, in a half century hence, issue the Emancipation Proclamation as a military necessity and invoke the "gracious favor of Almighty God" and ask for the "considerate judgment of mankind," thus announcing the freedom of four million slaves, both North and South would have regarded this seer either as an imposter or a madman. But Time, that greatest of all historians, would fulfill that prophecy.

The story of this wilderness-born son of Thomas Lincoln and Nancy Hanks, with his rise to fame and power, has no parallel in the Old World, and only some two or three instances in American history approach this. Without a name and even the right to have a name; born on a level with a dog's nose and a cow's horn; unschooled; with no family background other than that of undistinguished or second families; homely, uncouth, and ungainly; and then by and by becoming the occupant of the White House and the ruler of a great nation, his life therefore excites both admiration and wonder, and strangely his unexampled fame still rises.

Lincoln did not write or speak in glorified ways about the place of his birth. Indeed, Lincoln scarcely had a memory of his birthplace. From June the first, 1861, to April 1865, he could not have visited his birthplace without risking his life.

Millions of the followers of the Nazarene each Christmas season make much of the scenes of the nativity at Bethlehem. There is, on the whole, comparatively little interest from the public in the birthplace of Washington. The major interest in the Father of our Country appears to be confined to Mount Vernon, where he long resided and where he died and where he lies buried. The same thing is substantially true concerning all of our other presidents—save Lincoln.

In Lincoln's case, there is almost equal interest in his birthplace and the place where his ashes repose—Springfield, Illinois. We of course do not overlook the noteworthy fact peculiar to Washington, Jefferson, and Lincoln that our citizens visit pretentious monuments erected to these great men in the nation's capital. But the birthplace of Lincoln continues to claim universal interest and that beyond all others.

The fact that Lincoln was born in a one-room log cabin with marked evidence of poverty is likely responsible, in part, for this unusual interest. Writers and speakers from time to time compared Lincoln's nativity to that of our Savior—at least, mention is made of the log cabin with its dirt floor in comparison to the stable and the manger cradle of Jesus.

We must not overlook the fact that a number of our presidents were born in log cabins. Among these were Andrew Jackson, Andrew Johnson, James A. Garfield, and U. S. Grant, but the fact that Lincoln wrestled with poverty throughout the whole of his formative years and on down to his later manhood has made for a widespread feeling that beyond all others Lincoln in particular belonged to the common people or, as he himself was accustomed to call them, the plain people.

As has been true of others, Lincoln's public life and labors were far removed from the spot where he was born, but this did not and does not lessen the interest in that little log cabin, which was preserved at least in part and sacredly guarded by the national government.[2]

Perhaps no single year during the past two and a half centuries, and for that matter through the whole of the past, gave to the world so many distinguished men as did the year 1809. In statesmanship there was William Ewart Gladstone and Hannibal Hamlin; in literature, Oliver Wendell Holmes, Edgar Allan Poe, and Alfred Lord Tennyson; in invention, Cyrus Hall McCormick; and in ecclesiastical statesmanship, Pope Leo XIII. Then there was Charles Darwin, and the Fowler brothers, who popularized phrenology; Kit Carson, who was destined to occupy a large place in opening up the vast empire west of the Mississippi; and in this group of notables, Lincoln occupies a commanding place. The list may be extended so as to include a half dozen more.

All of these notables save Kit Carson possessed enviable educational advantages over Lincoln. In substantially every instance, all of these men were privileged to gain a running start in life while comparatively young. Lincoln was nearing fifty before he gained promising recognition.

Some of the Lincoln biographers introduced unfounded romance, as well as certain unreliable purported facts, concerning the birth of the president. Some of the writers introduce some-one locals called "an old granny woman," who is represented as a frontier midwife who brought Lincoln into the world. One of the writers identifies this old woman as Peggy Walters, a neighbor of the Lincolns. This Peggy Walters stated in interviews in later years, when she was in fact at that time an elderly lady, that she was present on the occasion of Lincoln's birth. Her own state-ment and her years show conclusively that if she was present at all she was then a young lady and not at all "an old granny woman."[3]

I interviewed a lady in 1901 who was born in 1830 near the Lin-coln cabin. This lady claimed that her grandmother, whom she well remembered, was present in that Lincoln cabin on 12 Febru-ary 1809, when Lincoln was born. My informant was a lady of good standing and character. I was her pastor for some years and thus knew her quite well. This lady reviewed a number of state-ments made from time to time by her grandmother concerning circumstances connected with the birth of Lincoln. She described the evidence of poverty—the rude bedstead, the one-room log cabin—the bearskin placed on the bed by Tom Lincoln, and such other things that doubtless characterized that scene. Whether this reputed grandmother of my informant was indeed present on that notable occasion or not, I am not at liberty to say, but one thing is clear beyond dispute—no physician was present. It is reasonable to suppose that someone other than Tom Lincoln and Abe's two-year-old sister, Sarah, were there when Abe was born.

If we are to accept Dennis Hanks's story of the event—and I see no reason why we should have occasion to question this—we are quite certain that Betsey Sparrow did not arrive at the Lincoln cabin until after the birth had occurred. Thomas and Betsey Spar-row resided near the Lincolns and, according to Dennis Hanks and Tom Lincoln, came to the Sparrow cabin with the news of Abe's birth and requested Betsey to hasten to Nancy. However, boy-like Dennis Hanks, who was in his tenth year, cut out for the Lincoln cabin to see his new cousin before Tom Lincoln and

Betsey began their journey. Betsey responded to this appeal and remained in the Lincoln cabin for some days, journeying back and forth between her home and that of the Lincolns.

In the light of the foregoing, it is therefore possible and even probable that my informant's grandmother, who, as represented lived nearby, was in fact in that Lincoln cabin.

She was not "an old granny woman," but she was a mother, and if correctly reported, this woman could render helpful service.

After all, it does not matter who, if anyone, was present on this occasion, but it does matter to neglect Tom Lincoln unjustly, as has been done by certain historians. There was no negligence on the part of Nancy Hanks's husband in this matter. I think Tom Lincoln did see to it that some nearby neighbor lady was present, and it is quite probable that time did not permit his long ride to town for a doctor.

Many thousands of visitors throughout the nation have made pilgrimages to this little log cabin in which Lincoln was born. Three of our presidents have made official visits to this historic place and in their official capacity addressed the multitudes. These were Woodrow Wilson, Theodore Roosevelt, and William H. Taft. Doubtless in the future other chief executives will journey to this historic shrine. It is a good place to spend a glorious hour or a full day.

Those who gaze on that little log cabin at Hodgenville can, if thoughtful, appreciate quite fully what America really means. But it is regrettable—to put it mildly—that the site's visitors receive misleading and erroneous conceptions of Lincoln's childhood due to inaccurate inscriptions appearing on the walls of the Memorial Building that shelters that little log cabin. If one accepted these inscriptions literally, it would follow that Lincoln spent not only the whole of his Kentucky years in that cabin; likewise he would be surprised to learn that Lincoln was nearing his majority before he left Kentucky! And certainly, as you read these inscriptions, you are made to feel that this cabin was his home for years.

The simple fact is that Lincoln was in that cabin for two years. He left it as a mere toddler when the family removed to the Knob Creek farm some miles distant. Then, too, instead of Lincoln spending his young manhood in Kentucky, he was but a mere lad when the family quit the Knob Creek cabin for Indiana.

In substantially every instance, Tom Lincoln's Knob Creek neighbors, like himself, belonged to undistinguished or second families. This likewise holds true for little Abe's schoolteachers, Zachariah Riney and Caleb Hazel, and undoubtedly the pastors of Little Mount Baptist Church in no single instance belonged to what is so often spoken of as the upper class or first citizens of Kentucky. This future president may never at any time during his Kentucky residence have seen or heard a representative of that "better" or "upper" class, either in conversation or on the platform.

The one and only claim that can be made on behalf of Kentucky in giving to the world Abraham Lincoln is to be found solely and only in the fact that he was born on Kentucky soil even though the whole of his lineage on both sides of the house was that of Virginia—unless it should be found that the father of Nancy Hanks was a Kentuckian, and even if this could be established, it would be ascertained that he was born elsewhere than in Kentucky. Doubtless this unknown, too, was a Virginian.

I deem it proper here to inquire what would have been Lincoln's career had he remained a citizen of Kentucky. Undoubtedly he would not have been given much consideration—perhaps something akin to that of Dr. Robert Breckinridge or Cassius M. Clay and others.[4] And had he remained a citizen of Indiana, it is probable that no inviting political career would have been opened to him, at least nothing comparable to what subsequently occurred in Illinois. The Illinois field was, in its way, a made-to-order arena for the Rail Splitter.

Indiana accepted him when he was a mere child, and as I shall endeavor to point out did much for him throughout those fourteen years. Illinois, receiving him in his twenty-second year, administered to him in many ways, and helped to mold and fashion him for his brief four years in the White House, and when the assassin laid him low, it was quite fitting and proper that his ashes should rest in the bosom of the state that gave him to the nation, rather than a burial in Indiana where his "angel mother" sleeps and where he spent the whole of his formative years, or at Hodgenville, Kentucky, where he was born.

NOTES

1. This suggestion that Hardin County blacks equaled whites in population lacks support in available records. The 1800 Hardin County population was 3,653, according to the Second Census of Kentucky: 3,317 whites, 325 slaves, and 11 free blacks.

2. Over fifty years after Abe's death, the Lincoln Farm Association commemorated his birth on the family's land at the top of a low hill in what is now Abraham Lincoln Birthplace National Historic Park. Although a "symbolic" log cabin sits encased in a grand neoclassical temple, the featured cabin differs substantially from the original Lincoln home. The National Park Service initially accepted the cabin as authentic, but the president's only surviving son, Robert Todd Lincoln, called it a "fraud" (Sellars, "Lincoln's Logs"). See also Pitcaithley, "A Splendid Hoax." For a discussion of typical construction in this era and geographic setting, see Kniffen and Glassie, "Building in Wood in the Eastern United States."

3. Peggy's legal name was Margaret LaRue Walters. She was born on 11 December 1789, the youngest daughter of John LaRue (the namesake of LaRue County, Kentucky). By the time of Lincoln's birth, Peggy was twenty years old and married to Conrad Walters. Though she died on 26 October 1864, by all accounts she retained a clear memory until her death (Barton, *Paternity of Abraham Lincoln*, 171, n1).

4. Dr. Robert Breckinridge was both a politician and Presbyterian minister. Cassius Clay was a Kentucky planter, politician, and emancipationist who sought the abolition of slavery. He also founded the Republican Party in Kentucky.

FOUR

—ᴍ—

KENTUCKY CHILDHOOD

THERE WAS NOTHING IN THE childhood of Lincoln especially different from any other normal Kentucky boy in that
Knob Creek community. He was normal in size and was not at
all precocious, and so far as is known, he did not at any time say
or do anything out of the ordinary—certainly nothing at all that
became prophetic of his later greatness.

It is safe to assert that Abe's Knob Creek cabin years were more
or less humdrum, with now and then some little event occurring
in the home or at the church and perhaps at the log schoolhouse
that made for variety and thus served to relieve the monotony.

He performed chores, ran neighborly errands for his mother,
and assisted his father in small ways in the fields. He himself
recalled, when in the White House, how he dropped grain in
the furrowed ground and helped to shell corn for grinding at the
grist mill. He carried ashes from the big open fireplace, and when
the ash was hickory, he was instructed to place this in a special
receptacle for soapmaking or smoking meats.

He and Sarah carried water from the spring, both for the usual
household needs and for filling the big iron kettle that swung on
a pole resting in forks embedded in the ground. In season he re-
plenished the smoldering smokehouse fire with chips where side

meat, hams, and shoulders were cured. He learned to ride horse-back as he accompanied his father to and fro in his field work. He trudged beside his mother in her neighborly visits to other cabins.

Boy-like, he entered into the usual children's games with his sister, Sarah, about the cabin and later was active in the school-ground sports. During his last year at Knob Creek, he had a little dog called Joe. This little mongrel was merely a house dog, but Abe thought so much of him that he insisted on taking him along when the family immigrated to Indiana.[1]

Nancy Hanks was accustomed to reading Bible stories for Abe and Sarah, and many believe she was wholly responsible for ob-taining a copy of *Aesop's Fables* and Bunyan's *Pilgrim's Progress*. These books were probably purchased at some public sale for a mere pittance, but these two books, together with some half dozen later purchases, were destined to produce lasting and de-termining results in Lincoln's life.

There are good reasons for believing that these books were obtained during the later period of the Knob Creek residence. In any event, we do know that Abe had sufficiently mastered por-tions of them so as to read them before small groups. Someone had to do more or less coaching in Abe's reading, especially with some of the proper nouns. We also know that when the family left Knob Creek for Indiana, these three books were taken along.

Abe could probably read before attending school, at least the last session. Since Thomas Lincoln was never a ready reader and was at no time a believer in "edication" beyond readin', 'ritin', and 'rithmetic, we can assume that Nancy Hanks was Abe's home teacher. One Lincoln biographer introduces Dennis Hanks as Abe's teacher, but in light of the well-known illiteracy of Dennis, Abe probably received no sort of worthwhile help from his cousin Dennis.[2] Additionally, Abe and Dennis were separated at this time by some miles and rarely saw each other, if at all.

The log schoolhouse Abe and Sarah attended for two brief ses-sions was located nearby down the road from the Lincoln cabin.

Abe's schooling under Zachariah Riney was negligible and was in fact more in the way of keeping Sarah company as well as having some place to go, rather than a place for study.[3]

Certain writers have made much ado over the fact that Riney was a Catholic. Some of these writers have gone so far as to state that Riney was a Roman Catholic priest. The purpose and aim of these writers was to show that Catholic teaching and Catholic influence early in Lincoln's life made for certain later attitudes. Riney was not a priest, and there is no sort of proof that he ever attempted to introduce religion in his teaching. The fact that Riney was a member of the Catholic Church was not a thing then or now to occasion wonder or surprise. Riney merely exercised his fine American right in worshipping God according to the dictates of his conscience.

Abe's second school session under Caleb Hazel, although brief, enabled some degree of progress in the matter of reading and spelling. It is well known and definitely established that when the family reached Indiana, Abe could both read and write well. He was then in his eighth year.

Caleb Hazel probably did not depart from the usual school-room procedure in those days in order to discuss current events such as the War of 1812, which was near its close. The fact that soldiers from the general neighborhood of the Knob Creek community in some instances had been in battle engagements such as New Orleans would perhaps occasion at least playground discussion. It is certain that such events became a subject of fireside discussion in Tom Lincoln's cabin. We are told that little Abe met up with a returned soldier on at least one occasion not far from the creek where he and his sister, Sarah, had been fishing. Having been taught by his parents to be kind to the soldiers, Abe gave this soldier a fish. This was a little thing to do; nevertheless it not only discloses that Abe remembered the second war with England; it also indicates his early appreciation of soldiers.

The fact that the Knob Creek cabin of Thomas Lincoln, as well as the log schoolhouse, was located near the highway over which

there was comparatively much travel from Louisville to Nash-
ville, Tennessee, made it possible for little Abe to witness the
passing of the many travelers to and fro. Doubtless in this way
Abe caught glimpses of the big world that he now began to hear
about.

Tom Lincoln's cabin was much the same as the cabins of his
neighbors. The reciprocity of neighborliness in that Knob Creek
community represented a marked equality. It is true that a number of those citizens owned slaves. Tom Lincoln and Nancy
Hanks were sufficiently prosperous to have owned servants, but
they were both alike opposed to the system of slavery. Only one
Lincoln ever owned slaves—the president's Uncle Mord, and he
disposed of these.

It should be noted that the phrase "poor whites" was a term
coined by the slaves—at least they in particular made frequent
use of that phrase. Whatever else it may have meant, it was especially meant to apply to those who did not own slaves. That other
phrase, "white trash," was closely related, if they do not mean the
same thing, in denoting a man as a poor white. No fine distinc-
tions were made between those who, although financially able
to own slaves but elected not to do so, and those who were not
blessed with means to purchase slaves. At least that was the case
in the Knob Creek community.

In later years, Lincoln pointedly said: "I cannot remember the
time when I did not hate slavery."[4] To take him literally we must
therefore conclude that his hatred of the system dated back to his
Knob Creek days, his childhood.

In any comprehensive view of Lincoln's later attitude toward
the system, we must recall that he did see slavery in a vicious
form in Kentucky elsewhere, at least onboard steamboats plying
up and down the Ohio.[5] In the well-known letter to his friend
Joshua Speed of Louisville, who upheld the system, Lincoln takes
occasion to remind him of a scene witnessed by both men where
a number of slaves were chained together. Lincoln specifically

voices his opposition to all of this by saying: "The memory of that scene robbed me of my sleep."[6] Doubtless Lincoln's hatred of slavery grew with his years, but we cannot escape the conviction that the beginnings of his hatred of it as a system hark back to his Knob Creek childhood.

There was no nationwide slavery agitation in 1815. The same thing was true concerning the liquor issue or, for that matter, lotteries. Of course here and there were found individuals and whole communities who were opposed to slavery, as well as other evils mentioned.

During the period that the Lincolns resided at Knob Creek, the Little Mount Baptist Church, to which the Lincolns belonged, divided over the matter of slavery. It is true that in those early days everywhere many little matters in the way of differences became serious enough to occasion church trials, but this division on slavery was not a minor matter.

It is interesting to note that this slavery dispute, which necessitated a moderator or peacemaker, led to the choice of Thomas Lincoln. That choice is deeply significant. Tom Lincoln owned no slaves and was known as an opponent of the slave system. Even so, both the opponents of slavery and the slave masters unanimously agreed on Tom Lincoln as moderator. This suggests that he had not been looked on as an agitator and points to his reputation for fairness, honesty, and judgment.

It would have been strange indeed had an alert and active boy such as we must believe Abe to have been at this time not have manifested some degree of interest in this quarrel. Doubtless Abe was present and was an ear- and eyewitness of this dispute. Even if too young at the time to have appreciated the deep significance of this quarrel over slavery, he at least later came to see in this some of the deeper meanings, and it may have entered into his later phrasing when he said that his parents left Kentucky "partly on account of slavery."[7]

The Little Mount Baptist congregation "hired" no pastor. The United or Separatist Baptists did not believe in paid preachers or salaried men. In fact, there were no settled pastors either at Little Mount or at Jonesboro, Indiana. It is true that certain men served with more or less regularity in both churches, but they were not hired. The preacher resided in no parsonage or manse, and he was not in fact a pastor in the present-day sense of that term. This statement does not mean that the minister did not indeed minister to the membership, for he did, but it does mean that often at least and indeed usually, the man in the pulpit was a citizen of the community, usually a farmer who labored through the week as did his Sunday hearers. Then, too, it must not be supposed that since they did not hire or pay a minister that it would follow that he was not the recipient of many helpful things, for these pioneers were generous and took extreme delight in sharing with their pastor such things as they themselves enjoyed. This was true at Little Pigeon Church in Indiana as well as on Knob Creek in Kentucky. These gratuities were viewed as the biblical method of procedure in carrying on the work of the Lord.

The Little Mount congregation comprised hearers who were, like the preacher himself, unschooled. As a congregation they were stoutly opposed to an educated ministry. A college or seminary graduate would have been voted as uppish, one who thereby belonged to the high-hat group. That which was true of the Knob Creek or Little Mount Baptist group during Tom Lincoln's day was likewise true a bit later of the membership of Little Pigeon Church at Jonesboro, Indiana. Thus it will be seen that this was the character of the preaching heard by Abe in his childhood as well as the kind of preaching heard throughout the whole of his formative life.

It is unlikely that the little boy Lincoln ever conversed with an educated person during his Kentucky years. If he did, it was an exception, and it is equally improbable that he ever at any time during his childhood listened to an educated preacher in the Little Mount pulpit. It is true that there were educated people in Elizabethtown and there was an academy located there. Since

Abe was but a child, the presence of this academy meant nothing to him personally.

It must not be supposed that since Tom Lincoln was in common with substantially all of his neighbors—certainly those who made up the membership of Little Mount Church—he was therefore stoutly opposed or "agin" all education. That would be an erroneous supposition.

Tom Lincoln and all of his neighbors were enthusiastic about having their children master readin', 'ritin' and cipherin'. Anything beyond this was regarded as superfluous and led to worldly pride.

On Sundays when the father and mother attended the church services, little Abe and Sarah accompanied them. This must have been a genuine red-letter day in Abe's calendar, at least the journey to and from the church, and some other things as well. He saw the people, and that was something. Then, too, he enjoyed the horseback ride behind his father. Sarah rode astride behind her mother, but no woman in those days was ever known to ride astride except the typical mountaineer. Perhaps such a performance would have become a matter for the church board to mull over.[8]

The church services meant preaching and singing. This branch of the Baptists was opposed to Sunday schools. The entire church program was built around the grown-ups. Children had no place or vital part in it. Later in life, Abe voiced his criticism of this procedure and more especially voiced his opposition to the ranting, singsong pulpit efforts. The custom of constantly discussing controversial subjects of small moment proved especially distasteful to Abe—at least, this was true of him in Indiana.

In those early days a sermonette was an unheard-of performance. Two and even three hours were deemed necessary to discuss what might have been said in thirty minutes or less time. Two hours was an exceedingly long time for a little boy to sit on one of those backless puncheon benches with his feet some inches up in the air.

If the pioneer dress was severely plain with its homespun and deerskin, this was in keeping with the unadorned church walls. There were no carpeted aisles, and the rostrum was likewise bare. The roof of the church had no spire or belfry, and why should it have a belfry since there was no church bell? There was no organ and no choir loft. The devil was in the fiddle! And he might in some ingenious manner get into a church organ! Even the leader's tuning fork was frowned on, all because of its suggestive shape; hence it was spoken of as the devil's pitchfork.

The singing would not cause a little boy like Abe to offer any helpful contribution. Besides, Abe, even during his youth, was never a singer, and certainly as a man he rarely ever pitched a tune. Abe probably received very little uplift during these services.

I have no sort of a disposition to speak lightly of these frontiersmen, and certainly I am not disposed to leave the impression that these frontier pulpit men with their illiteracy and other shortcomings were below the standards in Indiana. Indeed, some of these very preachers served for a time at [Spencer County, Indiana], where conditions were about the same as at Knob Creek.

These ministers were delightfully sincere, and I am not disposed to question their transparent good intentions; much less do I hold them up as representative of what was usually spoken of as the ruling or upper class of Kentucky. But they were, on the whole, God fearing, truthful, and honest citizens.

The Kentucky contribution, save for such schooling as Abe received and his association with representatives of a dependable class, up to his seventh year, may be stated in a single brief phrase—Abraham Lincoln was born on Kentucky soil.

NOTES

1. Some early source material suggests the dog Joe was actually a pet of Thomas Lincoln and that Abraham had no special affinity for the animal.

For a story recounting how Abraham may have indirectly killed the dog, see Wilson and Davis, eds., *Herndon's Lincoln*, 28n. See also J. Rowan Herndon to William H. Herndon, Quincy, IL, 21 June 1865, in *Herndon's Informants*, 51, ed. Douglas and Davis.

2. Whichever "Lincoln biographer" Murr refers to here actually relies on Dennis Hanks's own assertion that he taught Lincoln; as Murr notes, this assertion is unlikely true.

3. Lincoln first attended school in Knob Creek, Kentucky, in 1815 at age six. His teacher was Zachariah Riney, originally from Maryland, who came to Kentucky and taught in a windowless, one-room school with a dirt floor.

4. Lincoln's actual quotation comes from an 1864 letter to Albert G. Hodges, in which he wrote: "I am naturally anti-slavery. If slavery is not wrong, nothing is wrong. I can not remember when I did not so think, and feel" (Basler et al., *Collected Works of Abraham Lincoln*, 7:281). Earlier, in an 1858 speech in Chicago, Lincoln stated: "I have always hated slavery, I think as much as any Abolitionist. I have been an Old Line Whig. I have always hated it" (Basler et al., *Collected Works of Abraham Lincoln*, 2:492).

5. The Lincoln home at Knob Creek rested over thirty miles from the Ohio River. It is unlikely that Abraham saw steamboats while living here, at least certainly not with any regularity.

6. This reference to losing sleep over slavery does not appear to be an exact quotation, but it does generally summarize Lincoln's views as he relayed them to Joshua Speed in a letter dated 24 August 1855. Lincoln and Speed met in Springfield, Illinois, during the 1830s and remained friends throughout life.

7. Basler et al., *The Collected Works of Abraham Lincoln*, 4:61, 62.

8. Riding a horse "astride," in a sidesaddle fashion, allowed female riders to sit with both legs on one side of the horse rather than one leg on either side. Thus, women in skirts could ride modestly in fine clothing.

PART II

LINCOLN'S INDIANA YEARS

FOLLOWING YEARS OF RESEARCH AND conversations with Lincoln's neighbors and those who knew them, Murr published a three-part series in 1917 and 1918 on Lincoln's life in Indiana for the *Indiana Magazine of History*. Aptly titled "Lincoln in Indiana," the series ran in issues dated December 1917, March 1918, and June 1918.

FIVE

INDIANA UNCLE AND COUSINS

If I send a man to buy a horse for me, I expect him to tell me his
"points"—not how many hairs there are in his tail.[1]

THE REMOVAL OF JOSIAH LINCOLN, uncle of the President, to
Indiana was some four years prior to the admission of the State
into the Union. It appears that he, like many others who lived in
slave territory, hearing of the fine prospects in the "Indian country to the north," joined the tide of emigrants coming up from
the south, and with no particular objective in view journeyed
out into this wilderness, not knowing whither he went save that,
in common with substantially all of the pioneers, he did not stop
until the great oak forests in the hills were reached, where there
were abundant, ever flowing springs of clear water.

The location chosen was in Harrison County, where, at the
little town of Corydon, was then located the seat of government
of the territory, which four years after his arrival became the
capital of the State. The land which he selected was originally
covered with a heavy growth of timber, was well watered and
doubtless was considered a good location by the pioneer; but it
is now largely barren and comparatively valueless.

Thomas Lincoln, father of the President and younger brother of Josiah, came on a visit to this section of the State a short while prior to his own removal from Kentucky to Spencer County, Indiana.[2] The inhabitants of the territory at the time of Thomas Lincoln's visit were looking forward to its early admission into the Union. It was while visiting his brother that Thomas Lincoln decided to seek a home in the wilderness of Indiana, making choice of a place a few miles farther west.

Comparatively little is known of Josiah Lincoln.[3] However, what is remembered possesses at least some value as setting forth certain family traits. In personal appearance he somewhat resembled his brother Thomas, being rather rugged, compactly built, of dark complexion—as were all of his descendants. Moreover, he had a broad, hearty laugh and was given to storytelling. The writer personally knew the older descendants of Josiah Lincoln, as well as those of the generation following.

All of the Lincolns in Indiana during the campaign of 1860 were Democrats and voted for Judge Douglas for President in preference to their illustrious kinsman, with the single exception of Benjamin. He was early influenced politically and otherwise by his mother's relatives, who were Republicans, and this accounts for the support given to his relative rather than any ties of consanguinity or mere family loyalty. Moreover, the larger portion of the younger Lincolns have ever been and are now Democrats. Only one of this branch of the family became a Civil war soldier, and he, Warden Lincoln, having volunteered and been mustered into the ranks under the excitement of the times, found occasion later, as claimed by some of his relatives, to express regret at having enlisted, but he made a good soldier, serving as a private. He had the misfortune of being taken prisoner and for a time was in Libby prison, but being later placed on Belle Isle, was exchanged and reached home. Doubtless, had it been known by those in authority at the prison that he was a cousin of the Abolitionist in the White House, he would not have been granted his freedom.

Mordecai and Joseph, brothers of Warden, were drafted. Mordecai, not desirous of personally serving, sent a substitute, while Joseph, entertaining the same attitude in the matter, and not being possessed of sufficient means to obtain a substitute, took French leave, so his relatives assert, of Indiana and succeeded in eluding the authorities by repairing to the State of Illinois until after the close of hostilities.[4] The political attitude of these Lincolns toward their kinsman in the White House and their criticism of the conduct of the war by the administration were in keeping with the attitude of many of their neighbors in southern Indiana and indeed of many throughout the entire North.

In Southern Indiana and southern Illinois, both having been very largely peopled from the South, it was not strange that there was a large element whose sympathies were favorable to the Southern Confederacy. But there were large numbers in both States, many of them friends and supporters of Judge Douglas, who were intensely loyal to the Union.[5]

Illinois, however, was more fortunate than was Indiana in one very important particular, in that General John A. Logan, a Democrat up to the fall of Fort Sumter and for some time thereafter, resided in that section of the State, and being loyal to the flag wielded a salutary influence over his followers.

The southern portion of Indiana did not possess a leader of the prominence of Logan to turn the tide in favor of the Union in this crisis. There is small wonder that the Knights of the Golden Circle and kindred disloyal organizations flourished.[6] But notwithstanding this, the majority of soldiers who went out from first to last during the great war from southern Indiana were Democrats.

The writer's father was a Douglas Democrat, casting his vote for the "Little Giant" in preference to the "Railsplitter," and never manifested at any time any partiality for Lincoln. While he saw no military service, being an invalid, three of his brothers served the Union.

Practically all of the numerous descendants of Josiah Lincoln were and are rather short of stature, maintaining to the latest generation those characteristics manifested in their progenitor, which may be said to be distinctively Lincoln traits.

They almost uniformly have coarse black hair and dark eyes, and are somewhat given to humor which in certain instances has been quite marked. For the most part they have been small farmers, the exception being that two of them for a time, like their cousin Abraham, attempted to keep a general store, and it was attended with about as much success as was his venture— "it winked out." One of the younger generation, Joseph, the son of Mordecai, is an auctioneer, and he especially possesses some degree of wit and humor.

This branch of the President's family has always been regarded by their neighbors as good citizens, possessing splendid neighborly qualities. All of them have been and are poor, yet honesty has ever characterized them. They have always had the reputation of being peaceful and inoffensive, possessing in substantially every instance a high sense of honor; and if any liberties were attempted with this, or intentional provocation in any form given, it was met with a challenge to a personal encounter. The absence of personal fear or cowardice is very marked among them, and in certain ones there was a venturesome spirit. The writer well recalls hearing "Mord" Lincoln say, "My rule for fording Big Blue when she's on a tear is: watch for the hosses' ears and as long as I c'n see 'em, I'm all right."

While none of the Indiana Lincolns possessed unusual physical strength or marked mental ability, they were generally hardy and rugged, and occasionally there was one who in the common schools gave evidence of possessing more than ordinary ability. However, their schooling has been confined to the grades in substantially every case.

They have maintained certain family names such as Mordecai, Joseph, Thomas, and Benjamin, but there has never been an Abraham among them, and it is highly probable that there never will be.[7] It should be stated, however, that one son of Warden, who served in the Union army during the Civil war, is called "Abe," not by the family, but by his schoolmates and others merely as a nickname.

During the Civil war when there were those in this section of the State accustomed to indulge in caustic criticism of the administration at Washington in conducting the war and of Mr. Lincoln in particular, calling him "the Black Abolitionist," etc., none of his Indiana relatives resented this; and while they did not agree with their kinsman in the White House politically, they refrained from indulging in the use of severe and clearly objectionable personal remarks themselves. Yet they were pleased rather than not when others pointed out mistakes of the administration.

After the close of the war they assumed an attitude of silence to the rising fame of the President, neither manifesting pleasure nor indicating any displeasure, and this attitude has been kept up to the present time, so much so, in fact, that in almost every instance when approached and engaged in conversation concerning the Great Emancipator, they assume a listening attitude, apparently proud of the great fame of their kinsman Abraham, but loath to say anything themselves. The writer does not recall ever hearing an Indiana Lincoln indulge in any language that could by any possible construction be construed to mean a boast of his relationship to the President.

It may be said, therefore, that the attitude of this branch of the Lincolns toward the President is that they are proud of the fact that their kinsman became illustrious and made for himself a great name, but they are in every case quite content to look upon this [achievement] in common with the millions, not desirous at all of receiving any notoriety by reason of their kinship to him. This rather exceptional disposition is not due to any petty jealousy, certainly not attributable to ignorance or any remnant of antebellum political prejudice, but is rather due to a distinctive family trait so remarkable as to be true of all of them: that is, they possess a mingled modesty and honesty which forbids undue personal exaltation or any disposition whatever to reap where they have not sown.

The political predilections of the Indiana Lincolns is not a thing to be regarded as at all strange or such as to occasion wonder since the earlier members of the family, including Thomas, father of the President, and even the President himself, were all Democrats in politics originally. Before his leaving Indiana for Illinois, Abraham was a pronounced Jacksonian Democrat, priding himself in this; and John Hanks is the authority for saying that he offered to whip a man in Illinois soon after their arrival in that State who was speaking rather disparagingly of Jackson.[8] So pronounced was Lincoln's attitude during the Adams and Jackson campaign that some of the old pioneer friends recalled a couplet or two of a song that "Abe" and Dennis Hanks were in the habit of singing:

> Let auld acquaintance be forgot,
> And never brought to mind,
> And Jackson be our President,
> And Adams left behind.

The manner of life of the older members of the Indiana Lincolns, their personal appearance, their contentment and indeed joy amid struggles with poverty bear a marked similarity to that of Thomas, father of the President, so that it may be said that their life was lived on a somewhat similar plane to his. Although the location of the President's boyhood home in Spencer county is but a few miles from where Josiah Lincoln settled and where may still be found many of his descendants, yet none of these has ever visited this section, and not one of them was present on the occasion of the unveiling of the Nancy Hanks Lincoln monument in the year 1902.[9] Likewise, none of these Indiana relatives has ever made a pilgrimage to Springfield to see the grave of the President or gone to the nation's capitol.

If there is discerned in the President's paternal relatives a reticence somewhat exceptional, as well as a disposition to avoid any accusation of desiring to take advantage of or in any way profit by the good fortune of a kinsman, it certainly stands out in bold contrast to the behavior of all of his maternal relatives, the Hankses, who straightway importuned Mr. Lincoln to befriend them on his accession to the Presidency, a thing, however, which he failed to do. The Indiana branch of the President's family never so much as wrote him a letter or in any other way attempted to communicate with him for any assistance looking to the liberation of Warden Lincoln from a southern prison, where he was known to be undergoing all of the usual discomforts of prison life, perhaps suffering some indignities by reason of his name and blood.

In seeking to account for Mr. Lincoln's greatness, it is therefore not at all necessary to resort to certain doubtful expedients or envelop his fame in mystery, as some have been disposed to do. Such persons have gone to the extreme of lightly esteeming both his maternal and paternal ancestry, and have attributed his uncommon endowment to the example and influence of his stepmother, Mrs. Sally Bush Lincoln. Others, by reason of the obscure origin of his mother, Nancy Hanks, have supposed that his greatness is traceable to this source; and yet still others, going on the theory that it was necessary to have a great ancestry in order to account for such a remarkable man as was Mr. Lincoln, eagerly sought to trace some connection with the noted Lincoln family of the East; and when it became apparent that they were of common origin this was seized upon and became all that in their estimation had hitherto been found wanting.

The proper attitude concerning the matter, it seems, would be that Mr. Lincoln was indebted equally to both the Lincolns and the Hankses for certain well-known traits of his character. But since the Lincoln traits unquestionably predominated in him and his connection with the Massachusetts Lincolns has been established, the historian is relieved from the temptation of overshadowing his life with certain elements of mystery. For no matter what currents swept into his blood, and whatever in his character may be attributable to these, the fact remains that the President possessed those well-marked family characteristics, both physical and mental, so peculiar to the Lincolns.

NOTES

1. Carpenter, *Six Months at the White House*, 254.

2. No other evidence supports Murr's assertion that Thomas Lincoln visited his brother Josiah in Indiana just before the family's permanent move to the state. Murr, a native of Josiah's Harrison County, may promote a biased theory or conflate a later trip.

3. Thomas Lincoln's siblings include Mordecai Lincoln (1771–1830), Josiah Lincoln (1773–1835), Mary Lincoln Crume (1775–1832), and Nancy Lincoln Brumfield (1780–1845).

4. *French leave* refers to an unauthorized or unannounced departure, often without permission.

5. "Judge Douglas" is a reference to Stephen A. Douglas (1813–1861), one of the Democratic Party nominees for president in 1860. Douglas previously beat Lincoln in the 1858 Illinois election for the US Senate. Douglas advocated popular sovereignty, contending that each territory should determine whether to permit slavery within its borders.

6. Knights of the Golden Circle was a secret society in the mid-nineteenth century whose members, often racists, advocated secession of slave states.

7. Although no other "Abraham" may have existed among the Indiana Lincolns, the future president's grandfather—Abraham Lincoln (1738–1786)—did carry that name.

8. Although Murr's assertions about Lincoln's originally identifying as a Democrat may ring true, the autobiographical fragment Lincoln wrote in 1859 characterizes his life in public affairs with the comment that he was "always a whig in politics" (Basler et al., *Collected Works of Abraham Lincoln*, 3:29, 512).

9. In 1879, wealthy Hoosier businessman Peter E. Studebaker paid to erect a marble stone on Nancy's presumed gravesite; it still stands today. In 1902, J. S. Culver carved a massive stone monument and had it placed in front of the Studebaker marker. The unveiling Murr mentions concerns the Culver stone, but in 1933 the Culver monument was moved to a new location on a nearby trail.

SIX

—◊◊◊—

LINCOLN'S POVERTY

A friend came to him to borrow a "biled" shirt. "I have only two,"
said Lincoln, "the one I have just taken off, and the one I have on;
which will you take?"[1]

THE ELDER ABRAHAM LINCOLN, FATHER of Thomas, appears
to have been a man of passing wealth for that day. On reaching Kentucky from Virginia in the year 1780, he entered on large
tracts of land, and was apparently destined to prosper; but subjected as the pioneers were to the depredations of marauding
Indians, he fell a victim to these vindictive and merciless foes in
the year 1788. The story of the manner of his death and some of
the attendant circumstances have often been related by biographers of his grandson.[2]

This story was one of the legacies of pioneer days bequeathed
to his sons by Josiah Lincoln. This and other stories, they allege,
were often related by him about the fireside on winter evenings,
describing somewhat in detail this particularly tragic scene.
He told of the father being shot and killed from ambush by the
bloodthirsty savages while he was laboring in a clearing a short
distance from the house, accompanied by his three sons, Mordecai, himself, and Thomas, the father of the President. When the

shot was fired and the father fell, both Mord and Josiah immediately fled, Mord going to the house to secure a gun. Taking deliberate aim at an ornament on the breast of an Indian brave, who, with uplifted tomahawk, was in the act of dispatching his baby brother Thomas, he fired, killing him instantly. Josiah having left his brother Mord to the protection of the two sisters and his mother, ran for neighborly aid, which he straightway procured, and on their return all the Indians had departed, save a wounded one, who had crawled into the top of a fallen tree. No quarter was shown to this unfortunate, and while the circumstance produced in Mord such ungovernable hatred for the redskins as to cause him to slay them on the least provocation, or no provocation at all, ever afterward, yet it does not appear that it so affected either Thomas or Josiah.

Although the elder Lincoln possessed large tracts of land, yet the old law of primogeniture caused his entire estate to pass into the hands of his eldest son, Mord, who, it appears, did not in any way aid his brothers. He managed so poorly as to possess but little more than either Josiah or Thomas on the occasion of his removal from Kentucky, which date is not certain, but is known to have been after approaching old age.

At the time of the father's death in the year 1788, Thomas, the fourth child and youngest son, was ten years of age. Thus left fatherless at the same age that his illustrious son was bereft of a mother, he led a somewhat checkered career. He became more or less a wanderer, for we catch glimpses of him visiting and laboring as a "hired man" for his uncle Jacob on a tributary of the Holston river in Tennessee; then in Breckenridge County, Kentucky, where at one time he whipped a noted bully in "just three minutes," coming out of the encounter without a scratch. In 1803, at the age of twenty-five, he purchased a farm, and in the year 1806 he was in Hardin County, learning the carpenter's trade with Joseph Hanks. His vagrant and wandering career had given him a plentiful supply of anecdotes and yarns, which it is said he could tell very cleverly, and which was perhaps one of the best, if not the only, trait ever certainly bequeathed by him to his son, Abraham.

The father of the President has been described by numerous writers as being in person comparatively short and stout, standing five feet, ten inches in his shoes. His hair was dark and coarse, complexion brown, face round and full, eyes gray, and nose large and prominent. He weighed at different times from 170 to 196 pounds. He was so "tight and compact" that Dennis Hanks declared, "He never could find the points of separation between his ribs, though he felt for them often." He was a little stoop-shouldered and walked with a slow, halting step. He was sinewy and brave, but his habitually peaceable disposition once fairly overborne, he became a tremendous man in a rough-and-tumble fight.

At the time of his marriage to Nancy Hanks, June 12, 1806, Thomas Lincoln could neither read nor write, an accomplishment his wife possessed, thereby causing her to be esteemed and looked upon with more or less wonder by the illiterate pioneers.[3] This circumstance, by way of contrast with her husband's deficiency in this and certain other things, unfortunately caused many of her son's biographers, in attempting to eulogize the wife and mother, to esteem lightly whatever of excellence Thomas Lincoln possessed.

It has been the fashion of many of these biographers of President Lincoln to speak disparagingly of his father, and no word in any caricature of his supposed shortcomings has been used more often than that of "shiftless." They have accused him of improvidence, made the occasion of his learning the carpenter's trade a mere pretext, and refused to allow that he was anything more than a pretender with tools after actually learning the trade and doing more or less work. They have found fault with his lack of ambition. They charge him with inability to pay for a farm of some two hundred acres which he purchased at the age of twenty-five years, three years prior to his marriage. They have professed to

see in his three removals in Kentucky, his going from that State
to Indiana, thence to Illinois, and two or three changes of location in that State, nothing but evidence of a confirmed nomadic
wanderer. These and many similar accusations against him have
been made from the first biography of his son to the last.

When the governor of a certain State on one occasion expos-
tulated with his aged mother for granting certain indulgencies
[*sic*] to his little son, she straightway admonished him by saying: "When you, sir, shall have reared as good and great a son
as I have, then you may come to me with your theories and they
shall receive due and proper consideration, but not before." So in
like manner, when these ruthless, not to say heartless, critics of
Thomas Lincoln, father of the President, shall take into consideration the fact that while he did have certain defects of character,
even to the point of being actually shiftless, yet be it said to his
everlasting credit that no man since the world began has ever
been father of such a son.

It is submitted that for a boy fatherless at ten, "kicked and cuffed
about from pillar to post," with no money nor influential friends,
with absolutely no school advantages—certainly not having the
chance that his son had, and yet accomplishing certain things—
he deserves some credit at least. He appears to have been steady
enough and sufficiently settled in life not only to learn a trade,
but also to become the owner of a farm at twenty-five, which fact
alone indicates at least that he had some native ability and force of
character. It is related that he possessed the best kit of carpenter's
tools in his county. He was regarded as a man possessed of sufficient ability to warrant the civil authorities in appointing him
road surveyor or supervisor, which, while a position of no great
moment, meant something in the way of leadership and respon-
sibility. When all these facts are taken into consideration, it must
be said that Thomas Lincoln was a man of some ability, certainly
not deserving the treatment that he has received at the hands of
the biographers of his son.

Some time during the late summer of the year 1816, Thomas Lincoln built a raft on Rolling Fork of Salt river, on which he loaded most of his effects, consisting of a tool chest, a number of barrels of whiskey, and such other things as he possessed, save a few lighter and more needful household articles which his family would make use of in his absence. He proceeded to make a journey down Salt River to the Ohio River and thence to Indiana, where he had decided to seek his fortunes in an effort to better his condition.

That the elder Lincoln was of a restless and roving disposition is beyond dispute, and his repeated removals "to better his condition" to some extent justify the many charges of his biographers of his being a mere wanderer and squatter. In spite of the apparent justness of these accusations, most of these proposed ventures promised well, and certainly in some one or two instances there was abundant excuse for the venture made. We have the best of authority—his illustrious son—for believing that he was actuated by good and sufficient motives for his removal from Kentucky to Indiana; and it appears that no better reasons were ever offered by any pioneer for a change of location than those in favor of Lincoln's removal from Indiana to Illinois in 1830. President Lincoln, in discussing the reasons for their leaving the State of Kentucky, said that it was "partly on account of slavery, but chiefly on account of the difficulty in land titles in Kentucky."[4] It should be remembered also that for some seven generations the family had been pioneers in as many States or counties, and Thomas Lincoln was but manifesting the same disposition that appears to have possessed his forbears.

Being a carpenter, the elder Lincoln had no difficulty in constructing a craft that under ordinary circumstances would prove seaworthy. It is believed that in view of the fact that he had made at least two flatboat trips down the Mississippi river to New Orleans, he was a fairly good waterman. On this trip soon after entering the Ohio from the mouth of Salt River his boat or raft capsized, causing the loss of the larger part of his cargo. We are told, however, that he succeeded in righting the raft, fishing up some of the whisky and tools, and contenting himself as best he could with the loss of the remainder, he continued his journey, finally docking at Thompson's, now called Gage's Landing, a short distance below the town of Troy, Indiana. His reason for choosing Spencer County rather than settling near his brother Josiah in Harrison County was largely due to the fact that he was dependent upon the river for conveyance of his effects to a new location, and having "run the river," he had some knowledge of this region where he eventually located.[5]

After making his lonely journey and effecting a safe landing at Thompson's, he placed his cargo under the care of a settler by the name of Posey. Since this man preferred the river front to the interior and could make use of the boat, it was sold to him, and the pioneer "struck out on foot" in the wilderness in search of a new home. After going inland some fifteen miles, he met with a man by the name of Carter, with whom he had more or less acquaintance. (Lincoln City is in Carter township.) This circumstance seemed to have largely determined his choice of the location which he made in the "midst of the bush." There were seven families residing in this region when Thomas Lincoln made choice of his future home.

The site chosen by Thomas Lincoln was admirable from every standpoint save one, and that defect outweighed all of the splendid advantages it otherwise possessed. It did not have a never-failing spring; in fact, there was not at that time any water on it.[6] Later, as Dennis Hanks stated, "Tom Lincoln riddled his land like a honeycomb for water, but did not succeed in finding it."[7]

Although Lincoln proceeded to take possession of the quarter section of land in true pioneer fashion by cutting and piling brush at the corners, he became in fact a squatter until the month of October 1817, when he journeyed to Vincennes and formally entered the land, although the patent was not issued until June 1827.[8]

The site chosen for his "camp" was on a rather high knoll sloping in every direction. In ten days after landing his craft at Posey's he announced that his "half-faced camp" was ready for occupancy, having in that time cut the poles or logs and notched them, doubtless being assisted by Carter and others. Crossing the Ohio, he walked back to the old home in Kentucky—a distance of about one hundred miles—and securing the friendly aid of his brother-in-law, who supplied him with two horses, he took his little family, consisting of his wife; his daughter, Sarah, aged nine; and son, Abraham, aged seven; and "packed through to Posey's."[9]

The town of Troy was at this time a place of some importance; indeed, of all those towns in the southern and western portion of the State, it was second only to Vincennes in size. In the year prior to the coming of the Lincolns, a settler by the name of Hoskins had been employed to blaze a trail from Troy to the village of Darlington, the county seat town to the west, in order that "the mail carrier might not get lost." This blazed trail passed through the region where Gentryville was a little later laid out, and it was over this trail, a "bridle path," that Thomas Lincoln moved his family and household effects to his new home. A wagon had in some manner been procured for this purpose although such vehicles were not at all common, for the first wagon brought to this part of the State was by one John Small, a Kentuckian, in the year 1814.[10]

After encountering considerable difficulty on account of felling trees and removing logs, making their comparatively short journey of fifteen miles a very tedious and trying one, they at length reached the half-faced camp. The time of the arrival of the new "settlers" was during the last half of the summer of 1816. At any rate, it appears that sufficient time was left after their arrival to enable them to cultivate "a few vegetables and a little corn."[11]

The new home to which Thomas Lincoln took his little family was a singular one indeed. As has been indicated, it was made of small sapling logs or poles and had but three sides closed, the fourth being left open, where a bonfire or log heap was kept burning during cold weather, and not only served to ward off the wintry blasts, but afforded the only means they had for cooking. The little, one-room, pole cabin was fourteen feet square, without windows, ceiling, or floor, and of course there was no necessity for a door. The household and kitchen furniture was only such in name. Aside from a small amount of bedding, a Dutch oven, a skillet, and some tinware, there was at first nothing with which to furnish the home. A rude bedstead was constructed in one corner, and in another corner a pile of leaves gathered from the surrounding forest constituted the couch of the future President.

The woods surrounding the cabin furnished an abundant harvest of wild grapes, crab apples (Johnny Appleseed had unfortunately never reached this section), service berries, blackberries, and strawberries were plentiful.

The writer recalls hearing his grandmother (who came from the South a short while after the coming of the Lincolns) tell of the abundance of wild strawberries in this region. They drove through acres of these berries, and so luxuriant were the vines and so plentiful the harvest that the limbs and even portions of the body of a white horse were discolored, as if the animal had waded in blood. There were nuts of various sorts to be had in the forest such as hickory, pecan, hazel, and the white and black walnut. Moreover, the virgin forest was a hunter's paradise, there being bears, deer, and choice wild fowls such as turkeys, geese, and ducks. In addition to these, there were the smaller game birds and animals. Any undue amount of pity and sympathy bestowed on pioneers dwelling in such a land of plenty is wasted. While not perhaps flowing with milk and honey, yet in so far as the mere matter of supplying the larder was concerned, it could scarcely have been more highly favored. There is small wonder that Dennis Hanks was moved to exclaim in his old age, when recalling these years spent in Indiana, "I enjoyed myself then more than I ever have since."

The first winter spent in Indiana was, so far as bodily comfort was concerned, the most trying time in the life of the future President as he lived quite on the level, if not below, that of thousands of slaves whom he afterward liberated. With one side of their little cabin open to the elements and the rebellious smoke again and again sweeping into the camp, it furnished not only a striking contrast to the later life of the President, but so far surpassing anything in history as to leave little chance for a parallel.

The elder Lincoln has been censured from first to last for his failure to provide better accommodations during the first year of his Indiana life, and is charged with continued improvidence and neglect, being called *lazy* by many of the biographers of his son. It must be remembered in speaking of Thomas Lincoln's poverty that while he was poor indeed, yet poverty was quite the rule of all the pioneers of this early period. Though it cannot be claimed that he was especially "work brittle" and ambitious enough to go out and seek labor, yet he never avoided work offered. He seems to have rested upon that passage of Scripture which says to let every day provide for itself. Nevertheless, the writer failed to find among his pioneer neighbors any charge that Thomas Lincoln, and his son, Abraham, in particular, were "lazy." On the contrary, it was asserted that while the elder Lincoln lacked initiative, taking life quite easy, he was content if perchance crops were abundant and labor to be had. When the morose and gloomy made doleful prophecies as to a hard winter and failure of crops, he was buoyant in spirit, optimistic, laughing and even joking with his neighbors concerning their fears. Although not regarded as a hard-working man for himself, he made a "good hand for others" and was at work almost continually.

So much has been said concerning the poverty of Lincoln's youth that it is proposed here to examine the evidence from an angle hitherto not taken. One of the boyhood friends of Lincoln, Wesley Hall, some two years younger than the President, related

a number of incidents concerning this period, and one in particular bearing upon his poverty.

Wesley Hall's father was a Kentuckian who had moved to Indiana, settling some four miles from the Lincoln cabin, but reaching this section some time after the coming of the Lincolns. The
elder Hall was regarded as quite prosperous for one in those days.
Furnishing some justification for this claim, he operated a tanyard in addition to owning and cultivating a large farm, making
shipments of leather by way of the river to southern markets. This
necessitated at certain times the employment of a number of men,
and he frequently employed both the elder Lincoln as well as his
son, Abraham.

On one occasion during the early winter, Wesley Hall was sent
to mill beyond Gentryville, a short distance from the Lincoln
cabin. But since the Halls lived to the east some four miles, it was
more than a five miles' journey. According to the pioneer custom,
no favors were shown youth or age in certain things, and the rule
especially obtained in the matter of going to mill, for each one
had to "take his turn." Such was the law.

Young Hall found upon his arrival on this occasion that a
number of men and boys had preceded him, and by the time
his turn came the entire day had almost passed. During the last
half of the afternoon, a severe snow storm had set in, and by the
time the miller carried out his "grist" and assisted him to mount
preparatory to making the homeward journey, some inches of
snow had fallen. This alarmed the pioneer lad, lest some mishap
should befall him and he should lose his way through the forest,
become a prey to wild animals, or succumb to the cold. More
especially was he so impressed since nightfall was fast approaching and the snow was driving furiously in his face. On reaching
the turn in the road leading up to the Lincoln cabin, he decided
to go there for the night. Riding up in front of the silent, snow-
mantled house, he hallooed in true pioneer fashion a time or

two: "Hel-lo! Hel-lo!" Just here it will be proper to permit Mr. Hall to tell the remainder of his story:

Bye and bye I heard the door begin to creak on its wooden hinges, and then through the storm I saw old Tom a shadin' his eyes with his hand a tryin' to see who I wuz. And purty soon, satisfying himself that it wuz me, he leaned back and laughed a big broad laugh, and then a startin' out to where I wuz he says, says he: "Is that you Wesley? You get down from thar and come in out of the weather." So I commenct [sic] to git ready to slide off my sack and by the time I got ready to light, old Tom wuz there and helped me down. Then a turnin' around lookin' towards the cabin, he calls out a time or two, big and loud: "Abe! O, Abe! Abe!" And he ain't more'n called till I seen Abe a comin' through the door, and when he asked what wuz wanted, and seein' who I wuz at the same time, old Tom says: "Come out here and git Wesley's grist while I put his hoss in the stable. Wesley's mighty nigh froze I reckon." Then he laughed again. Well, I wuz cold I c'n tell you fer I hadn't had anything to eat ceptin' parched corn since mornin'. Well, as I say, old Tom told Abe to come and get my sack, and I noticed as Abe come out to where I wuz he hadn't but one shoe on, and thinks I to myself, what's up with Abe fer I saw Abe wuz a walkin' on the ball of his heel so's to hold his big toe up which wuz all tied up, and by this time I reckon there wuz mighty nigh six inches of snow on the ground. Yit Abe's foot wuz so big and long it didn't make no difference if the snow wuz that deep. Abe hadn't any trouble about a keepin' his sore toe above the snow line. When I asked him what wuz the matter with his foot, he told me he'd split his big toe open with an ax out in the clearin' that day. Well, Abe then wuz as big and stout as he ever wuz and so he jest reached over and took that sack of meal with one hand and layin' it across his arm, him and me went into the house while old Tom put the hoss in the pole stable.

I set down in front of the fireplace and commenct [sic] to thaw out, and in a little bit old Tom come in, and a settin' down by me a slappin' his hands together and then a rubbin' 'em so, like he allus' done, he says, says he: "Wesley, you got purty cold I reckon,

did you?" And when I commenct to say I did, Mrs. Lincoln come
in and she says, after we'd passed the time of day, she says, says
she: "Wesley, I reckon you're hnugry." And I told her I wuz; and
then I told her about the parched corn. And she says: "We haint
got no meal to bake bread. We're out just now," but a pointin' to
the big bank of embers that I'd already noticed in the fireplace
and of course knowd what it meant, she says, says she, "We've got
some potatoes in thar a bakin' and we'll git a bite fer you purty
soon." At that I spoke up and I says, says I: "Mrs. Lincoln, jist help
yerself out of my sack thar." And so she done as I told her.

Well, old Tom and Abe and me went on a talkin' and purty soon
I heard a funny grindin' noise back of me, and I looked around to
see what it wuz, and it wuz Mrs. Lincoln a hollerin' out a big turnip.

Just at this point in Mr. Hall's narrative he paused and asked
the writer if he could guess what Mrs. Lincoln was "hollerin'
out that turnip fer." When some two or three attempts had been
made to solve this mystery and all proved to be clearly wrong,
to the evident amusement of the old gentleman, he resumed his
narrative by saying:

She was makin' a grease lamp. Course I'd seen a many one. She
hollered it out and cut a small groove in it on the lip, and after
she'd filled it with hog's lard and laid a wick in the notch, and lit
it, she handed it to me, and a butcher knife to Abe, and she says:
"Boys, go and get me some bacon." So me and Abe went out to a
little pole smoke house, and I held up the light while Abe cut a half
moon out of a side of bacon. So Mrs. Lincoln went on with gittin'
supper, and bye and bye she says: "Supper's ready." So when we
set down to it we had corn cakes, baked potatoes, and fried bacon.
After the supper dishes was mashed up old Tom, a slappin' his
hands together and a rubbin' em like I say, he says, says he: "Now,
Abe, bring out your book and read fer us." Old Tom couldn't read
himself, but he wuz proud that Abe could, and many a time he'd
brag about how smart Abe wuz to the folks around about. Well,
Abe reached up on a shelf where he kept his books and then a stir-
rin' up the fire on the hearth with some dry stuff he had piled in
one corner by the jamb, he commenced to read.

When the writer asked as to whether the narrator remembered what book it was that Abe read from, he straightway replied:

> Oh, yes! It wuz the life of Ben Franklin. He read to us till bed time, and that night Abe and me slept together up in the loft. We got up there through a scuttle hole in one corner of the ceilin', and to git up to it we had to climb up a peg ladder made by boring holes in the logs and insertin' wooden pins. I remember the bedstid [sic] which of course I saw many a time. It wuz a mighty sorry affair; still it answered the purpose. A hole wuz bored in the north wall and a rail-like piece wuz sloped off to fit this. The same thing wuz close on the west wall, and these two rails wuz brought together and fastened in the same way to an upright post out in the floor and then acrost these wuz laid split boards or whipped plank, or some thin slats rived out, and on these wuz a gunny sack filled with leaves gathered from the woods. On this Abe and me slept covered with bear skins.

Lincoln's bedfellow on this snowy winter night lived to see him in the White House.

NOTES

1. Whipple, *The Story-Life of Lincoln*, 151.
2. Abraham Lincoln's father, Thomas, witnessed the murder of his own father: In spring 1786, while Abraham worked in his Kentucky field with his three sons, a Native American attacked and shot him dead. Afterward, Native Americans became one of Thomas Lincoln's favorite subjects to discuss (Anderson, "Native Americans," 11–29).
3. Despite rudimentary reading and writing skills, Thomas Lincoln could sign his name.
4. Autobiography written for John Locke Scripps [ca. June 1860], in *Collected Works of Lincoln*, Basler et al., 4:61–62.
5. Murr suggests that Thomas Lincoln intended to cross into Indiana closer to his brother in Harrison County but landed farther southwest because of a capsized boat. But this assertion finds no other support in the historic record. Despite many local legends about where the Lincoln family crossed the Ohio River, most historians agree on Thompson's Ferry

(also called Anderson's Ferry), slightly downriver from Troy, Indiana (Bartelt, *There I Grew Up*, 16).

6. The National Park Service notes the Lincoln homesite offered "good water" and says the "Lincoln Spring was the main source of fresh water when the Lincolns lived here. The spring was one of the main reasons Thomas Lincoln chose this site for his homestead" (Lincoln Spring, National Park Service, accessed 25 April 2020, https://www.nps.gov/places/lincoln-spring.htm).

7. Lamon, *Life of Abraham Lincoln*, 21.

8. Thomas Lincoln's family arrived in Indiana in December 1816, and he filed his land claim on 15 October 1817, less than one year later.

9. We do not know what evidence Murr relies on to suggest that Thomas returned to Kentucky with Nancy's brother. Murr may confuse it with his return trip to Kentucky with the Johnston family.

10. Much of what we know about this trip comes from statements by Dennis Hanks to William Herndon. Hanks indicated the Lincolns came on horseback to the Posey farm and then borrowed a wagon to reach the new homestead (Hanks interview, 13 June 1865, in *Herndon's Informants*, ed. Douglas and Davis, 38–39).

11. Murr's assertion that the Lincolns arrived in summer 1816 is unsupported by other evidence. Most historians agree the family arrived in Indiana in December 1816. Even if Murr is correct and the family arrived in late summer, they would have lacked enough time to plant worthwhile crops.

SEVEN

—∿—

BOYHOOD ASSOCIATES

Gold is good in its place; but living, brave, patriotic men, are better
than gold. For my own part I have striven, and shall strive to
avoid placing any obstacle in the way. So long as I have been here
I have not willingly planted a thorn in any man's bosom.[1]

IN THE THOUSANDS OF PAMPHLETS and more extended no-
tices of the life of Abraham Lincoln there is, for the most part,
comparatively little said concerning the adolescent or formative
period in his career. Because of the universal interest in Mr. Lincoln's life, any contribution bearing upon any phase of his career
should be of interest and not wholly without value. Nevertheless,
it is true that there has been but meager notice of his youth since
those who have undertaken this task possessed but little data;
and thus in consequence the conviction inevitably forced itself
upon all that there was but little that transpired during Mr. Lincoln's youth particularly prophetic of the years that followed. In
many instances, therefore, the formative period in Mr. Lincoln's
life has been, in consequence of the meagerness of knowledge
and reliable data, dismissed as being commonplace. Professing
to see nothing exceptional during these formative years, his biographers in many instances have passed on to the days of his

early manhood and sought to call attention to what they regard the real beginnings of his remarkable career. In doing so, in their unwarranted haste to pass to the scenes of his public career, they do not fail to quote the well-known lines of the poet which Mr. Lincoln was accustomed to apply to himself: "My life was but the short and simple annals of the poor," as if this would prove a sufficient refutation of any charge of meager notice of the years prior to the day of his appearing on the prairies of Illinois.[2] To put it in another way, the Lincoln admirers have been made to believe that he was a Hoosier prodigal who came to himself about the time, or soon after, reaching the State of Illinois; and at this time or subsequent to it, there were certain super-added things affixed to his character that made for honesty, truthfulness, and fixity of purpose.

The fact of Mr. Lincoln's honesty, which was so prominent in his later life, is not doubted for a moment, but since substantially all the recorded instances of this trait of his character found their setting in some event in later life, there is a belief that this trait was not particularly noted in his early career, or if so, it was not sufficiently prominent to call forth especial attention, whereas, all of his early associates interviewed by the writer stated that this was quite marked, and so much so as to cause them to remember him by it.

The writer is convinced, by reason of some years' residence among the early associates of the great war President, that the boy Lincoln was father of the man.[3] We are indebted to the many biographers of Mr. Lincoln for so many things, and to some of these in particular, it would be something approaching sacrilege for one now at this late day to appear even to take any liberties with any long established beliefs concerning our martyred President. Happily this does not appear to be necessary. But however well meant the efforts were on the part of these numerous historians touching Mr. Lincoln's early career, unfortunately they have succeeded in focusing the gaze of the world either upon the spot in the State of Kentucky that gave him birth or upon the prairies of Illinois where he took his rise to fame, and where his ashes now rest. Those years in his life which he spent in Indiana from 7 to 21, which ordinarily make a period in the life of most men of momentous importance, have been more or less neglected. To undertake at this late day the task of correcting the perspective of the Lincoln admirers by focusing the attention upon his youth is an exceedingly difficult one and ordinarily would prove discouraging; but since it is believed that sufficient data is at hand to substantiate the claim, the task has been undertaken with a view at least of supplementing the work of recognized authorities in this field as well as rendering tardy justice to Lincoln's youth.

It is to be regretted that some of the earlier biographers of Mr. Lincoln did not make a greater effort to collect information touching his youth since the field was at that time white unto harvest, particularly soon after the death of the President, at which time some two or three biographers came to visit the scenes of Mr. Lincoln's boyhood and young manhood in Spencer County, Indiana. Some of the more recent writers met with experiences well calculated to discourage further effort in this field since they possessed erroneous notions of Hoosier manners and customs. In consequence of this handicap some very amusing, not to say ludicrous, things transpired during attempted interviews with certain ones of Lincoln's old associates. Many of the historians in speaking of the citizens now residing in the region where Gentryville is located regarded them as quite below the average, characterizing them as "listless," "poor," "free and easy," "devoid of ambition"; and reference has been made to the "antiquated business methods," "dog-fennel streets." With many other such statements they seem to pay a tribute to the wisdom and foresight of the Lincolns in having the good sense to leave that region, since the country and its inhabitants at the present time do not meet with their approbation.

That there is apparent justification for such a characterization of both the inhabitants of that section today, as well as the region itself, is quite true, and perhaps this would more especially appear so to strangers although it may be permissible to suggest that these allegations are particularly in bad taste relative to the country itself since they were made by those who happen to reside in that section of the United States where abandoned farms are the rule, whereas there are few abandoned farms in Spencer County, Indiana. Appearances are often woefully deceptive, and it is believed that a better knowledge of Hoosier manners and customs, particularly among the pioneers, would in itself serve a splendid corrective in certain things.

It may be true that Gentryville and Lincoln City are "dog-fennel towns," yet there are several hundreds like them in Indiana. Gentryville is much the same place that it was during the boyhood of Lincoln. One may still see the Saturday group of loungers seated on dry goods boxes, whittling and chewing favorite brands of tobacco, and "swapping yarns," from which point of vantage they gaze betimes down the little streets to the barren knolls in the distance. The scene is common and to be met with not only in this section of the State of Indiana, but also in certain portions of Kentucky and Illinois. Such scenes are not particularly inspiring and are not calculated to impress a visiting stranger with the belief that from such an environment there would come forth any youth who could by any possibility rise to fame; yet, just such places have produced, and may yet be destined to produce, some of our most eminent men. Some two or three incidents and circumstances are here related that occurred within the Lincoln zone, all of them of comparatively recent date and coming under the personal observation of the writer.

A man with long gray locks, somewhat loose and disheveled, was seated in the witness chair in the circuit court. It was during the month of January, and the weather was cold. He wore a pair of "eastern" boots whose heels had a predilection for rolling over and upward as if in sport of one another. His "foxed" trousers were baggy and tattered, and whether the bottoms were too badly worn for service or whether it was merely a habit of the owner, no matter; in any case they were crowded down into the boot tops. A faded, brown, hand-me-down overcoat, held to its moorings by a bit of binder-twine looped through the torn buttonhole and about the button, served to keep out the cold, this being the only outer garment worn over a shirt not too immaculate. On his knees rested a somewhat dilapidated hickory-straw hat, with the preponderance of evidence in favor of its having done service for at least two summers and certainly until far into mid-winter.

An attorney (now holding a government position of national importance) from a distance, with evident preconceived notions concerning the old gentleman, was cross-examining the witness.

"Mr. Witness, can you read and write?"

"No, sir."

"You spoke of the payment of taxes" (resting his eyes for a moment upon the boots). "Do you own property?"

"Well, yes, sir."

"Now then, just state to the jury what your holdings consist of, whether real estate, etc., etc."

"Well," began the witness, looking down as if greatly embarrassed, "well, I own a leetle land in this county and some in the county a-jinen."

"You own a little land, you say, in this and the adjoining county?" (Another glance at the boots, which on taking its leave swept past the straw hat and then fixed itself steadfastly upon the apparently disconcerted face of the witness.)

"Now, sir, just tell the jury about how much land you own."

"Well," still looking down, "well, sir, I've got a leetle the rise of three thousand acres here in this county, and some time back I got hold of a leetle jag of money, and not havin' any place jest then to put it, I bought a few hundred acres over in tother county. Besides what leetle land I own, and a few hundred head of cattle, horses and sheep, I've off and on ever now and then been loanin' a leetle money an' ginerally took mortgages on land, so I've got plasters you might say, mountin' to nigh on to right about $30,000 or better, and I've got government"—

"That will do, Mr. Witness, that will do."

The witness here referred to was about the same age as Lincoln and lived but a few miles from Gentryville. The writer was present on the occasion referred to and remembers the chagrin and crestfallen air depicted upon the countenance of the imported attorney, and furthermore he recalls the apologetic remarks subsequently made by the attorney, he being more especially induced to do this on learning that the witness was not only a fine type of old fashioned honesty and truthfulness, but was the wealthiest man in the county.

The old gentleman was not a miser nor yet miserly. He merely continued the habits and customs of the pioneer days. His dress as above described, which is not in the least exaggerated, was subject to a marked change on Sunday; that is to say, the soiled linen was replaced by a garment destined to do duty until the next Sabbath. With slight variation in the matter of dress—on the whole somewhat better but in all other points essentially the same, the foregoing description would be that of the father of a man born in this region during the Civil war, who today occupies a chair in one of the great universities of our country.

A case was being tried in the Federal court. A number of witnesses were subpoenaed, among them being an elderly man with a snow-white crescent encircling his chin. His shoes, originally black, were now brown. He wore no such conventional apparel as a collar or necktie, and his clothing otherwise was not at all pretentious. He had spent most of his life in the school room and was quite generally addressed by all classes of citizens in this Lincoln country as "Professors"; and being well known to the officer of the court, that officer very naturally called the witness by such address. An attorney, thinking to make capital out of this circumstance, especially since he noted the character of his dress, began his examination of the witness by requesting to know why he was called "professor."

"I do not know, sir, why I am thus so regarded and so addressed, for I make no claim whatever to that honorable title. It is true that I have been a teacher for some time, in fact nearly all my life; but I do not suppose that I am at all entitled to such consideration."

The attorney, not yet satisfied, pursued the matter further.

"Well, professor, you are a graduate of course and can doubtless read Latin." (Not at all supposing that the witness was a graduate or possessing such knowledge as the question implied.)

"Yes, sir," replied the professor, "Yes, sir, I am a graduate of our State University, and in obedience to your desire to know whether I possess ability sufficient to enable me to read Latin I should say that in addition to my mother tongue, I speak French and German rather fluently, Spanish only indifferently well, but I read Hebrew, Latin, Sanscrit [sic] and Greek quite well. Indeed, I have even been told by those who have manifested a decided partiality for me that I could have been a linguist had I taken up this study, say at your time of life, but I attribute this great claim of my friends to some little acts of kindness which I have rendered them from time to time through a somewhat lengthened life, rather than to any real excellence that I may possess."

It was within a half-dozen miles of Gentryville that a stranger was impertinent enough to ask an old Hoosier who had an extraordinarily large-sized nose: "How does it happen that you have such a big nose?"

"I kept it out of other people's business, sir, and let it get its growth."

As an aid to credulity and at the same time serving in part at least as a fair excuse for the treatment here offered, it may be stated that the writer was born among and reared with later generations of the Lincolns.

It does not appear to be generally known that all three sons of the elder Abraham Lincoln, grandfather of the President, eventually emigrated to Indiana. The first to come was Josiah, the second son, who settled on Big Blue River, in Harrison County, Indiana. This was in the year 1812. To this wilderness home came Thomas Lincoln, father of the President, on a visit, and in part at least his removal from Kentucky to Indiana a little later, in the year 1816, was due to the persuasions of his brother, Josiah. His reasons for leaving Kentucky are given elsewhere in this narrative, but on deciding to leave Kentucky he was induced by his brother to try his fortunes in the new State north of the Ohio river.

The writer's forbears came up from the South to this section of Indiana, also settling in Harrison County, and were neighbors to Josiah Lincoln. Thus the writer grew to manhood with the descendants of the uncle of the President.

Later the writer resided for some years in that region where the future President spent his childhood and boyhood and attained his majority. Here he personally knew a number of Mr. Lincoln's boyhood and girlhood friends and associates. Repeated interviews were obtained with these pioneers, some of whom up to that time had never so much as been interviewed by a newspaper reporter, much less by any of the biographers of Mr. Lincoln. It may be said, however, that this latter statement, apparently incredible, is to some extent accounted for by reason of the fact that these in particular had removed from the Spencer County home to other points in the State and, in one or two instances, to other States.

Some of these boyhood friends of Lincoln here referred to were parishioners of the writer or were members of his congregation, and in a few instances he officiated at their funerals and the funerals of members of their families.

It is believed that much confirmatory information was obtained from quite a number of the older citizens, who, while being mere children during the residence of the Lincolns in Spencer County, yet being children of the neighbors of the Lincolns and accustomed to hear the fireside discussions concerning the great President, especially after his rise to fame, what they related was in certain instances quite as valuable and trustworthy, and perhaps in an instance or two even more so, than was that offered by some who spoke from personal knowledge.

With no well-defined purpose of ever making any use of the data obtained beyond personal gratification, having been reared a Democrat in the belief that Douglas was transcendently great as compared to Lincoln, and having had a gradual political "conversion," my interest in Lincoln grew accordingly. Much time was thus pleasantly spent in interviewing those who either personally knew Lincoln as a boy, or those who were mere children during his stay in Indiana, or those who were born about the time of his leaving the State in the year 1830.

Considerable care has been exercised to distinguish between matter-of-fact truth and mere tradition. Of this latter there was considerable, and occasionally there was an intermingling of fact and tradition. The traditions in every case came but little short of well-established facts, and some of these were quite as interesting and suggestive as any statement based upon personal knowledge.

The mooted question as to the President's maternal ancestry was altogether in favor of the position taken by almost all of his earlier biographers, particularly by Herndon. With no desire whatever of attempting to reopen a discussion that appears to be closed, a statement or two is made. In every case when Lincoln's pioneer neighbors were asked as to the obscure origin of Nancy Hanks, the reply was invariably the same—that she was the daughter of Lucy Hanks and a Virginian.

On one occasion after the writer had delivered a lecture on Lincoln in the region where the President had lived as a boy, and having some of Lincoln's old friends in the audience, he was approached by a rather elderly lady who requested an interview on the following day. This was gladly granted. After some questions as to what "the books said concerning the origin of Nancy Hanks," the following statement was made:

> I am the daughter of a woman who was about the same age as Lincoln and lived neighbors to the Lincolns both in Kentucky and in Indiana. My grandmother and Nancy Hanks were girl friends, and my grandmother often told me that she was present at the birth of President Lincoln. I've heard both my mother and grandmother tell many incidents concerning Nancy Hanks and the Lincolns and Abraham in particular. As to Nancy Hanks's origin, I've heard my grandmother say again and again that Lincoln's mother was a fine lady and wasn't to be blamed for some things; that she was the daughter of Lucy Hanks and some unknown man in Virginia. My mother said that was what the other people told her, and no one ever said anything to the contrary.

Inquiry was made as to the reliability of the testimony offered, and it not only appeared abundantly trustworthy, but also was corroborated by the statements of others. In no case among the pioneers was there a disposition to accept any other story relative to the origin of Lincoln's mother. That Mr. Lincoln himself held to this belief concerning his mother is certainly true. Herndon, *Life of Lincoln* states, "Beyond the fact that he (Lincoln) was born on the 12th day of February, 1809, in Hardin county, Kentucky, Mr. Lincoln usually had but little to say of himself, the lives of his parents, or the history of the family before their removal to Indiana. If he mentioned the subject at all, it was with great reluctance and significant reserve. There was something about his origin he never cared to dwell upon."

Herndon further asserts that on one occasion while he and Lincoln were driving across the prairie in a buggy, the statement was made to Herndon by Lincoln that his mother, Nancy Hanks, was the daughter of Lucy Hanks and a well-bred, but obscure Virginia planter or farmer. He argued that from this last source came his power of analysis, his logic, his mental activity, his ambition, and all the qualities that distinguished him from the other members and descendants of the Hanks family.

A biography of Lincoln was prepared by Mr. Scripps for campaign purposes. Lincoln was asked to submit data for this, which he rather reluctantly did. In a letter to Herndon after Lincoln's death Scripps stated, "He (Lincoln) communicated some facts to me concerning his ancestry which he did not wish to have published then, and which I have never spoken of or alluded to before."

What these facts were we, of course, do not know, but presumably they must have had to do with this obscurity. Dennis Hanks, a son of Nancy Hanks, aunt of the mother of Lincoln, was ever insistent that the mother of President Lincoln was named Sparrow instead of Hanks. Certain it is that both she and Dennis Hanks were for a time in the home of the Sparrows, who, after the marriage of Nancy to Thomas Lincoln and her removal to Indiana, also removed to that State, taking the irrepressible Dennis with them. It was these Sparrows who occupied the half-faced camp abandoned by the Lincolns, and, when seized with milk-sick, were removed to the Lincoln cabin and both died there. Their deaths took place at the same time as that of Lincoln's mother.

It is passing strange that these pioneers should all be of one mind concerning the obscure origin of Nancy Hanks if there was no foundation for such belief.

However reliable may be the statements of discoveries made by Mrs. Hitchcock, a descendant of the Hanks family, relative to the origin of the President's mother, there never was, and is not now, just ground for any accusation against these pioneer neighbors of the Lincolns for entertaining and freely expressing the belief since it was indisputably credited by her illustrious son, and by the elder Hankses and others whose testimony is a matter of record.[4]

NOTES

1. Basler et al., *Collected Works of Abraham Lincoln*, 8:101.

2. Scripps to Herndon, 24 June 1865, in *Herndon's Informants*, 57: "Why Scripps" said he, on one occasion, "it is a great piece of folly to attempt to make anything out of my early life. It can all be condensed into a single sentence, and that sentence you will find in Gray's Elegy:
'The short and simple annals of the poor'
That's my life and that's all you or anyone else can make of it."

3. This phrasing occurs in other Lincoln contexts as well. In the center of Lincoln Bicentennial Plaza (unveiled in 2009), located inside Lincoln State Park (Indiana), is this quotation: "The child is the father of the man." The line, from an 1802 poem by William Wordsworth titled "My Heart Leaps Up," is the theme of the plaza.

4. Over the years each of the various theories about Nancy Hanks's origins acquired support—until a mitochondrial DNA study published in 2015 ended the century-old debate and proved Lincoln's mother was, indeed, one of Lucey Hanks's two illegitimate children. The results proved, too, that Lucey Hanks Sparrow was a daughter of Ann Lee Hanks and was *not*, as some believed, a descendant of the Shipleys. Nearly all Lincoln historians now agree that Lucey Hanks was Nancy's mother and Abe's grandmother (Shuda, "DNA Study Helps Solve Lincoln Lineage Debate").

EIGHT

—∿—

MANNERS AND CUSTOMS OF HOOSIER PIONEERS

Quarrel not at all . . . Yield larger things to which you can show no
more than equal right; and yield lesser ones, though clearly your
own. Better give your path to a dog, than be bitten by him in
contesting for the right. Even killing the dog would not cure the
bite.[1]

A PROPER UNDERSTANDING OF THE manners and customs
of the pioneers of Lincoln's youth and young manhood is essential to appreciate some qualities of his mind and peculiarities of
belief and practice which appeared when later he was associated
with the learned and skillfully trained statesman and politicians
who were for the most part reared under an altogether different
environment. The pioneer was more or less given to superstitious beliefs and committed to the trustworthiness of tokens and
dreams. While this characterized substantially all classes during
the formative period of our country, yet these strange and weird
beliefs in particular found a congenial, abiding place in the minds
of the pioneers who came from the South and settled in this wilderness. Indeed, the belief in the efficacy of tokens and dreams,
and the faithfulness and almost religious zeal with which signs
have been observed, have ever characterized the frontier line.

These strange beliefs inevitably begot still stranger customs. This was especially true of the people in and about Gentryville. If in this section there may yet be found some of those strange beliefs still lingering among those of that earlier period, it need not be regarded as strange since in other centuries the will of the Almighty was determined by the presence or absence of dew upon a sheep's pelt, and kingdoms were lost or won by the casting of lots. It may well be doubted whether there is not yet clinging to most of us, like barnacles upon a ship's hull, some of the age-long beliefs of our fathers. While we are living with the light beating full upon our faces, yet there is discerned in some an indication that these fireside memories and nursery teachings of that dim and distant past so possess us as to lead to the conclusion that it would not at all be difficult to revert to the practices and beliefs of other years. Bishop Matthew Simpson, one of the greatest forensic orators of his time, and an educator of national prominence, himself a pioneer and a great friend and confidential adviser of Lincoln, ever felt a strange and unaccountable pleasure and delight on seeing the new moon over his left shoulder.[2] A certain United States senator from Lincoln's boyhood state on more than one occasion in the midst of political campaigns refused to ride in a carriage drawn by black horses.

Abraham Lincoln was so indoctrinated with many of these beliefs during his youth that they clung to him until the day of his death. He always believed in the trustworthiness of dreams, one of which in particular was viewed as a good omen because he dreamed it prior to the victories of Antietam, Vicksburg, Gettysburg, the naval battle between the *Monitor* and the *Merrimac*, as well as just before the surrender at Appomattox. This dream and others he with a strange simplicity related to cabinets and, doubtless in the very simplicity of his belief, failed to realize that these gentlemen viewed such as exceptional, if not indicating a decided weakness.[3]

Advantage is taken of the opportunity here of calling attention to a fact not especially enlarged upon by any, yet which is patent and known to all; that is, we do not take liberties with Lincoln as we do with many other great men. We laugh with him, but we do not suffer any criticism of him without registering a vigorous protest. This is not true even of Washington.

To the pioneer in Lincoln's day, the carrying of an edged tool, such as a hoe or an ax, through the house was an omen of bad luck, foretelling a death in the family during the year. The breaking of a mirror was another sign of death within that period. The plaintive howling of a dog meant that the morrow would tell of a death somewhere. The crossing of the hunter's path by a dog meant bad luck in the chase unless the hunter locked his little fingers until the dog was out of sight; or, what was regarded as better still, if he returned to the point of starting and began his journey anew, all ill fortune occasioned by the bad start would not be reckoned against him. The writer has frequently witnessed these circumstances.

Friday was a day in the calendar to be avoided in instituting any new departure; that is to say, beginning anything new such as plowing, sowing or reaping in the fields, or making a garment, unless the labor could be completed during the day.[4] A bird alighting on the window or coming into the house was a sure sign of sorrow. All planting, sowing, fencing, and preparation for the same was to be governed by certain signs of the moon. Plants such as potatoes, maturing beneath the surface of the soil must be planted in the dark of the moon. And in like manner tomatoes and beans must be planted in the light of the moon.[5]

Clapboards on the roofs of buildings would cup and curl if the sign was not right. The fence would settle and sink or creel if there was a failure to consult the almanac for the proper sign. They believed in witches of various sorts, quite as much as they of New England ever did. Although there was no disposition to burn them, they were feared and guarded against. They especially believed that some evil-disposed old witch could work evil upon a child.

The writer has a distinct child's recollection of being caught up from his innocent play into the arms of a frightened lady and hurriedly carried away to a point of supposed safety from a reputed old witch who it was presumed was working her spell over him preparatory to actually bewitching him. It is not believed that this old witch in reality succeeded in her efforts at this time or at any subsequent period, but the writer frankly confesses that while he escaped all of the influences and beliefs so generally prevalent in his youth, nevertheless he finds more satisfaction and contentedness than do some if there is never a hoe or an ax carried through his house. Truly the beliefs of our grandmothers live after them.

Although there was no physician nearer than 30 miles to the Lincoln home, yet this settlement had a "doctor" of a doubtful sort, one "Cy" (Josiah) Crawford, for whom Lincoln and his sister, Sarah, often labored as "hired man and girl." "Cy," or "Old Blue Nose," Crawford, as Lincoln later named him, was what was usually spoken of as a "yarb and root" doctor. As a diagnostician he doubtless did not excel, but it was small matter since his prescriptions were few and generally harmless, even if sometimes unpleasant to take. If there was evidence of inflammation, "a counter-irritant was slapped on," and generally "a heroic, old-fashioned, Baptist foot washing" was urged just before the hour of retiring. Blue mass pills were used on the least provocation although if these were not to be had a substitute was suggested. The writer recalls one instance when "shoemaker's wax" was in an emergency made into plaster and the patient lived to praise his saviour, if not his remedy, in his effort to remove the same. Crawford, in lieu of there not being even a traveling dentist, was an extractor of teeth. Heroic methods were used for a time; but his services being so much in demand, he obtained a "twister" pair of forceps, and thereafter the surgery was more scientifically performed. A conversation with some who sat under his "prying, twisting, and gouging" revealed the fact that laughing gas would have been more than welcomed.

Since bleeding was quite generally practiced in that day by reputable physicians, Crawford, always abreast with the times, obtained a lancet and thus added this accomplishment to his practice. Generally speaking, every settlement had a man or woman who could stop bleeding in cases where a vein or artery had been severed, without resorting to the barbarous practice of ligating or cauterizing. This was done by pronouncing certain cabalistic words. The secret of possessing such power was on no account to be conveyed to another unless under proper direction and orderly procedure. A man was forbidden, on penalty of losing his skill, to convey to his brother the secret; but he might with perfect safety admit a woman into the secret, and she in turn could with equal safety initiate a man. At the perilous risk of losing forever whatever cunning and skill the writer may possess in this regard, he dares here to put it to a test by indiscriminately publishing the secret. It will be at once apparent that this conveyance is only possible to ladies. The remedy is simplicity itself and consists in thrice repeating the sixth verse of the sixteenth chapter of the Prophecy of Ezekiel.[6]

Faith doctors were implicitly believed in. Long journeys were made to them, their charms invoked and their skill put to a test. In substantially every case these men behaved something after the manner that Captain Naaman supposed the prophet Elisha would have done in his case. They refused to make any charge for services rendered, but if exceedingly provoked by some who were the beneficiaries of their healing powers, they suffered them, on taking their departure, to leave a token of their appreciation as a thank offering.

There was a commendable reciprocity of neighborliness prevailing among the pioneers. Much of their work was shared in common, particularly such as raisings, huskings, and rollings. Associated with these labors by the men, which may not inappropriately be styled field sports, the women of the entire neighborhood assembled to prepare the sumptuous feasts consisting of venison, turkey, pigeon potpie, hominy and corn-dodger.

Spinning contests were indulged in, and the hand-made loom was much in vogue; and if there chanced to be the finishing of a blanket or coverlet, or in some instances a quilt, all the young ladies—and some not so young—would surround this, holding on with both hands, while someone from the crowd of men who were interested onlookers would throw puss, the now thoroughly frightened house cat, into the bagging center. Well might there be manifest interest, for who could tell which way a cat might jump under such circumstances and thus indicate the next bride?

Play parties and dancing (hoe-downs) were much in favor, and the mere announcement of a neighborhood wedding meant an invitation for all to attend who cared to do so. Spelling matches were held every Friday night during the school term, and school-house debates invariably attracted large crowds. Old-time school exhibitions, where dialogues were recited and "pieces" declaimed, were frequent. Sometimes these were weeks in preparation and the program so lengthy as to last half the night. Religious services prior to 1820 were conducted in private homes, usually by some chance itinerant preacher. Lincoln never saw a church until he was 11 years of age, and he helped in its erection.[7]

The dress of the pioneer would appear quite as strange to us as some of the modern fashions would have been to him. No woolens were worn in and about Gentryville until the year 1824. Buckskin breeches, sewed with whang, thus making an ornamental fringe, a loose-fitting blouse, and a coonskin cap with the tail hanging down was the usual garb of the men. This was Lincoln's dress during his entire Indiana residence, save that he managed in some manner to get possession of a white shirt a short while before his removal to Illinois.

In all of these farm and community labors, social gatherings, exhibitions, and religious worship, Lincoln was a familiar figure.

He particularly enjoyed the schoolhouse debates and exhibitions. The *Kentucky Preceptor* furnished the major portion of the declamations as well as subjects or themes for debate. Some of these latter which were debated by young Lincoln and others were "*Resolved*, That fire is more destructive than water"; "Who has the greater right to complain, the negro or the Indian?" Such themes were very gravely discussed not only by the younger generation, but also by the older men as well. It is said that young Lincoln in these debates was calm, logical, and clear. He, however, often became quite humorous, causing great laughter by his peculiar antics and original remarks, but his aim appeared to be to cause his side to win. At such times two captains stood forth in the presence of the assembled crowd in obedience to the demand of the society and proceeded to "choose up." A stick some three feet in length, often a walking cane, was tossed into the air by one of the captains, the other captain catching it in one hand, and the first in turn grasping it. They placed their hands alternately in position until one became the possessor of the stick. This was repeated three times, the two best out of three deciding first choice of a debater or the side of the argument—depending upon the original agreement. After the house had been divided, the "jury" was selected by the president, usually from three to five members. Sometimes ladies were privileged to sit as judges. It will be seen that Lincoln's method in debate was such as to win "the jury."

One of his old friends, Nathaniel Grigsby, usually called "Natty," although Lincoln called him "Nat," said that when Lincoln appeared in company, "the boys would gather and cluster around him to hear him talk. He was figurative in his speeches, talks, and conversations. He argued much from analogy and explained things hard for us to understand, by stories, maxims, tales, and figures. He would point out his lessons or ideas by some story that was plain and near to us in order that we might instantly see the force and bearing of what he said."[8]

Young Lincoln was a great mimic, entertaining and amusing crowds quite as much in this manner as in any other. The humor of any situation or a mirthful and ludicrous turn seemed to criss-cross with smiles his face, which even at that time his associates alleged was "shrivelled and wrinkled." His smiles and laughter spread in humorous confusion over his countenance long before the vehicle of speech had presented the object or subject of his humor to his auditors.

In his reading he devoured anything and everything that came in his way, never stopping to inquire what it was so long as it furnished his active mind something on which to labor. In like manner the subjects of his mimicry were as varied as occasion might offer, ranging from peculiarities in gait or speech of a neighbor or passing stranger to the pulpit efforts of the backwoods, hard-shell Baptist preacher. He was much in the habit of repeating the Sunday sermon to the men and boys in the field on Monday. If perchance he made a rare find, and his Monday audience appeared to appreciate his efforts, he repaired to the Gentryville store at night after the days' labor was done, and there repeated it, embellishing, revising, and enlarging as occasion seemed to warrant.

The Little Pigeon Baptist meeting house was erected in the year 1820.[9] The elder Lincoln was the boss carpenter, superintending its erection; and, while Abraham was but 11 years of age at this time, it is said that he assisted in felling the trees out of which the building material was obtained. This church was a story and a half high, and, while its proportions were not great— being 26 by 30 feet—for that period it made a rather pretentious house of worship. It had two windows, each 20 by 36 inches, and was heated in extreme weather by means of two old-fashioned fireplaces, there being two mud-and-stick chimneys, one at either end of the building.

The church was more or less regularly served by pastors duly called, but there were long intervals when the little congregation was largely dependent upon "local" ministers or some chance

ministerial visitor. The regular ministry, while more or less helpful, was in the main but little beyond the major portion of their
parishioners intellectually. Since most of them were illiterate,
and some of them painfully so and much given to certain pulpit
mannerisms, they afforded the critical student of human nature,
young Lincoln, a fine field for the free play of his powers of mimicry, and his mirth-provoking efforts at preaching were such as
indelibly to fix these in the memory of his boyhood associates
many years afterward.

Matilda Johnson, his step-sister, said "he was an indefatigable
preacher." It was his usual custom when his father and mother
went to church and he and other members of the family remained
at home to take down the Bible, read a verse, give out a hymn, and
after this had been rendered he proceeded to "preach" a sermon.
On one occasion when in the midst of Lincoln's sermon-lecture
in the grove near the cabin, John Johnson, his stepbrother, and
others who had doubtless heard the Sunday morning sermon
out in the fields during the week, came up with a land terrapin
which they had picked up in their morning rambles along the
creek, and desiring to witness the quick but clumsy movement
of the creature, placed a coal of fire on its back. Young Lincoln
remonstrated, but in the midst of the fun occasioned by the fran-
tic efforts of the fire-bearing creature to escape its tormentors,
Johnson picked it up and hurled it against a tree, breaking its
shell. As it lay quivering and dying the preacher quickly adapted
himself to his audience and began an exhortation on "Cruelty to
Animals," saying among other things that "an ant's life is just as
sweet to it as our lives are to us."

Young Lincoln was in the habit of delivering the Sunday sermon to his stepmother when for any cause she was not privileged to attend worship. The entire family would sit and listen
to Lincoln, who would repeat not only the sermon, but the text,
and in almost every way reproduce the morning effort, even
to the amen. Mrs. Lincoln greatly enjoyed these reports and

professed to think that she derived more benefit from Abe's ser-
monizing than she did from the minister himself.

The Lincoln home was the stopping place for the ministers.
This furnished such an opportunity for Lincoln to argue that
he invariably availed himself of it. On one occasion he had "cor-
nered" an illiterate preacher on some point in the story of Jonah,
and in the midst of his confusion Lincoln suddenly asked him
who was the father of Zebedee's children. The pastor confessed
that he did not know. This Zebedee witticism was one of Lincoln's
earliest attempts, although the first recorded humorous effort was
when going to mill and witnessing the slow grinding of the old
horse mill, he remarked that "his hound pup could eat all the meal
it would grind in a day and then bawl for his supper."

It was in the pulpit of this Little Pigeon Baptist meeting house,
Mr. Herndon states, that young Lincoln witnessed an amusing
incident which befell one of these transient preachers, an incident
that Lincoln in later years frequently related, and is as follows:

> The meeting house was located in the woods a mile and a half
> from our home and some distance from any other residence.
> Regular services were held only once each month. The preacher
> on this occasion was an old-line Baptist and was dressed in
> coarse linen pantaloons and shirt of the same material. The trou-
> sers were manufactured after the old-fashioned style, with baggy
> legs and flaps in front, commonly spoken of as "barn doors,"
> which were made to attach to the frame without the aid of sus-
> penders. A single button held his shirt in position, and that was at
> the collar. He arose in the pulpit and in a loud voice announced
> his text: "I am the Christ whom I shall represent today." About
> this time a little blue lizard ran up underneath his roomy panta-
> loons, and the old preacher not wishing to interrupt the steady
> flow of his sermon slapped away on his legs, expecting to arrest
> the intruder; but his efforts were unavailing, and the little fellow
> kept ascending higher and higher. Continuing the sermon, the
> preacher slyly loosened the button which held the waistband of
> his pantaloons, and with a kick off came the easy fitting garment.

Meanwhile Mr. Lizard had passed the equatorial line and was exploring the part of the preacher's anatomy which lay underneath the back of his shirt. Things by this time were growing interesting, but the sermon kept grinding on. The next movement on the part of the preacher was for the collar button, and with one sweep of his arm off came the tow linen shirt. The congregation sat for an instant as if dazed. At length one old sister in the rear of the room rose up and, glancing at the excited object in the pulpit, shouted at the top of her voice: "If you represent Christ, then I am done with the Bible."

On another occasion a traveling minister happened in the settlement one Sunday morning and was invited to preach. It appears that his pulpit mannerisms, gestures, and platform eccentricities were quite out of the ordinary. He had the habit among other things of rolling his eyes not unlike the old-time colored preacher; and when he warmed up to his theme, he pounded the Bible and the hymn book mercilessly, accompanied by certain pauses that might have been eloquent but for the fact that the speaker's zeal got the better of his judgment, for just at this juncture he introduced sundry groans and windy suspirations which no doubt he supposed would greatly aid in fastening the word as a nail in a sure place. In addition to the foregoing, the preacher possessed an unfortunate physical defect, perhaps acquired, which was so characteristic of not a few public speakers. He had a mingled sybillant, sonorous, nasal twang, which he pitched into that peculiar key in rendering his sing-song address.

Lincoln was present on this occasion, as were many others of his age, and some of these boyhood friends of Lincoln, among whom was Nat Griggsby, related that young Lincoln again and again repeated this sermon to the farm hands and the group of loungers at the Gentryville store, and so faithful was the presentation not only in words, but also in pulpit mannerisms—the rolling of the eyes, pounding of the Bible, and the nasal twang—that it was the judgment of those who heard Lincoln's effort as well as the original presentation that it was impossible to tell wherein the one differed from the other.

It will become at once apparent from some of the foregoing incidents that there never was any justification for the position taken by some of Mr. Lincoln's biographers in assuming, as they did, that he was inclined to make sport of the church or religion as such. The attitude assumed by some of his biographers was based not only upon this habit of Lincoln in repeating the Sunday sermon, but also upon some poetic effusions composed "in Bible language," usually after the manner and style of the ancient Chronicles, wherein he caricatured "Sister Gibson and Brother Gibson," members of the Little Pigeon church, who had been derelict in duty and in consequence had been called upon to undergo the ordeal of a church trial.[10] After diligent inquiry touching Mr. Lincoln's religious convictions, nothing whatever was found indicating any tendency toward infidelity or atheism, certainly no semblance of a disposition to criticise or lightly esteem the church or religion. This position of his earlier biographers, who were themselves personally so inclined, is absolutely without any foundation.

When it is recalled that young Lincoln's habit of mimicry and his subjects and objects of caricature were promiscuous, there is small wonder that these crude efforts in the pulpit were seized upon by him as quite the best for the exercise of his powers, since this field was more inviting than any other that presented itself and he very naturally availed himself of it.

Being naturally more or less a comedian and adapting himself to his audiences, he gave way to buffoonery indiscriminately, making selection of anything especially appealing to him. He not only mimicked the noisy traveling preacher who was much given to polemic discussion, but also was in the habit of repeating any public address heard, whether on the stump or before the bar. If the address appealed to him as being eloquent or possessing any excellence in any other way, he brought into play his exceptional powers of memory, repeating such portions with evident attempt at seriousness, noting their effect, taking this opportunity to "hear his voice," of which his associates maintained that he was especially vain. Not that his vanity led him to suppose that his voice was musical or fitted for public address beyond others, but his consuming ambition to become a public speaker gave free play to his fancy; and in such boyish efforts he flattered himself into the belief that he was preparing against the day when he could and would take the stump in real earnest.

He early manifested a desire to indulge himself in public address. If the school exhibitions may be taken into account, his age was about eleven years when he began on his own account. This disposition grew upon him through the years, until by the time he had reached 17 he was continually "on the stump." His stepmother stated that after a few efforts before boys of his age he at length ventured to try his powers before larger groups. He particularly made choice "of the hands in the fields" until, as she put it, "it soon became an amusing sight to see and hear him make these speeches." She further confessed that her "husband was forced to break it up with a strong hand" since it kept the men from their work.[11]

There appear to be few such characters as Shakespeare, Burns, and Lincoln who, if left to dwell apart and follow the plow or make use of the ax and maul, deprived of the privilege of a university or college, develop those great faculties which nature has so abundantly endowed them with, who happily reach their destined goal by a route, if circuitous and accompanied by exacting and patient toil, which is nevertheless apparently best suited to them.

Perhaps if Lincoln had been privileged to enjoy the curriculum of a great university, we would doubtless have had a master mind so skilled and trained as to have enabled him to occupy a commanding and enviable place in history, but it may well be doubted whether or not the very discipline imposed by such a course of training would not have marred or altogether lost to the world some of those rare qualities of mind and heart which were so prominent in him and which above all else distinguish him from most great men of his time.

Since Lincoln was destined to rise by the sheer force of his own personality and imperious will and to develop the great qualities of mind in this almost unbelievable manner, it was his good fortune to spend those years of strange preparations among a simple-minded, yet honest and patriotic folk, hedged in by a wilderness, but freed thereby from those conventional restraints and hindrances that older and more settled communities usually impose. At the same time he was removed from the blighting effects of vice which, had he been subjected to them, might have prevented the maturing of a character embodying all of the essential basic elements of the plain people. Lincoln did not, as some have supposed, live the cabin life in the White House so much as he lived the White House life in the cabin.

Any attempt to analyze his character or in any measure seek to account for the sustained, universal interest in him by substantially all classes of people, as well as youth, and claimed by all political faiths, leads to the fact that in him was embodied all of the essential and vital elements of manhood as well as the willingness and sincerity of purpose to give executive expression to the wishes of the people. There is discerned in this universal admiration of Lincoln not only an unconscious expression of resentment of such encroachment, but also an indication of an instinctive desire to throw off all mere artificialities of life. We recognize that in him dwelt the fullness of the simplicities of life to the extent that he became the apotheosis of the plain people.

Leonard Swett, a political friend and associate of the great President, stated that Lincoln in speaking of his Indiana life, always spoke of it as the story of a happy childhood. There was nothing sad or pinched about it and no allusion to want in any part of it. His own description of his youth was that of a happy, joyous boyhood. It was told with mirth, illustrated by pointed anecdotes, and often interrupted by his jocund laugh.[12]

If the Civil War crisis in our national life necessarily demanded a leader who was the embodiment of all that the people themselves stood for or desired, then Providence anticipated this by making choice of a youth without a distinguished name; reared him in the seclusion of the wilderness, just as He has almost all of His great leaders; and when he appeared, he so far met the high expectations of the Almighty and received the gratitude and applause of mankind that Major John Hay, his private secretary, voiced the sentiment of many when he said: "Abraham Lincoln was the greatest character that has appeared in the history of the world since Jesus Christ."

NOTES

1. Basler et al., *Collected Works of Abraham Lincoln*, 6:538.

2. Matthew Simpson (1811–1884) was indeed a trusted adviser to President Lincoln. He was with the Lincoln family at Lincoln's death and preached the sermon at his funeral in Springfield.

3. In great detail Murr describes various superstitions among those in southern Indiana, perhaps a reflection of Murr's own spiritual interests as a pastor. The degree to which Abraham Lincoln adopted these superstitions remains a matter of debate. Yet, on at least one occasion, Lincoln admitted, "I always was superstitious" (Abraham Lincoln to Joshua F. Speed, 4 July 1842, in Lincoln, *Speeches and Writings*, 95). Herndon published a letter in 1885 in a spiritualist magazine noting Lincoln was "in some phases of his nature, very, very superstitious" (William H. Herndon to the editor, 4 December 1885, *Religio-Philosophical Journal*, 12 December 1885).

4. This Friday superstition may trace to Jesus's crucifixion on that day of the week.

5. Gardening by the moon, or, more specifically, according to the phases of the moon, is an ancient practice not unique to southern Indiana. Roman historian Pliny the Elder, in his *Natural History*, offers advice on planting by moon phases. *Farmers' Almanac*, which began publication in 1818, has always followed the lunar-planting philosophy. See Jaime McLeod, "Why Do We Garden by the Moon?" *Farmers' Almanac*, accessed

31 August 2019, https://www.farmersalmanac.com/why-garden
-by-the-moon-20824.

6. In the King James Version this verse reads, "And when I passed by thee, and saw thee polluted in thine own blood, I said unto thee when thou wast in thy blood, Live; yea, I said unto thee when thou wast in thy blood, Live."

7. Although many church services were held in private homes on the frontier in the early nineteenth century, there is no other historic evidence to support when Lincoln first saw a distinct church building.

8. Nathaniel "Natty" Grigsby (1811–1890) was a good friend of Abraham Lincoln and attended school with him. Natty's brother, Aaron Grigsby, married Lincoln's sister, Sarah.

9. A plan to build a new Little Pigeon Baptist Church was organized in 1821, and that same year Thomas supervised its construction.

10. No Gibsons appear in the index to the Little Pigeon Church minute book, nor are any Gibsons buried in the church's cemetery.

11. Murr offers no sources for these quotations, and their origins remain unclear.

12. For more on Swett's comments, see Eckley, *Lincoln's Forgotten Friend*, 36. See also Rice, *Reminiscences of Abraham Lincoln*, 468.

NINE

LINCOLN, A HOOSIER

I am not afraid to die, and would be more than willing. But I have
an irrepressible desire to live till I can be assured that the world
is a little better for my having lived in it.[1]

ALTHOUGH MR. LINCOLN WAS BORN in Kentucky, it is not
possible by any proper method to classify him as a Kentuckian
in the sense that he stood forth as typical and representative of
the citizenship of that great State. The extreme poverty of his
parents, together with their utter lack of social standing with that
dominant class usually regarded both in Kentucky as well as by
those without as possessing those distinguishing traits that dif-
ferentiated them from citizens of other States, makes any attempt
to exalt one of Lincoln's class as typical or representative in any
way of Kentucky, but little short of preposterous.

Kentucky, as has been stated, has not only produced many
great sons, but has been especially fortunate in adopting others.
It may be said to her credit that she has been quite as kind to the
one as to the other, but the class whom she has delighted to honor
has not been that one to which Lincoln belonged. Henry Clay,
an adopted son, was more nearly representative of the genuine
Kentuckian in the estimation of Kentuckians themselves, and

certainly by those without the State, than any whom Kentucky
has ever produced.

If it be true that in him were to be found those distinguishing
traits more prominently than in others—traits which historians
and writers generally have regarded as peculiarly differentiating—
then it may be said that there are discerned even today among the
class to which he belonged these same marked traits; and being
generally true as it is of her citizens, and so much so as to justify
the pride they have in such a heritage, it would appear that but for
the unprecedented fame of Lincoln, there would have been great
hesitancy to classify him as one of their number in view of the fact
that he possessed nothing in common with the ruling portion of
them. Certainly there was nothing in common between Lincoln
and Henry Clay save their political predilections; for on the social
side and in all that distinguished Clay in addition to his brilliant
genius, Mr. Lincoln bore absolutely no resemblance. Lincoln was
awkward, ungainly, and homely to a marked degree; uneasy to the
extent of being bashful in the presence of ladies; lacking culture,
ease, and grace; a total stranger to many of the conventionalities of polite society. And thus had he been destined to remain in
the State of his birth, he would have more nearly represented the
mountaineer type and such as they, rather than that other class so
accustomed to such a man as Clay.

Clay was a Chesterfield in the drawing room, a Marlborough in
dignity and bearing before public assemblies; so polished and re-
fined in his manners, so brilliant and fascinating in conversation,
and so prepossessing in personal appearance as scarcely to have
an equal; withal a statesman the peer of any and all of his day, and
so persuasive, convincing and eloquent an orator, with a voice so
charming as to awe vast assemblies, command listening senates
and cause his one-time enemy, John Randolph of Roanoke, who
sat in his invalid chair, to exclaim to his attendants: "Lift me up
so that I may hear that voice once more." Henry Clay, and such
as he, will ever be regarded as embodying those eminent traits

bespeaking the genuine Kentuckian rather than will Abraham Lincoln, who would have been the last person to assert such a claim for himself.

Without, therefore, a purpose to make invidious distinction against any, it cannot be justly charged that the claim degenerates to the level of a mere puerility when it is asserted that Abraham Lincoln was a typical Hoosier rather than a Kentuckian, and he was such not only during his residence in Indiana, for one fourth of his life, but it is further asserted that he remained a Hoosier throughout his great career.

State lines, of course, do not ordinarily mark the boundaries of racial characteristics or peculiarities in manners and customs of representatives of the same people, save perhaps in those instances where large rivers or mountain ranges form the boundary lines. Hence the change of residence of Mr. Lincoln to the Sangamon River country was not such as to occasion any difficulty in adjusting himself to the purely local manners, habits, and customs of the people. But it is nevertheless true that there was a marked individuality and certain well-defined characteristics in speech and in habits of life typical of the Hoosier. These dominant traits of character which Mr. Lincoln acquired during a residence in Indiana of 14 years clung to him to the day of his death.

In his pronunciation (he began his Cooper Institute address by saying, "Mr. Cheerman"); his peculiar idioms, homely illustrations, figures of speech; his quaint humor and rare wit; his personal appearance; his refusal—at least failure—to conform readily to mere conventionalities in dress; and many other things of that sort were pre-eminently characteristic of the pioneer Hoosier. Mr. Lincoln's hands had held the ax and maul so long as to prove rebellious when the conventionalities of men attempted to glove them. His custom was to carry his gloves on occasion, but he rarely wore them.

The genius and all that has made for fame in Indiana has in the main been south of the National Road, which runs through the

State centrally from east to west. The Hoosier north of this line was as a rule an Eastern product—a Yankee—while the southern half of the State was peopled by Carolinians, Tennesseeans, Virginians, Kentuckians, and a few Yankees, the latter class coming by way of the Ohio River. If there is apparent contradiction to the foregoing statement in the pride that the State of Indiana has had or now has in such men as General Lew Wallace, Senator John W. Kern and Vice-president Thomas R. Marshall and others, let it be remembered that their blood and lineage are wholly that of the southern Hoosier; the tide of emigration coming up from the South merely carried them somewhat farther north than it did others.

That there was marked illiteracy during the pioneer period goes without saying, and that there was a sad lack of refinement and culture is also quite true. But it seems to have escaped the earlier writers' notice for a time that the blood which peopled the southern portion of the State in particular was for the most part quite as good as any in the New World; and since it was this strain that was destined to produce the first typical American, Abraham Lincoln, there is the highest reason for asserting that it was of the best.

Prior to the Civil war the eastern portion of our country looked upon the West somewhat after the manner that Europe viewed the New World, in the matter of letters, up to the time of Washington Irving. The country had been accustomed to look to the Atlantic coast for leadership in substantially everything, and so strongly intrenched was this notion in the minds of the people generally that even the people of the West themselves were slow to realize that it was this section of our country that was to produce the typical American. During the formative period of our country's history, the Atlantic coast was of necessity but Europe transplanted to the New World. So it became necessary to allow the tide of emigration to reach that region somewhat remote from these influences to bring forth "upon our new soil" this real dominant Americanism.

As great as was Mr. Lincoln in the estimation of the East, there are certain sections today that have never yielded the ancient notion of the East's own rightful leadership, and they refuse to allow that any good thing can come out of the West, which surpasses or even equals the East. Not that there is any vulgar opposition to the claim made by the West, so much as there is a dogged disposition to ignore the West to the point of thinking in terms of the East, and apparently not at all realizing that what we as a nation had been unconsciously striving for has been in fact consummated west of the Alleghenies.

That southern Indiana was of all places best suited to rear this great character destined to furnish the nations of the earth an example of the possibilities of the plain people is the position here taken. The odium, not to say the shame, of being a Hoosier has, as heretofore indicated, undergone a marked change since Lincoln's time. While Mr. Lincoln was a resident of this portion of Indiana, or soon after his reaching Illinois, there were many domiciled in log cabins in this Indiana wilderness who were afterward to become famous.

It is significant that the private secretary to Mr. Lincoln, Major John Hay, who later became one of our greatest Secretaries of State, was born a few miles north of where Lincoln lived;[2] and in 15 miles from the birthplace of Hay and a few miles to the east of Lincoln there lived Walter Q. Gresham, afterward an eminent jurist, a great soldier, and also a Secretary of State.[3] Here resided Eads, of Eads jetties fame; and it was from this portion of the State that there came Generals Harrison, Hovey, Wallace, Burnside, Rosencranz, and others of Civil War fame; the Lanes—James, Joseph, and Henry S.—and what shall we say of Generals Jefferson C. Davis, John Tipton, Governor Jennings and Joaquin Miller; of writers, jurists, orators, educators, and statesmen who subdued this wilderness, fought valiantly at Shiloh, Vicksburg, Antietam, Gettysburg, or marched with Sherman to the sea?[4] Among such a people capable of producing and rearing these and such as these, Mr. Lincoln spent those years between 7 and 21. If we may be permitted to assume that the Almighty desiring early to surround his destined leader through a terrible Civil War with those influences best calculated to bring about the deliverance of a people in bondage, as well as preserve the unity and continuity of a great nation, by taking him to a free State among a people who had strong convictions against human slavery, then we may see no departure from His ancient methods in dealing with His chosen.

Jefferson Davis, who was born in a slave state, within a few miles of Mr. Lincoln, and reared in the belief of the justice of such an institution, said by way of rejoinder to President Lincoln's Emancipation Proclamation, in a message to the Confederate congress, that "it was the most execrable measure ever recorded in the annals of guilty man." Thus we may perhaps be allowed to surmise that had Lincoln continued to reside in Kentucky, his attitude, if not favorable toward slavery, at least might have been so lenient as to have eliminated him from leadership in the nation's crisis. The Indiana residence, while freeing Mr. Lincoln from that favorable inclination that seems usually to have prevailed with those reared under its sway, was at the same time in close juxtaposition, and thus permitted him to look occasionally in upon its cruelties. It is quite generally understood that Mr. Lincoln's first view of slavery after reaching maturity was on the occasion of his celebrated flatboat trip down the Mississippi river with Allen Gentry, this being when he was 19 years of age.

The writer, while residing in Spencer County, Indiana, a number of years since, serving a church there in the capacity of minister, had in his congregation a number of elderly men and women who remembered very well that Lincoln, while a ferryman at the mouth of Anderson Creek, accompanied their neighbor, Mr. Ray, a flat-boatman, down the Mississippi River some two years prior to the celebrated trip with Allen Gentry.

The circumstance and the occasion of the trip were as follows: Lincoln, while serving as ferryman at the mouth of Anderson

Creek, had cultivated a crop of tobacco on the site of the present little village of Maxville, some three fourths of a mile below the town of Troy. The tobacco field had been planted and cultivated by Lincoln during the lull of business as a ferryman, and while the tobacco had ripened, had been cut, cured and otherwise prepared for the market, Mr. Ray, well known to Lincoln, "was building a flatboat up the mouth of Anderson" preparatory to making the southern trip. Accordingly Lincoln, thinking that he saw a way for marketing his "two hogsheads of tobacco," proposed to Ray that they "strike up a trade," and on Ray asking "what sort of a trade he meant," Lincoln replied, "I've got my tobacco crop cured up and ready for market, and I've got no way to get it south unless I send it by boat, and it struck me you'll need hands. You and me might get together some way. I'll tell you what I'll do. I'll go along with you at the oar if you'll take my tobacco and then pay me the difference." This proposition appealed to Ray, and the bargain was accordingly made, Lincoln going along as a hand "at the oar."[5]

William Forsythe, for many years a businessman in Grandview, Spencer County, born and reared in the town of Troy, remembered "long Abe," the ferryman. He often related to the writer the circumstance of his having been "set across Anderson by Lincoln." He stated that the boys of Troy would frequently go down to the mouth of Anderson creek to hear "Long Abe talk and tell yarns." While he failed to recall any of "Long Abe's yarns," he stated that when the boys had "prowled about town" and time hung heavily on their hands, some one would at such times speak up and say, "Let's go down to Anderson and listen at Long Abe talk." Usually this suggestion was acted upon, and they would straightway repair to the ferry. When asked as to what Long Abe talked about, he replied, "He would just set down and the boys 'd all get around him and he'd say things that would make them all laugh." Forsythe often related the circumstance of Lincoln's making the flatboat trip down the Mississippi River with Ray.

Jefferson Ray, a son of the flatboat-man, was likewise a business-man; and he, as was Forsythe, was officially connected with the church of which the writer was pastor. Thus these and many others—some having personal knowledge and others relating the circumstance as received from Ray—establish beyond any doubt that Lincoln looked in upon slavery at least two years earlier than we have been accustomed to suppose.

The fact that Lincoln thus had an earlier view of slavery than is generally believed is, of course, of no great moment in any ef-fort made to establish his opposition to that institution. That he possessed a life-long conviction that all men should be free is indisputably true; but if he did in fact, as here recorded, make this flatboat trip south at such an impressionable age (that of 17), and it is as clearly established as anything could well be, then it does become more or less valuable not only as furnishing him a more extended view of the effects of slavery, but doubtless in no small measure served also as a preparation for the two later journeys south in more mature years, thus enabling him to profit during the interval by meditation and reflection such as must have nec-essarily arisen on the occasion of the journey made in the earlier period of his life.

In addition to the foregoing, the fact of Lincoln's having made this journey south should be told now since the earlier biogra-phers have failed to record it, and the passing of all those who could supply data and subject matter precludes the possibility of any future historian being able to glean in a field which is of course now largely, if not wholly, barren.

It should perhaps be stated in this connection that the writer found no authentic account of any definitely expressed convic-tions by Lincoln covering this period on the question of African slavery. However, James Gentry, when interrogated as to this par-ticular, exclaimed: "Why, Abe always was against slavery!" And then he added: "But Abe followed Henry Clay around wherever he'd go in mighty nigh everything, and old Harry's notions was responsible fer Abe a bein' so slow to send out his Emancipation Proclamation. Abe'd a done it long before he did, I reckon, if his head hadn't been so full of Henry Clay's notions."

That Henry Clay was Lincoln's political ideal and possessed marked influence upon him is true, and to no small extent justifies the conviction here expressed by his old boyhood friend and associate. Lincoln, naturally conservative and of the Clay school in politics, not only saved the border States to the Union during the Civil War, but on the other hand was able sufficiently to modify his Clay notion of gradual emancipation to issue finally the Emancipation Proclamation when it appeared to be warranted by military necessity.

NOTES

1. Speed, *Reminiscences of Lincoln*, 39; Speed to Herndon, Louisville, 7 February and 13 September 1866, in *Herndon's Informants*, ed. Wilson and Davis, 197, 337.

2. John Hay (1838–1905) was born about seventy-four miles away in Salem, Indiana.

3. Walter Gresham (1832–1895) was born in Lanesville, Indiana.

4. Jefferson F. Davis (1808–1889), president of the Confederate States, was born in Fairview, Kentucky, less than one hundred miles southeast of Lincoln's birthplace in Hodgenville, Kentucky.

5. Lincoln never mentions this trip in any recollections or accounts of his time in Indiana, a fact that undercuts its credibility. Indeed, Lincoln stated his first trip of this nature occurred at age nineteen. Lincoln's two flatboat trips to New Orleans, the first in 1828 with Allen Gentry and the second in 1831 with John Johnston and John Hanks, formed the longest journeys of Lincoln's life up to that point and were his only visits to the Deep South.

TEN

ONE-FOURTH OF LINCOLN'S LIFE SPENT IN INDIANA

I tell my Tad that we will go back to the farm where I was happier as a boy when I dug potatoes at twenty-five cents a day than I am now.[1]

MENTION HAS BEEN MADE OF the fact that in many instances those who have undertaken the task of writing extensively concerning the life and character of Mr. Lincoln have professed to see comparatively little which appeared to justify special treatment beyond a few anecdotes and stories in the events of his career prior to his becoming a resident of Illinois. It is strange indeed that in this day, when educators are calling attention particularly to the adolescent period of youth, that there has not been some effort beyond that hitherto attempted to note particularly this period in the life of our martyred President.

The failure to do this, especially in more recent times, is doubtless attributable in part to the fact that those who have attempted to gather suitable data have generally made hasty journeys to this field; and meeting with comparatively little success, they have yielded to the belief that this period was so elusive as not to warrant any extended effort.

In view of the fact that Lincoln is so generally regarded as a model in the higher reaches of statesmanship, politics, and morals, and possessing as he did substantially all of the cardinal virtues, so that writers and speakers, both on the platform and in the pulpit, editors of magazines, the press, educators in the great universities, the schoolmaster in the "little red schoolhouse," and the plain people in the highways and about the firesides in millions of homes are accustomed daily to recount his virtues, laud and magnify his name; therefore, if it can be shown with any degree of certainty that the formative years had much to do in shaping Mr. Lincoln's unprecedented career, then it would appear that a somewhat extended investigation of this period of his life is not without considerable interest. Moreover, if these neglected years may be made to yield a fruitful harvest, then it is but just to the memory of Lincoln that this be done, especially since he reached the heights of fame from a lower level than any other great character in history.

The only great men in American history comparable to President Lincoln by reason of early disadvantages are Horace Greely, Henry Wilson, and Benjamin Franklin.[2] If in the judgment of some there be yet others, distinctively American, deemed worthy of such comparison, these named are at least representative. They were all born in a zone of alluring chance and opportunity as compared with Lincoln. Greeley and Wilson were each within a three-days' tramp of educational centers while Franklin was born and lived in one. The beaten path of travel crossed their horizon. There was no lack of incentive and inspiring examples of patriotic men prominent in public affairs while Lincoln's youth was far remote from any and all of those influences calculated to uplift and inspire, things usually deemed so essential in attaining unto excellence.

Lincoln's poverty, like Franklin's and Wilson's, was exceedingly great, but was in his case more easily and contentedly endured than the more exacting thing of being deprived of a chance to quench his consuming thirst for knowledge. His youthful ambition to rise in the world was native, dominating, and irresistible.

Denied as he was the privileges of school, access to libraries, and the association of the educated and learned, it was left for him to demonstrate the possibility of going forth to conquer, unaided by artificial and external means, save a borrowed library of seven books and becoming as he did such a master of them as to enable him in turn to master men, cope with rising events, and challenge the admiration of mankind. So great were his achievements and so enduring his fame that he staggers royalty on its road with burdens of oppression into soberness and justice and provokes and inspires by his illustrious deeds along the path from the dust-covered floor of his wilderness cabin to the nation's capital, the peasant's son to hope. The boy Lincoln needed no incentive to acquire knowledge. To know with him was, from the first, a passion. He did not wish so much for examples of what learning might accomplish or produce as he did for the necessary tools with which he might fashion the boy of his day, himself, into the man he really believed himself capable of becoming.

He early learned to believe in himself, implicitly, trustfully, and overwhelmingly; and no one thing was more conspicuous throughout his entire career than this, save perhaps his honesty. No President of the United States ever received more advice and listened to it more patiently than he, but no man who ever sat in the executive chair of the nation needed it less or used it more sparingly. This was characteristic of him as a youth. He gave a patient hearing to all and then followed his own counsel. He was quite self-contained and abundantly resourceful, accustomed as he was in youth, and later in his public career, to be much on the stump, yet his caution was so great as to make him a rather poor extemporaneous speaker. He must first think it over and then he was ready without fear or favor. He never doubted his ability to meet any emergency or master any task, and he cared but little for precedent although he established more precedents than any other President in American history. He wrote his first inaugural address without consultation with anybody and read this "as if he had been delivering inaugural addresses all his life."[3] He kept his own counsel. In mature years he rarely confided in his most intimate friends. He never did fully in any of them. In youth this trait was noticeable. He was diffident on occasions and impressed all of his associates with the idea that what he said on any given subject was but little as compared to much that he could say. He never left any one in doubt, however, as to any position taken on any subject. From the day of his youthful opposition to intemperance down to the "house divided against itself" speech and the famous letter to Horace Greeley wherein he stated that his "paramount object was to save the Union," he stood out in the open. He rescued politics from the charge of trickery and double-dealing and restored it to a place of honor, and if it has at any time since sunk down into the "mud and scum of things," it is no fault of his.

What Lincoln purposed doing or saying in any given case he carried out to the letter. Where most others jumped at conclusions, he patiently reasoned his way; and when once he reached it, no one could by any possibility, either by persuasion or force, move him. Mrs. Lincoln once said of him, "When he has made up his mind, no one can change him."

As a youth his obstinacy would have passed for stubbornness but for the manifest fairness and justness of the position taken. This, together with the fact that his sense of justice and honesty ever caused him to make amends for any mistake in judgment which he made, caused him to be invariably chosen by his associates to adjudicate differences.

Any boyhood quarrel leading to fight ended by Lincoln's opponent becoming his friend. He "got mad," but was a stranger to malice. When he said in a great state paper—his second Inaugural Address—"with malice toward none, with charity for all," he was not voicing a thing learned during the terrible four years' war; he was but announcing to the world that his lifelong disposition to hold no malice; after having been tried in the fires of four years of Civil War, he had come out unchanged. Had General Andrew Jackson been in his stead and given utterance to such a sentiment, we would perhaps have deemed it so at variance with his accustomed manner as to call it hypocrisy. Jackson, however, would never have uttered this sentiment at the close of a great war for the preservation of the Federal Union. It may be doubted whether we have ever had any other President who would have done so.

Young Lincoln had a fight with William Grigsby when 16 years of age, and not only did they "make up" and become friends, but also during the Civil War on one occasion when party spirit ran high, a man in Gentryville was freely indulging in criticism of Lincoln and "Bill Grigsby hauled his coat off and made him take it back." The Lincoln critic was a local bully, and after the trouble, when Lincoln's honor had thus been saved by proxy, Grigsby exclaimed: "No man can talk about Abe around here unless he expects to take a lickin'."

The great Lincoln lecturers such as Bishop Charles Fowler, Vice-president Schuyler Colfax, and Col. Henry Watterson, listened to with attention and great profit by multitudes, always placed the emphasis upon other periods in Mr. Lincoln's life rather than upon the formative years. Indeed, it cannot escape the notice of the least observant that substantially all that has ever been said upon the platform concerning Mr. Lincoln's youth, especially as pertaining to or influencing in any way his public career, has been very largely confined to those years (the first seven) spent in Kentucky, the State of his birth.

Some of his biographers, in desiring to have him secure the supposed benefits of a longer residence in his native State than it was his fortune to have, took some liberties with certain incidents occurring at a later period and gave them a Kentucky setting. Two biographers at least distinctly assert that Lincoln was called "honest Abe" while yet a resident of Kentucky; and some of them attribute to him the ability [to] read and write while a mere infant, making much of his schooling in that State, and otherwise making assertions that are incompatible with reliable testimony.

The boy Lincoln learned to read quite young, while yet a resident of Kentucky. He was, however, indebted to his mother for this skill rather than to Riney or Hazel, his two teachers there. The attendance at the Riney school was at the age of four, only for a very brief time, and he went simply to accompany his sister, Sarah. He was seven years old when he attended the next term. Evidently he was greatly profited and made rapid progress during this session.

Col. Henry Watterson in his great lecture on Lincoln, as well as in other public addresses where incidental reference to Lincoln is made, invariably speaks of him as the "great Kentuckian," making no mention whatever of that period in Mr. Lincoln's life spent in the State of Indiana.[4] But as if fortifying himself against the possibility of this assertion being called in question, since the whole of that life save the first seven years was spent outside Kentucky, he straightway asks, "For what was Springfield, Illinois, but a Kentucky colony?"

In view of the foregoing logic, what would be the claim in behalf of Henry Clay, who was a bearded man from the State of Virginia when taking up his residence in Kentucky? And to use the interrogatory of Colonel Watterson, and apply it to Mr. Clay, we may ask, "For what was Kentucky but a Virginia colony?" Again in the case of Gen. Albert Sidney Johnston of New England lineage, that great military captain who came so nearly planting the Stars and Bars on the banks of the Ohio River, does it follow that he was a Puritan when his impressionable years of training were spent among Cavaliers? And yet again, because the last remaining member of the old school of brilliant editors, Col. Watterson himself, honored as he is throughout the nation, and ever regarded as a truly great Kentuckian, because he himself happened to be born elsewhere than in the State of Kentucky, does it in the least lessen the just claim to such distinguished consideration since he like Mr. Clay is the very embodiment of all of those eminent traits bespeaking a Kentuckian?

When the bill before the United States Senate proposing to appropriate $2,000,000 for the erection of a Greek memorial temple to the memory of Lincoln was under discussion, Senator Ollie James of Kentucky, in speaking in behalf of the measure and in opposition to the proposed substitute, that of erecting a memorial highway from Washington City to the battlefield of Gettysburg, spoke of Mr. Lincoln as "that great Kentuckian" and suggested that if it was deemed advisable to construct a Lincoln roadway anywhere, it would be more fitting to build one from Lincoln's birthplace in Kentucky to the State of Illinois. The presumption is that in that event this highway would pass through Indiana, although, as usual, no mention was made of that State.

Ex-Presidents Roosevelt and Taft both visited the birthplace of Mr. Lincoln in official capacity, and both of them, in addresses on those occasions, did not fail to note the fact (and very properly so) that Mr. Lincoln was a Kentuckian by birth, but no mention was made of the fact that when Illinois received him he was a bearded man, and when Kentucky dismissed him he was a mere child, departing with little more than a memory of his native state.

Colonel Roosevelt in particular spoke of Mr. Lincoln as "the great Kentuckian," and associated him with the Kentucky pioneers. Indeed, some of Mr. Lincoln's biographers have repeatedly denominated him as a Kentucky pioneer, whereas his parents were both Virginians; and while he was born in Kentucky, in leaving that State while yet so young, he cannot rightly be claimed as in any sense a Kentucky pioneer. As Colonel Roosevelt asserts, he was associated with these pioneers although but very briefly and merely as a child. However, some of his Indiana neighbors were Kentuckians.

A search through numerous addresses delivered on great public occasions, in lectures, periodicals, and books reveals the unmistakable fact that but small space has been allotted to those years in the life of the great President spent in Indiana, but much has been said by the many concerning Mr. Lincoln's birthplace and a labored effort made to account for his greatness by the mere fact of his having had a Kentucky origin. The reasons for this are perhaps not difficult to ascertain, at least some of them.

Kentucky had the proud distinction of early producing or adopting many great men. Being the gateway to the North through which the emigrant tides poured to the newer states and territories, she took toll of these, often selecting the best, but not always. As a slave State fostering an institution that materially contributed to the creation of a regime generally prevailing over a large portion of the state, although not all, Kentucky lodged with this favored class all the political power, as well as the intellectual, financial and social prestige. It was this class that was met with and spoken of; and being especially fortunate in her adoption of Henry Clay, Kentucky saw the world without readily coming to regard Clay and such as he as typifying Kentucky as a whole.

Her mountaineers and poor whites did not at that time disturb averages as they now do. They were then content to enjoy their feudal rights. The currents of life swept around them. No John Fox Jr. was at that period portraying their life and character, but whatever was said in song or story was of the other dominant and ruling class.[5] So true was this that when Stephen Collins Foster from farther north looked in upon this scene, he was induced to locate "The Old Kentucky Home" in the Blue Grass region with "darkies gay" and pickaninnies playing on the cabin floor.

Indiana was not so fortunate in some particulars. During the pioneer period of her history, and therefore while Lincoln was a resident of that State, the term *Hoosier* was given to her citizens, a name at that time and for a considerable period thereafter conveying the idea of, whatever else it may, inferiority, boorishness in manners, deplorable ignorance, and crudity; and thus the name was indicative of that something bespeaking an inhabitant of a State whose community life was believed to be faithfully portrayed by Edward Eggleston in the *Hoosier School Master*. Eggleston perhaps never meant that his fictitious portraiture of the early pioneers was to be taken so seriously, but fiction though it was and portraying as it did the life and character of the pioneer type of that day, not only in the State of Indiana but also throughout the Middle West, no matter-of-fact history was ever more faithfully and literally received. It is believed that in remote sections of our country there are those today who still hold to the ancient belief, and apply it to the present generation of Hoosiers. Therefore, for one seeking to eulogize a great character, and particularly such a one as Lincoln, deficient as he was in the training of the schools, certainly anything else but polished in the manners and customs peculiar to the older and more settled communities, and above all, one who apparently by nature was so democratic in his tastes and appetencies, there is small wonder that the earlier historians and eulogists (all of whom save one were from without the State) studiously avoided the Hoosier period in Mr. Lincoln's life, save that in tracing his itinerary they bridged these formative years spent among Hoosiers with a few incidents and anecdotes of more or less interest and briefly noted the beginnings of his career, then passed on to the more active years of his manhood in the State of Illinois.

At this late day when we are so far removed from those things once generally prevalent, when the title *Hoosier* has become quite as honorable as that borne by the citizens of any State in the Union, and more especially when we come to consider the life and services of such a world character as was Mr. Lincoln, some things may be justly asserted concerning the Hoosier period in his life with a reasonable expectation that adequate emphasis be allowed and it in consequence be placed in its proper relation.

Three states—Kentucky, Indiana, and Illinois—helped produce, rear, and offer the world this great character. It is a distinguished honor that the State of Kentucky has in being able to point with pardonable pride to the spot that gave birth to our greatest American. This spot has been highly and very fittingly honored by the expenditure of a vast amount of money in the erection of a suitable memorial building. This has caused Presidents, congressmen, governors of States, and multitudes of the plain people to make pilgrimages there and thus pay homage to his memory.

The prairie State of Illinois that twice offered Mr. Lincoln as her successful candidate for the Presidency, and in whose soil his body now reposes beneath a costly and imposing monument, has just cause for pride. But if Kentucky gave Mr. Lincoln birth, it was as if she deemed that quite sufficient honor and speedily dismissed him at the tender age of seven to be received by the new State of Indiana with a pioneer's welcome. Here amid the heroic frontier hardships he reached his majority, spending 14 years, or just one fourth of his entire life on Indiana soil.

In an address to an Indiana regiment of Civil War soldiers President Lincoln said, "I was born in Kentucky, raised in Indiana, and now live in Illinois." Since it is particularly with these years spent in Indiana with which we have to do, the inquiry is here made: What period in the life of any man is of as much interest or ordinarily calculated to influence and shape the destiny as those years between 7 and 21? What happened during those formative years in Mr. Lincoln's life? Was his stay in Indiana a mere chance, one of the accidents in the fortune of a roving, nomadic father, or is there rather discerned a leading of Providence?

It may not be inappropriate here to raise the question, would his career have been what it afterward became had he spent these formative years elsewhere, even in the State of Illinois? Or, reversing the order of history, had he been born in Indiana, spending the first seven years there, removing to the State of Kentucky, remaining there until attaining his majority, and then going to Illinois as he did, would his career have been what it was? It is believed that certain influences would have produced marked changes in him, and so much so as to have prevented Lincoln from becoming the great antislavery advocate and leader. Moreover, it cannot be doubted that had he spent all of these 14 formative years in Kentucky, even though born in Indiana, his greatness would have almost wholly been attributed to a residence and rearing among Kentucky pioneers, and the accident of his birth would have doubtless received somewhat less consideration than it has. Unquestionably, had Mr. Lincoln been reared elsewhere than in Indiana, particularly in a slave State, the plans and purposes of his life might have been hindered or defeated altogether. In raising such questions we are not wholly in a field purely conjectural.

NOTES

1. Whipple, *Story-Life of Lincoln*, 567.
2. Henry Wilson (1812–1875) was vice president under U. S. Grant and senator from Massachusetts.
3. Lincoln sought and received ideas from several others on the draft of his first inaugural address, including soon-to-be secretary of state William Seward, who suggested softening the original tone; Seward also contributed to the speech's closing.
4. Henry Watterson (1840–1921) worked as a prominent journalist in Kentucky and served as a Confederate soldier in the Civil War.
5. John Fox Jr. (1862–1919) was a popular novelist and short-story writer.

—⚋—

ELEVEN

THE EVERYDAY LIFE OF LINCOLN

I personally wish Jacob Freese, of New Jersey, appointed colonel of
a colored regiment, and this regardless of whether he can tell the
exact shade of Julius Caesar's hair.[1]

MANY PEOPLE HAVE FROM TIME to time expressed a desire
to know somewhat more in detail concerning the every-day life
of Lincoln's youth; something as to his manners, habits and customs; whether he possessed vicious tendencies; whether he was
given to idleness or not, as has been alleged; whether he was of a
quarrelsome nature; and many other things of this sort, so that
some adequate idea might be formed as to just what extent, if
any, there was a basis for supposing him at that time making any
preparation, however unconsciously, for the unprecedented career that awaited him.

A painstaking effort was made covering this field of inquiry,
and it is believed that these repeated interviews with his former
associates elicited information which will aid in reaching conclusions as to the influence some things transpiring in his youth had
in shaping his destiny.

It should be stated first of all that Lincoln himself was accustomed to assert from his fifteenth year onward, in a sort of

half-jest, half-earnest way, that he didn't always expect to grub, dig, and maul. When asked at such times what he expected to do, he invariably replied, "I'll do something and be somebody," and often closed by saying, "I'll be President, I reckon."[2] If Lincoln possessed visions of a future altogether different from the ceaseless round of menial toil, which did not particularly promise to better his condition since he failed to receive remuneration commensurate thereto, his boyhood associates in no single case asserted that they at any time anticipated the great career of Mr. Lincoln. As we now look back upon Mr. Lincoln's career and witness his rise to fame, it appears so utterly at variance with all that is deemed essential to achieve greatness as to occasion momentary doubts of the truthfulness of history. Had he lived in an earlier age, his life story would have speedily passed into romance and fiction.

Contrary to the usual representation, a number of these boyhood friends, while not especially schooled, were quite well informed, and many of them had prospered until they possessed at least passing wealth. No better citizens could be found anywhere than the Gentrys, Larmars, Halls, Forsythes, Brooners, and others. These men asserted that "Lincoln as a boy was jokey and lively, entering into all of their boyish sports heartily." These sports and games consisted of jumping half hammon (now called hop, step, and jump), the broad jump, running, slap jack, town ball, stink base, wrestling, I spy, etc.

On one occasion when quite a number of the young folks had gathered at the Lincoln cabin and were engaged in a game of "hide and go seek," Lincoln among them, Granny Hanks came to the door with a Bible in her hands, and calling to young Lincoln, said, "Abe, I want you to come in hyar and read a chapter for me out'n the Bible. I aint heard it read fur a right smart spell." It should be stated that it is not certain just who this old lady was, but there was a lady called "Granny Hanks" who, for a time at least, resided with the Lincolns. These pioneer neighbors of the

Lincolns frequently alluded to her in conversation. No mention has ever been made of her by any of Mr. Lincoln's biographers, and it is quite immaterial for our purpose to establish the identity, save that there might arise the charge that this character was purely fictitious. That substantially all of the immediate relatives of Nancy Hanks followed her to Indiana is the statement made by the Hankses themselves, and thus there need be no scruples as to the identity of this particular lady.

We are accustomed to believe that in those days respect on the part of young folks for old age was especially characteristic. At any rate, in this case Lincoln immediately quit the game when so requested and went into the house followed by all the rest of the young folks. The future humorist and wit, who read a chapter from Artemus Ward to members of his cabinet just before announcing his intention of publishing the Emancipation Proclamation, now gravely seated himself opposite the old lady and presently began thumbing the leaves of the book which had been handed to him in search of a suitable chapter. The young people had crowded into the room, some being seated on the backless bench, some two or three on chairs, and a number standing about the room. Presently the reader began a chapter, presumably in the Prophecy of Isaiah, but he had not read very far until he began making use of Bunyan's *Pilgrim's Progress* and such other volumes as he was familiar with, all this time making solemn but ill-concealed, sly observations as to just how this rendering was being received by Granny Hanks. After a number of verses had been read the old lady's suspicion became aroused; and finally when the reader ventured to make a rather free translation, she suddenly interrupted him by exclaiming, "Abe, I've heard the Bible read a great many times in my life, but I never yit heard them things in it afore." Lincoln, perceiving that he was fairly caught, threw off his make-believe solemnity and abandoned himself to guffaws of hearty laughter, at the same time lifting the book high above his head and occasionally striking his knees a resounding whack with the free hand. After indulging himself in this manner for a time and occasioning more or less merriment among the older boys and girls present, his laughter at length subsided and he remarked, "Granny, you caught me that time, didn't you?" He then began deliberately reading again, this time following the text.

The character of Lincoln's humor and his disposition to make free use of it at the least provocation by associating it, as in this instance, with the more serious things of life were apparently prominent enough at an early period readily to account for some of the surprises produced in the minds of cabinet officers and others high in authority during the days of his occupancy of the White House.

It is exceedingly difficult for those of this century and age of plenty, accustomed to the numerous conveniences of modern life, to appreciate adequately the social standing, self denial and lack of the many things once regarded as luxuries, but now considered as necessities and which in many instances are now to be had merely for a trifle. Moreover, the early settlers, particularly in Lincoln's day, had to contend with some things which their descendants are free from altogether. In addition to the afflictions peculiar to the pioneer period as well as the danger of being exposed to wild animals, there were many annoyances to which the people were subjected. They had the mosquito without the modern conveniences of meeting his attacks; the woods tick still met with in certain sections; burrs such as the "stick tights," "Spanish needles," cockle, and "beggar's lice"; venomous serpents such as the deadly rattlers and copperheads—the latter being, if not quite as venomous, certainly more treacherous; chiggers and numerous inconveniences. In addition to the foregoing there were the body and head lice, particularly the latter. It was Lincoln's favorite poet, Burns, who wrote a poem "on seeing a louse on a lady's bonnet." Had the Scotch bard been a resident of this section in the early days, he would have had occasion to witness the "crawlin' beastie" again and again, for no term of school ever closed without a siege by this species of vermin.

Wesley Hall stated:

> One morning bright and early Abe came to our home, and after being seated and asked by my mother in true neighborly fashion, "How are all the folks?" he replied, "They are all well, Mrs. Hall, but mother thinks the children have got the creepers, and she sent me over here this morning to borry your fine-tooth comb." When this information was imparted, Mrs. Hall threw up her hands and exclaimed, "My Lordy, Abe, d'ye reckon it's a fact?" Whereupon Abraham observed that "he reckoned they had, but not having a comb with teeth close enough together to ketch 'em, he had been dispatched on the hunt of one that would."

The accommodating possessor of this household article brought it forth and knowing that her own children, and Wesley in particular, had been at play with the Lincoln children, she suddenly suggested the possibility of the "creepers" having found lodgment on the heads of the younger members of her own household and, desiring to verify her supposition, she put it to the test by proceeding to comb the head of young Wesley and found abundant evidence to justify all of her suspicions. After young Hall had been subjected to this rigid examination, with Lincoln seated near, occasionally offering humorous remarks, Mrs. Hall made bold to suggest the possibility of the "creepers" being upon Lincoln's head; whereupon he acquiesced to the effect that there was a possibility of this being true. Then Mrs. Hall further pointedly suggested that she be privileged to make examination. Lincoln got down on his knees before her and bent his head over, facing a newspaper spread out on the floor so that it was not long before all concerned were satisfied that the investigation was timely.

Lincoln was given to indulging himself in the sport of fishing, coon and opossum hunting at nights, but found sport distasteful if he had to stalk a deer cautiously, approach a flock of turkeys, or sit quietly on the bank of a stream without a companion. Such distaste grew out of the fact that it divorced him from his companions or necessitated refraining from conversation. His enjoyment of the night-hunting was attributed to the fact that on such expeditions there was small need of refraining from hilarious conversation; and since it placed him in company of a goodly number of men and boys, he engaged in this particular diversion quite frequently. His overmastering desire to be found in the company of others—the more, the better—led him to attend all social functions of the neighborhood such as weddings, corn-huskings, log-rollings, and raisings. In fact, he could usually be found mingling with the crowd no matter what had called it together. His presence, therefore, on some of these occasions, was not due to any especial interest in the things done, but because he loved the fellowship of men. He frequented all horse races held in the settlement; and if a fight between two bullies was scheduled, he was invariably present. These horse races, of course, were nothing more than a test of speed of "brag horses" in that and adjoining neighborhoods, the owners having usually placed a bet and challenged one another to a test. They partook somewhat of the nature of Indian pony races rather than regular racetrack meets. The race was run on a straight-away, often a public road. Such gatherings afforded opportunity also to ascertain who was the champion "wrastler" and the best broad or half-hammon jumper. Foot races were indulged in; "town ball," "stink base," and "chicken" were played not only before and after the races, but also on many other occasions where crowds were gathered. Horseshoe pitching, throwing a heavy maul as a shot put, lifting a dead weight—usually a boulder or log—and many other such things tested physical endurance and prowess. In all feats of strength Lincoln excelled, as in throwing the maul and wrestling. Because he was exceedingly awkward, his movements, while surprisingly quick, were ludicrous and provoked more or less merriment. Fistic encounters were quite common, but resort to the use of a weapon such as a knife or gun was exceedingly rare. Men bearing any grudge against each other, or taking umbrage at any fancied slight or insult, would say, "I'll meet you Saturday at town, and I'll settle with you there." Hence Saturday afternoon fights were numerous. Usually the fight was fair, that is, "no gouging or biting" was permitted, and no interference on the part of the bystanders was suffered on penalty of a personal chastisement by a backer. If the underman "hollered enough," that was usually satisfactory to both the victor and onlookers, but if in the heat of passion other punishment was still meted out, there was no lack of friends and sympathizers for the underdog who speedily came to his rescue. Lincoln was much given to wrestling, but seldom fought. He was not averse to this, but his well-known strength for a youth—a minor—prevented difficulties with men; and since he reached his gigantic stature of six feet, four inches, when 16 years of age, and possessing great strength, he was "too big to fight a boy and too young to fight a man." It should not be inferred by any of these remarks that Lincoln was quarrelsome or usually disposed to "pick a quarrel." Indeed, the very opposite was true of him, but in the phraseology of the day, "he allus toted his own skillet." When provoked and jeered at by the uninitiated because of his awkward appearance, he received the banterings at first quite good naturedly, and his tormentors were easily led into the belief that he was a coward. When forbearance ceased to be a virtue, Lincoln stood up for his honor and invariably thrashed his assailant.

Rothschild in *Master of Men*, in speaking of Lincoln during this period, said, "He was the shyest, most reticent, most uncouth and awkward appearing, homeliest and worst dressed of any in the entire crowd."[3] This characterization in some particulars is not in accordance with the facts as detailed by many of Lincoln's early friends. Young Lincoln was not shy of anything or anyone, save that he manifested more or less uneasiness in the presence of ladies. This was certainly true of him while reading law at New

Salem, Illinois, when it is related that he changed his boarding place because a number of strange ladies came there to take their meals. When called upon in Washington City to make an address before ladies, he stated that "he was not accustomed to the eulogy of women." Lincoln was not reticent at any time in life, and no more during his youth than at a later period, but if by reticence it is aimed to show that he could keep his own counsel and otherwise prevent encroachment upon his reserve, then no youth nor adult was any more reticent than he. But as a youth "he was a talker" and an incessant one although he was a good listener. He was not dictatorial or inclined to monopolize conversation, but so incessant a talker was he that he was charged, and doubtless justly so, by his associates as being "vain about hearing his own voice." However, it should be said that this allegation was made having in view his habit of preaching or stump speaking.

Major John Hay, his private secretary, asserted that Lincoln's intellectual arrogance and unconscious assumption of superiority was the one thing that such men as Senator Sumner and Governor Chase could never forgive. Secretary Seward, that astute politician and sage of Auburn, after three months of the untried Lincoln in the White House, wrote his wife that "the President is more than a match for us all."

When Mrs. Lincoln early in the administration said to her husband that certain politicians were asserting that Secretary Seward would "run things," Lincoln calmly remarked, "I may not rule myself, but certainly Seward shall not. The only ruler I have is my conscience, following God in it, and these men will have to learn that yet."[4]

Lincoln had a becoming respect for age—provided age set the example. A lady whom Lincoln had occasionally called on and accompanied to social gatherings, said,

> One evenin' Abe and me wus standin' out in the yard at our
> house a talkin', and we heard a clatter of horses' hoofs comin' up

the road that run past the house, and purty soon we seen who it was. It was a neighbor that wus always braggin' about his horses, a claimin' he had the fastest horse in all the country 'round, and he had a proud way of ridin' just to show off. So as I say, up he come, like as if he wus going after a doctor, and when he got opposite to us he stopped and begun as usual to brag about his horse, sayin' among other things that he could ride him in a lope all the way to Boonville and he'd never even draw a long breath, and a whole lot more things like that. Abe stood there and 'peared to listen to him like if 'twas the first time he'd ever heard him tell them things, and then when he finally got through, Abe up and says: "I've heard you say that time and again. In fact, your always a braggin' on what you've got and what you c'n do or a goin' to do. Now suppose jest for once in your life you quit your braggin' and blowin' around and really do something. Strike out for Boonville, and when you git there, take a right good look and see if your brag horse aint fetchin' some mighty short breaths."

As to Lincoln's being "the worst dressed youth in the crowd," that is an overdrawn statement, for they were all dressed about as nearly alike as coonskin caps, hunting shirts, or a blouse and buckskin breeches could make them. If there was any difference, it would be in Lincoln's favor on the score of cleanliness, for his mother frequently commented upon the fact of his being so careful with his clothing; and certainly no better evidence could be desired in such a matter than that of a mother. If the assertion that he was the worst dressed one in the crowd should be from the tailor's point of view, then there need be no difference of opinion concerning it. He appears to have always had more or less difficulty in obtaining garments large enough. His trousers were usually from 5 to 12 inches too short; and since he almost invariably wore moccasins or low-topped shoes, there was an unprotected area between the ankle and the knee that was quite large. Lincoln himself, in speaking of this when accused of being associated with the well-to-do and prosperous, said that this part of his anatomy "had been exposed to the elements for so long that his shin bone was permanently blue"; and he submitted that "there was nothing about the circumstance indicating aristocracy."

As has been clearly indicated, Lincoln was often selected by the uninitiated as a target for sport, and his good nature was frequently regarded as an indication of cowardice. On one occasion he was attacked as he stood near a tree by a larger boy with a crowd of others at his back. It was supposed, of course, that the big awkward boy would run when the charge was made, but not so. Instead, Lincoln quickly laid out the first, second, and third boys in rapid succession; and then placing his back against a tree, he turned tormentor, daring the remainder to make any further demonstration; and when they elected not to do so, he taunted them for being cowards.

There was at least one instance when Lincoln yielded to the temptation to deviate from his accustomed fairness, yet it would appear that there was some extenuation in the matter. Colonel Lamon, in his biography of Lincoln, relates what purports to be the correct version of this circumstance, but that there are some statements in it wholly incompatible with the general deportment of Lincoln, as well as in the subject matter itself, is the assertion of a number of eye witnesses of the affair. Wesley Hall, James Gentry, Redmond Grigsby, and Joseph Gentry were all living at the time that this incident was investigated by the writer. They were all present when the incident took place and were much given to relating this circumstance and for some cause reverted to it more frequently than any other that came under their observation during the early life of Lincoln.

A crowd of boys and young men had gathered for no particular purpose when Lincoln and William Grigsby, after a time, got into a dispute over the ownership of a certain spotted pup. Each alleged that a neighbor had promised to make him a present of this particular pup. The dispute finally assumed the proportions of a quarrel. Grigsby stepped squarely in front of Lincoln and angrily dared him to fight. Whereupon Lincoln said, "Bill, you know I can lick you so what's the use of you making such a proposition?"

Grigsby, of whom it was generally asserted feared no man and was a great fighter, replied: "I know you c'n whip me, but I'll fight you for the dog jest the same." Finally Lincoln said, "I'll tell you what I'll do, Bill. Although I know that pup belongs to me, and you know it too, I'm willing to put up John Johnson here in my place. He's more your size, and whichever whips gets the pup." This was readily agreed to by Grigsby, and "hauling their coats off as the boys formed a circle, they began the fight." They had not fought long until it became evident to all, and to Lincoln in particular, that Grigsby was having the best of the argument. Suddenly, without any warning, Lincoln stepped into the ring, seized Grigsby by the collar and trousers, and bodily hurled him over the heads of the crowd. He then "dared the entire Grigsby crowd to come into him." There being no disposition to do so, Lincoln's anger subsided quickly, and presently he was laughing and joking.[5]

Hall and the Gentry brothers asserted that "Abe always acted fair," and they couldn't understand at first why he should interfere as he did in this instance, until it was ascertained subsequently that the pup had in fact been given to Lincoln, and Grigsby knowing this, had conceived this plan of obtaining it. Both of the Gentrys and Hall stated that this altercation took place on the exact site of the railroad depot at Lincoln City, which stands 150 yards west of the Lincoln cabin site.

The assertion of Mr. Lamon in this instance, as well as in others, that "Lincoln drew forth a whiskey bottle and waived it dramatically above his head" on the defeat of Grigsby, or that he "was accustomed to take his dram," and such other similar statements, is not at all in accordance with any of the testimony given by Lincoln's early friends. They expressly stated that no such thing transpired during this fight as Lincoln exhibiting a bottle of whiskey, but they were unanimous in stating that Lincoln never at any time so much as tasted intoxicating liquor of any sort, nor did he use tobacco either in chewing or smoking.[6]

It was this same William Grigsby who later became such a warm friend of Lincoln that he offered during the Civil War to

whip any man in Gentryville who was disposed to speak disparagingly of his old friend "Abe Linkern." Amos Grigsby, brother
of William, a short while after the fight, married Sarah Lincoln,
sister of Abraham. At this time she was 18 years of age, and her
brother was 16. While they were very much attached to each other,
the Grigsbys did not like young Lincoln by reason of the affair
with William, and the wedding was arranged to take place in the
two-story log house of the groom's father. In fact, there was to be
a double wedding since one of the Grigsby girls was to be married
at the same time. Young Lincoln was not privileged to be present
and witness the marriage of his only sister in consequence of the
trouble aforementioned. Lincoln meditated revenge for this slight
in a manner quite unusual indeed and unheard of in this section.

Lincoln quietly sought an interview with a young man who he
knew was an invited guest at the double wedding and requested
that he do him a favor. "Certainly, Abe, I'll do anything for you.
What is it?" "Well, you know I'm not to be at that wedding. It
seems they don't care to have me around for some reason or other,
and I've picked you to look things over and somehow manage to
do the honors of conducting the grooms to the bridal chamber."
Careful and detailed instruction was given as to diplomatic procedure so that suspicions might not be aroused on the part of any.
It appeared that these were carried out to the letter and worked
admirably. When, according to the pioneer custom, the grooms
were escorted up the perpendicular sassafras ladder in one corner
of the room, which led up through a "scuttle hole" in the ceiling
to the now-darkened bridal chamber on the second floor, there
resulted more or less confusion for a time in ascertaining identity
just as Lincoln had planned.

Lincoln, considering this a clever practical joke, wrote an account of the affair in verse, calling the poem "The Chronicles."
These verses, recited by Lincoln on the least provocation to all
who would give him audience, gave the Grigsbys great offense.
When Lincoln ascertained that they were aggrieved, he went to

the Grigsby home and disclaimed having any purpose whatever
of casting any aspersion upon their character or good name, stating that he only purposed having some fun.[7] He closed by turning
over to them the original manuscript containing the objectionable Chronicles, accompanying this action with the promise that
so far as he was concerned nothing more would be said concerning them, a promise that he faithfully kept. This generosity of
character so appealed to the offended Grigsbys that they all became his friends.

As a sequel to this incident, it may be stated that James Gentry,
when some reference was made by the writer to the "Chronicles
of Reuben," laughed uproariously and straightway began reciting
certain portions of "Abe's poetry" in great glee. Gentry stated that
"when Abe wrote his *Chronicles* they kicked up a big hulla-ba-loo, but
finally it all got quiet when Abe handed them over to the Grigsbys."[8]

Redmond Grigsby was yet living at the time of the interview
with Gentry, and in the course of Mr. Gentry's remarks he incidentally mentioned the fact that only the day before this he had
met Grigsby and "they fell to talking about this double wedding
and the Chronicles in particular." Gentry remarked to Grigsby,
"Red, everybody's dead now but you, by gum! I'd let 'em come
out," meaning the publication of the *Chronicles*. But Mr. Grigsby
said, "Jim, there's plenty time fer that yet." It would appear from
this remark that the original document was in the possession of
Redmond Grigsby, a brother of Aaron. Mr. Grigsby died a short
while after this; and what became of the Chronicles, if he did in
fact have them in his possession, is not known.

NOTES

1. Basler et al., *Collected Works of Abraham Lincoln*, 7:10.
2. These quotations must come from Murr's own research and discussions with informants since no other available sources record them.
3. Rothschild is quoting a recollection of Major Alexander Sympson.
Rothschild, *Lincoln, Master of Men*, 2.

4. Wilson and Davis, *Herndon's Lincoln*, 307.

5. Louis Warren recounts this story in his seminal work, *Lincoln's Youth*, 196–197.

6. Ward Hill Lamon does cite this incident, but the quotations do not sync with Lamon's account; perhaps Murr quotes a different biographer. See Lamon, *Life of Abraham Lincoln*, 65–66.

7. Few other accounts, if any, include Lincoln's trying to explain himself to the Grigsbys. Murr may attempt here to provide cover for Lincoln.

8. Murr probably refers to James Gentry Jr. (1819–1905) since James Gentry Sr. died in 1840.

TWELVE

—⚏—

LINCOLN'S HONESTY AND TRUTHFULNESS

With malice toward none, with charity for all, with firmness in the right as God gives us to see the right, let us strive on in the work we are in, to bind up the nation's wounds; to care for him who shall have borne the battle, and for his widow and his orphan; to do all which may achieve and cherish a just and lasting peace among ourselves and with all nations.[1]

ALL OF THE DISCUSSIONS OF Lincoln's life make pointed reference to his uncompromising honesty and truthfulness. So prominent were these traits in his character as to induce his friends to denominate him "Honest Abe" while he was quite young.

Unfortunately, most of the emphasis has been so placed as to leave the impression upon the minds of our youth that Lincoln learned honesty sometime after reaching maturity, leaving the implication that either this trait was not noticed during his youth or, if so, no reliable and trustworthy evidence of it was obtained to justify specific mention of it at any length. This attitude is not only unjustifiable, judging by the facts and evidence testified to by his boyhood associates, but also at variance with all the generally accepted standards and theories of life governing such matters.

It is, of course, not charged that dishonesty characterized Mr. Lincoln's youth save in the single accusation made by some of the earlier biographers against him in recounting the advice given his flatboat partner, Allen Gentry, to pass counterfeit money for genuine money. When all the circumstances connected with this transaction are known, the inference and implication of doubtful honesty proves to be groundless.

In the days when Lincoln and Gentry made their celebrated flatboat trip down the Mississippi river "wildcat" money was quite as common as any other, particularly along the Ohio and Mississippi rivers.[2] Wildcat money was so frequently offered in payment in the smaller transactions at that time that it occasioned no more comment or concern than the depreciated "trade dollar," Canadian quarter, or dime did later in this section.[3] Thus, when Lincoln advised the passing of wildcat money received in the course of their bartering during the day, he was but following the custom practiced by the people of that time.

There never was any occasion for a revolution in Mr. Lincoln's character or a deviation in any particular from his youthful customs; he did not at any time practice deception or dishonesty. It may be said that whatever he may have learned or acquired in the State of Illinois, certainly honesty was not learned there. If his associates in that State, noting his steadfast adherence to the old-fashioned trait of honesty, denominated him "Honest Abe," it is but an indication that his early training in the Indiana wilderness was so rooted and grounded in him that he could not only withstand the social, business, and political temptations of life in Illinois as to challenge their admiration; but the inference is that he was much unlike most, if not all, other men in public life at that time.

Most men of mature years draw heavily upon the teachings of childhood and youth. To put it in a way calculated to meet with general acceptance, what a man becomes in morals and in the practice of the great principles of honesty and truthfulness is largely determined in childhood and young manhood. Never were these teachings better exemplified than in the life of Abraham Lincoln.

When Lincoln, a bearded man, walked down Sangamon River bottom, Illinois, for the first time, his character was already formed. He brought with him from Indiana his rare wit, humor, and inexhaustible fund of anecdotes. He possessed no bad habits. His school days were over. It is true that he took a post-graduate course in Shakespeare and Burns; and when John Calhoun, of Lecompton fame, offered him the position as assistant surveyor, this graduate of the Indiana wilderness, fresh from his reading of the classics—the King James version of the Bible, Aesop's *Fables*, lives of Franklin and Washington—reported to Calhoun in just six weeks for duty, having mastered this science in that incredibly short time, to the astonishment of his benefactor.

One of Lincoln's teachers in Indiana was a man by the name of Crawford. Lincoln was in his 14th year while in attendance upon this particular term. On one occasion the teacher observed that some liberties had been taken with the pair of antlers over the door of the school room, one prong having been broken; and on making this discovery he straightway instituted an inquiry to find the guilty culprit. Lincoln, being quite tall and seeing this prong presenting a temptation to swing upon, yielded, with the result that the prong failed to support his weight and fell to the ground. When the irate teacher asked who was guilty, Lincoln stepped forth and quickly volunteered the information: "I did, sir. I did not mean to do it, but I hung on it and it broke. I wouldn't have done it if I'd a thought it'd a broke."[4]

It is not at all necessary to suppose in attempting to show the honesty and truthfulness of Lincoln that there were no others in the school at that time who would have done as he did under similar circumstances. Indeed, in every little schoolhouse of the land today there are those who would do this; but since this circumstance did transpire as here related, it is important in that it sets forth the inherent trait at such a period in his life.

One of the neighbors of the Lincolns was Josiah Crawford, for whom young Abraham often worked as a hired man, and his sister, Sarah, worked as hired girl. "Old Cy Crawford," as he was usually called, was more or less given to certain peculiarities, being quite presumptuous and so penurious as to be called "tight" or "close" by his neighbors, but withal possessing many splendid traits. He was not an educated man; but being what was called "handy," he was able to do almost anything. He was a pioneer doctor and dentist, and in addition he was a farmer. In this latter capacity he frequently employed young Lincoln.

Crawford possessed a small library which, to some extent, accounted for whatever superiority he had over some of his neighbors. Lincoln borrowed all of these books, reading and re-reading some of them, one being Weems's *Life of Washington*. It was the custom of Lincoln to carry a book with him in the fields or in the clearing, and this practice was not dispensed with even when laboring for a neighbor. At every opportunity, whether at the noon hour or rest, or permitting a horse to breathe, he brought forth the book to read.

John Hanks, who lived with the Lincolns from 1823 to 1827, said, as recounted by Mr. Herndon, "When Abe and I returned to the house from work he would go to the cupboard, snatch a piece of cornbread, and sit down and read. We grubbed, plowed, mowed, and worked together barefooted in the fields. Whenever Abe had a chance in the field while at work, or at the house, he would stop and read. He kept the Bible and Aesop's *Fables* always in reach and read them over and over again."[5]

He kept up his daily custom of carrying a book with him and reading as he walked as well as reading until a late hour at night until established in the practice of his profession. During his boyhood on securing a new book, he frequently read until midnight. His artificial light for this purpose was made by gathering dry sticks and splinters and piling them beside the jambs so that when the fire died down he freely laid some of this tinder on the firestick and thus managed to read quite well. One night after having obtained the aforementioned copy of the *Life of Washington* from Crawford, he read until quite late; and on retiring to the loft he laid the book between two of the logs—the "chinkin and daubin had worn away." While he was wrapped in sleep, a rainstorm came and greatly damaged the leaves and warped the cover. On making this discovery the following morning Lincoln was mortified; and realizing the scarcity of books and keenly appreciating their value, he very naturally supposed that Mr. Crawford would be put out about it. Nevertheless, he took the damaged treasure home and related somewhat in detail the circumstances of the night before, proposing to do whatever the owner thought was right and proper to make amends for his carelessness.

Mr. Crawford was not averse to driving a bargain, for it was his custom with Lincoln to dock him when he failed to begin his day's labor early enough or for any cause lost any time. In this instance he proposed that Lincoln "pull fodder for three days and they would call matters even."[6] Lincoln entered no protest at the time and energetically went to work. In relating this circumstance to a gentleman in Rockport afterward, he stated, "At the close of the second day, my long arms had stripped every blade off old Blue Nose's corn, and I reckon Cy ought to be satisfied; at any rate I am, but I think he was pretty hard on me."[7]

We are indebted to Silas G. Pratt for an incident illustrative of Lincoln's mingled goodness, truthfulness and honesty:

> One morning when Lincoln, with his ax over his shoulder, was going to work in the clearing, his stepsister, Matilda Johnston, who had been forbidden by her mother to follow him, slyly and unknown to her mother crept out of the house and ran after him. Lincoln was already a long distance from the house among the trees following a deer path and whistling as he walked along. He, of course, did not know the girl was coming after him, and Matilda ran so softly that she made no noise to attract his attention. When she came up close behind, she made a quick spring

and jumped upon his shoulders, holding on with both hands
and pressing her knees into his back, thus pulling him quickly
to the ground. In falling the sharp ax fell and cut her ankle very
badly. As the blood ran out, the mischievous Matilda screamed
with pain. Lincoln at once tore off some cloth from the lining of
his coat to stop the blood from flowing and bound up the wound
as well as he could. Taking a long breath he said: "Tilda, I am
astonished. How could you disobey your mother so?" Tilda only
cried in reply, and Lincoln continued, "What are you going to
tell Mother about getting hurt?"' "Tell her I did it with the ax,"
she sobbed. "That will be the truth, won't it?" To which Lincoln
replied manfully: "Yes, that's the truth, but it's not all the truth.
You tell the whole truth, Tilda, and trust your good mother for
the rest." So Tilda went limping home and told her mother all the
truth. The good woman felt so sorry for her that she did not even
scold her.[8]

If, in speaking of honesty, we may make the term so broad as to
include not only right dealings in mere money or business transactions, but also fair-mindedness and an implied purpose and
intentional disposition to be such under trying circumstances,
there is much that may be said illustrative of the fact that Lincoln's life was the embodiment of truth and fair dealing. The
boyhood associates of Lincoln stated that his word was always
considered good and that he could be depended upon to do what
he agreed to do. He was generally trusted by his neighbors; and
if necessity seemed to justify his asking credit, as was sometimes
the case, this was granted.

It was generally conceded, however, by the old neighbors of
Lincoln and others who had personal acquaintance with members of the family concerned in one transaction that there was
one noted exception to the rule. The town of Gentryville was laid
out by Mr. Gentry in the year 1824. Gentry was a North Carolin-
ian who settled in this section in the year 1818, some two years
after the coming of the Lincolns. He was a man of some means
for that day, as evidenced in his entering 1,200 acres of land and

founding the town. He established a store, encouraged the purchasing of lots and the erection of houses, and offered certain inducements to artisans and trade-folks so that in a short while the little place became somewhat of a commercial center. Among those who had established themselves in business there was a certain Mr. Jones. On his proving to be prosperous and otherwise possessing advantages over Gentry, overtures were made to him, and he accordingly disposed of his business to Gentry. In a short while thereafter, he embarked in business again, locating this time a little distance from Gentryville, but near enough to cause the trade to follow him. On perceiving that the future of the town site was in jeopardy, Gentry proposed to Jones to move again to Gentryville. This he did, and it was his store that Lincoln frequented on Saturdays, rainy days, and evenings. Jones was a man of large influence, politically and otherwise. He early professed a great liking for young Lincoln and freely prophesied on more than one occasion that Lincoln would yet be heard from in the world. He was thought to be rather extravagant in some of his assertions and prophesies, however, and there is little wonder that the citizens should so think when they heard him venture to assert repeatedly that "Lincoln would someday be President of the United States." Jones was a man somewhat after the type of Denton Offut, the storekeeper with whom Lincoln was associated a few years later in Illinois. In fact, it appears that Lincoln's habit of frequenting these small stores invariably impressed himself so strongly upon the owners as to cause them to employ him. Lincoln drove a team for Jones, packed and unpacked boxes of goods, butchered and salted pork and at certain times performed some of the more menial services in the store proper such as the transfer of heavy and cumbersome wares from the cellar to the main floor. These labors, however, were not continuous, but merely occasional for a nominal sum as a wage—30 cents per day being the usual price. Jones was regarded as somewhat of a politician, and was a pronounced Jackson Democrat. At one time he was the only subscriber to the *Louisville Journal* in this place, and Lincoln availed himself of the privilege of reading it aloud—a habit which became fixed in him as in many another who was brought up in what was termed "blab schools," where every scholar studied his lesson by reading aloud during "books."

In later life Lincoln's practice was to read aloud, and he had difficulty in grasping the meaning of the printed page unless his ears heard as well as his eyes saw.

The fact that young Lincoln became a Jackson man was largely due to the association and influence of storekeeper Jones, and it was from this man that he obtained the *History of the United States*, one of the books that had so much to do in shaping his career. Just before the Lincolns left for Illinois and a short while prior to Lincoln's reaching his majority, he was in the store observing an extraordinarily large pair of shoes. They were so large as to cause him to think that they would fit him; and being greatly in need of footwear, he asked the privilege of trying them on. This, of course, was granted, and Lincoln found that they were just his size. He thereupon indicated his desire to purchase them, but stated that he did not have the money then and would not have it until a date which he specified. The storekeeper shook his head and refused the young man the desired credit.

Years went by, and Lincoln was to be inaugurated President. Very naturally some of his Gentryville friends were desirous of witnessing these ceremonies, and a little party of five made the journey to Washington, among them Jones, the storekeeper. No opportunity readily presenting itself to meet their old friend until after the inaugural ceremonies were over, they resolved to get in line and meet him at the general reception tendered. This suggestion was acted upon; and by a mere chance, not at all by design, the storekeeper Jones came last. As the first man of the little group approached, Lincoln, straightway recognizing him, greeted him with a beaming countenance, grasping the proffered hand in both of his and saying: "Howdy, Jim." He readily recognized each one as they approached, giving them a very cordial greeting; but when Jones approached, he was greeted with silence although Lincoln shook hands with him. The storekeeper, going on the supposition that he was not recognized, exclaimed, "Mr. President, I'm from Gentryville also. My name is Jones. I reckon you don't remember me." Lincoln inclined his body forward until his face was on the same level with the face of Jones and whispered in the ear of his old friend: "O yes, Mr. Jones, I remember you very well, and I remember that shoe transaction also," smiling and otherwise giving Jones evidence of his old-time friendship.[9] It is but just to say that a portion of this story was denied by Jones, who said that he never refused Lincoln the shoes, but that they were turned over to him when Lincoln asked for credit. The supposition is that, on seeing his old friend approaching him, Lincoln hit upon this plan to have a bit of his old-time sport even if the occasion was an inaugural reception. The story, however, as here recorded, received general credence by the old friends of Lincoln, and that it took place substantially as here detailed is doubtless true.

Nat Grigsby and the storekeeper Jones later on during the Lincoln administration called on the President at the White House. We have the best authority for stating the fact, the occasion, and the ludicrous results of that visit—the testimony of both Grigsby and Jones themselves. Nat Grigsby and Blue Nose Crawford had been caricatured by Lincoln in some of his doggerel poetry called the "Chronicles of Reuben." Grigsby, long afterward, confessed that at the time this occasioned considerable feeling on his part against Abe, but after a time all was forgotten. That this was true and that Mr. Lincoln thought quite well of Grigsby is evidenced by a circumstance that transpired on the occasion of Lincoln's visit to Gentryville during the campaign of 1844. Lincoln made speeches both at Gentryville and at Carter's schoolhouse. It was at the latter place that Lincoln, in the midst of his address, recognizing Mr. Grigsby who came in late, exclaimed, "There's Nat," whereupon he quit the speech and platform and went back to greet his old friend with old-time warmth and boyish enthusiasm, then returned to the front to continue his speech.[10] Whether it was this circumstance, or the numerous other evidences of Lincoln's partiality for him that induced Grigsby to believe Lincoln, as President, could and would appoint him to some federal position, it is immaterial for our purpose. At any rate, Grigsby was fully persuaded that he was amply competent to serve in some capacity (and he was a man of some ability). He very naturally presumed upon the old-time friendship of Lincoln and, accordingly, called upon Jones and proposed that he accompany him to Washington on a similar mission in his own behalf. This met with hearty approval on the part of Jones, and preparations were made for the journey. They resolved to see the President in person rather than to make formal application for a place in some other way. At length, the two old neighbors of the President appeared at the White House. Lincoln, being apprised of their presence, although many were in waiting, stepped into the room in which they were seated and greeted them quite as if he had met them at Carter's schoolhouse or Baldwin's blacksmith shop in Gentryville. Unmindful of who might chance to be in the room or what might be the construction placed upon his democratic demeanor, he said, "Howdy, Nat," and "Howdy, Bill," and otherwise by word and greeting conducted himself much as if he were oblivious of the fact that he was President of the United States.

Lincoln was never justly, at any time, accused of being hypocritical; but that he could act the part well calculated to carry out his purpose is much in evidence in this as in other instances. Major John Hay asserted that Lincoln "was a trimmer the equal of Halifax, but he never trimmed his principles."[11] There is discerned in this little circumstance with his boyhood associates an ability to manage men and deal with difficult situations in a way quite characteristic of him. After the warm greeting and hand-shaking with his old friends, accompanied by such familiarities as "the laying on of hands," and other evidences of appreciation of their visit, he requested that they both accompany him to an adjoining room. Going on the supposition that they were being taken to his private office where they could have the opportunity of presenting their claims, they quickly followed him and were ushered into a large room where Mrs. Lincoln sat. Neither of them having ever met Mrs. Lincoln, they were accordingly introduced by the President and, at the same time, dismissed or disposed of as follows: "Mrs. Lincoln, here are two of my boyhood friends from Gentryville, Indiana, Mr. Grigsby and Mr. Jones." Whether just at this point there was a sly wink or some other signal known only to the secret code of the President's family, is, of course, purely in the realm of conjecture; but the preponderance of evidence is much in its favor, for he straightway said after the formal introduction,

> Mary, you know I'm pestered and bothered continually by people coming here on the score of old acquaintance, as almost all of them have an ax to grind. They go on the theory that I've got offices to dispense with so numerous that I can give each one of them a place. Now here are two friends that have come to pay me a visit just because they are my friends and haren't come to ask for any office or place. It is a relief to have this experience. You know the room's full of folks out here (pointing) waiting to see me about something or other, and I want you to see that Nat and Bill here have a good time while they are with us."[12]

After the first Lady of the Land had given her promise to do as requested, Lincoln returned to his labors. It is not possible to know whether the President went to his private office and sought relief by giving way to unrestrained laughter or not, but he doubtless consoled himself with the fact that situations in the field of diplomacy, matters of great moment, could always be disposed of as readily as was true in this particular instance; he had reason to regard himself equal to any exigency that might arise. The two office-seekers, accustomed only to the dames and damsels of Gentryville gowned in linsey-wolsey, whose colloquial speech was quite their own, were suddenly found in the presence of a "fine lady," and there is no occasion for surprise when they asserted that both of them heartily agreed that discretion was the better part of valor and they accordingly beat a hasty retreat, returning to Indiana without so much as mentioning the real object of their visit to the capital. When twitted about their failure by some of their neighbors, they both confessed that "Abe was too much for them," especially after he had said what he did to Mrs. Lincoln about his old friends asking for office.

NOTES

1. This quotation is taken from Lincoln's second inaugural address delivered on 4 March 1865.

2. *Wildcat money* means worthless money formerly issued by state banks that became insolvent.

3. *Trade dollar* means the depreciated US silver dollar, used later in the nineteenth century, depreciated well below their dollar face value because of declines in silver's value.

4. Although this quotation appears in subsequent histories, Murr appears to be the original written source.

5. Herndon and Weik, *Herndon's Lincoln*, 43–44.

6. *Pulling fodder* means stripping the leaves from the corn stalk.

7. Although this quotation appears in subsequent histories, Murr appears to be the original written source.

8. Silas G. Pratt (1846–1916) is known primarily as a composer, but he also published a book in 1901 titled *Lincoln in Story*. This quotation appears on pages 11 and 12 of that book. For Matilda's account of this incident, see Bartelt, *There I Grew Up*, 73–74.

9. Jones and Lincoln spent time together in 1844 when Lincoln stayed at the Jones home in Indiana while campaigning for Henry Clay (Bartelt, "Aiding Mr. Clay," 29–39).

10. This interaction likely occurred at the Jones house, not the schoolhouse (Bartelt, "Aiding Mr. Clay," 29–39).

11. John Hay refers to ideas put forth by George Savile, Marquess of Halifax (1633–1695), who described a *trimmer* as one whose positions respond

to dominant fashion and balance them out. But Murr offers a summary of John Hay's statement rather than an actual quotation. The full text reads:

> In dealing with men [Lincoln] was a trimmer, and such a trimmer the world has never seen. Halifax, who was great in his day as a trimmer, would blush by the side of Lincoln; yet Lincoln never trimmed in principles, it was only in his conduct with men. He used the patronage of his office to feed the hunger of these various factions. Weed always declared that he kept a regular account-book of his appointments in New York, dividing his various favors so as to give each faction more than it could get from any other source, yet never enough to satisfy its appetite.

Herndon and Weik, *Abraham Lincoln*, 243.

12. Murr's source for this quotation is unclear.

THIRTEEN

—⁓—

LINCOLN'S FREEDOM FROM BAD HABITS

In it we shall find a stronger bondage broken, a viler slavery
manumitted, a greater tyrant deposed; and when there shall be
neither a slave nor a drunkard on earth, how proud the title of
that land which may truly claim to be the birthplace and cradle
of both those revolutions that have ended in victory.[1]

LINCOLN AS A YOUTH WAS remarkably free from bad or vicious habits. He was in general good favor with all of his associates and was dutiful and obedient to his father and mother. His
temperamental makeup was such as to win friends and to hold
them. He, as has already been indicated, never at any time in
his boyhood, used intoxicating liquors although this custom was
generally prevalent. Since Lincoln's habit was to frequent the gro-
cery store in Gentryville in company with Dennis Hanks, where
much drinking was indulged in, his refusal to drink intoxicants
is somewhat remarkable. He professed to have a distaste for intoxicants of all sorts and abstained as a matter of principle. In
later life he stated that "he had no desire for intoxicating liquors
and did not care to associate with drinking men."[2] His terrible
arraignment of the liquor traffic before the Washingtonian society is familiar to all, and it is highly probable that his strong

convictions expressed in later years on that subject were to some extent formed by noting, as he did while a resident at Gentryville, the evil effects of its use by many of his associates.

Wesley Hall stated that his father frequently employed both the elder Lincoln and his son, Abraham, to labor for him as carpenters as well as to perform work incident to the successful operation of a tanyard. Hall asserted that young Lincoln frequently pushed the plane at a workbench, preparing planks for the father's use in the construction of cupboards and other pieces of household furniture. In this connection Hall laughingly recalled a boyish act of his. On one occasion when Abraham was laboring at the bench with the plane, Hall crawled beneath the long bench and lay down upon his back just opposite Lincoln's feet. He was peculiarly struck with the great length of the young carpenter's shoes; and reaching forth, he selected a wooden ribbon and was busily engaged in measuring the foot when Lincoln noticed this performance and "yanked him out."

In the performance of the work connected with the tannery, the elder Hall frequently employed a number of men; and it was the custom, when weather permitted, to take the noon meal in the grove near the tanyard rather than to go to the house. Hall stated that when the food had been made ready and spread out on a rude table, and dinner was announced, Abe invariably walked to a certain large forest tree whose roots had grown in such a manner as to form a sort of rustic bench. There seating himself, leaning back against the trunk, he drew forth from the folds of his loose fitting waumus or blouse a book and began to read—rather than go to the table as the other men did to eat. When asked if Lincoln did not also eat the noon meal and why he did not do so with the others, Hall replied,

> Certainly Abe et dinner, but don't you know he never drank, and them times the black bottle would be passed around purty often, so Abe would say to me, "You see, Wesley, I don't drink and the

rest of the men do, and if I was to eat when they do and not drink with them, they'd think may be I was smart, and so I jest hit upon this plan of bringing along my book with me and reading while they eat. I eat after they get through—in plenty time to go to work when they do, and that-a-way I git to read some and at the same time I don't go against a custom that they think is all right even if I don't.

A diligent inquiry among Lincoln's boyhood friends for everything characteristic or peculiar to him elicited the fact among other things that he did not indulge in intemperate language. It might be alleged that there was an exception in the frequent use of the by-word *i-jings*, which seems to have followed him by way of Illinois to the White House.

That young Lincoln was extremely awkward and homely to a marked degree is evidenced by the testimony of all of his early friends. When Abe sat, his stature did not impress itself, but a close observer would note that his lower extremities were of such proportions that a marble or ball placed upon his knee would roll toward the body. His gait was exceptional and peculiar to him. He made rather long strides as compared to many tall men who, in attempting to keep step, form the habit of a jerky, premature stride. Lincoln lifted his feet squarely from the ground and in like manner planted them, so that the foot did not bend at the toes or the weight of the body rest momentarily upon the heel; however, he was slightly pigeon-toed. His walk therefore, while not to say cunning, was stealthy; and possessing great bodily vigor, he could walk long distances in a short while.

Mrs. Polly Agnew, whose maiden name was Richardson, and who was the mother of a number of children, some of whom became men of considerable local prominence—among whom was Doctor Mason, a physician well-known in his day throughout southern Indiana—often related a circumstance that took place on her arrival in Indiana, in which Lincoln bore a conspicuous part, and which furnishes a splendid field for a painter. The Richardsons were pioneers in Spencer County, floating down the Ohio River in a boat and landing at the site of the present beautiful town of Grandview. Their arrival was sometime after the coming of the Lincolns. The landing had been effected, and they desired to penetrate the interior some distance before locating. They had their ox-teams and wagon (save for the wheels), so the father and son felled a large gum tree; and sawing off blocks or circular slabs of such thickness as would prove suitable for wheels, they soon were ready to begin their journey through the unknown wilderness. No white man had as yet made settlement in this part of the country. The wagon was loaded with bedding, cooking utensils, and such other things as they would at first need; and with the mother and daughter, Polly, the narrator of the incident, they started on their tedious way, leaving behind them many things in the boat for which they had to make a second trip. The choice of a farm location was by midday decided upon. In the midst of the great forest they came upon a cluster of trees so situated as to enable them by cutting brush and laying these on poles placed in forks to erect a brush lean-to or brush house, which would serve them temporarily. The mother and daughter were left in the midst of the great forest alone while the men returned to the boat for another load. A storm came up, nightfall was approaching, and the wagon had not returned. In the midst of their anxiety there suddenly appeared out of the forest a stranger of gigantic stature, dressed in coon-skin cap, hunting shirt and buckskin breeches, and bearing a gun. He came up smiling and, by way of explanation for his presence, stated that he lived a short distance north, and having just learned that a new family was moving into the community he had come down to render any service needed. When informed by Mrs. Richardson that the men folks had gone to the river for another load and were expected to return at any time, the stranger remarked, "Well, ladies, I'm quite sure they cannot get back tonight for the rain has interfered, and so I'll just stay with you and see that no harm comes to you during the night."

This information and proffered help was anything but reassuring to the frightened ladies. The tall stranger, acting upon his own suggestion, now stepped to a large tree fronting the lean-to; and seating himself with the gun placed across his lap, he leaned against the trunk, thus evidencing his disposition to remain on guard. Seeing this, Mrs. Richardson stepped into the brush house and she and the daughter held a whispered consultation. It was agreed that while the stranger might prove to be more dangerous than any foe of the woods, yet the mother suggested that "he had a good face." After a few moments in conversation they observed that the stranger had laid down his gun and begun dragging a large limb toward the brush house. The mother and daughter both ventured out near him and requested to know what he meant by such procedure, whereupon he smiled and said, "Ladies, the woods around here are full of wolves and bears, and we've got to have a bon-fire tonight or they might give trouble." When the mother remarked that they entertained no fear of wolves, the man laughed right heartily and said, "You just wait and we'll see if there isn't about two women around here somewhere that'll get pretty badly scared before long." With that remark he began the search for dry branches and limbs of fallen trees, and this he continued doing until there was collected quite a pile.

When darkness had settled down over them and the wagon had not returned as the stranger had ventured to prophesy, the ladies became more or less reconciled to the presence of the man. He accepted the food they prepared, but refused to go into the lean-to. An hour or so had passed when the stranger, who all this time was watched from within with some remaining suspicion, called to them that they need have no fears of wolves who by this time were howling in the distance. Ere long these denizens of the night ventured quite near, and the ladies, thoroughly frightened, requested that he come into the lean-to. The stranger then approached the bonfire and requested Mrs. Richardson and her daughter to "step out and take a look at the green-eyes." This they did, and the daughter exclaimed in her fright, "Why, mother, there is a thousand of them. What would we have done alone?" The tall stranger laughed and said, addressing the young lady: "Miss, there is not more than a half dozen of the varmints, and every one of them is a coward. Now you just see if they are not." Taking a fire brand and waving it vigorously, [the stranger forced] the "green eyes" to vanish, and their howling was heard in the distance. The manifest danger confronting the ladies by the presence of such animals drew them nearer to their protector, and they acted on his suggestion to "go in and try and get some sleep while he kept watch." When morning broke, the stranger announced his intention of returning home, saying as he started, "I'll find out today if your men folks get back all right, which I reckon they will; but if they don't, I'll be back here tonight, and we'll keep the 'thousand pairs of green eyes' at a safe distance."

This was the introduction the Richardson family had to the future President, for the tall stranger who kept watch through the night was Abraham Lincoln. The Richardsons and the Lincolns became fast friends. It was William Richardson who stated that on one occasion when they were preparing to build a corn crib, and some heavy pieces of timber were to be put in place, the men engaged in doing this were making hand spikes with which to carry them. Lincoln chanced to come up and asked what they were going to do with hand spikes. When informed that they were being prepared to carry the heavy timbers, Lincoln remarked that he could shoulder and carry the sticks himself. And at once acting upon the suggestion, he actually performed the feat unaided. Richardson believed that it would have taken the combined strength of three or four men to do what Lincoln did.

It was this same Richardson who related another circumstance indicating the phenomenal strength of Lincoln. A chicken house was to be moved and some preparation was being made to do this when Lincoln picked it up bodily and carried it for some distance. Richardson thought that it "weighed at least 600 pounds, and maybe more."

Whether it was this romantic meeting of Polly Richardson in the brush lean-to, or whether it was due to certain traits of character discerned in her by Lincoln, particularly her considerate kindness of heart in befriending him in certain ways, that attracted him, in any case he often "kept company with her." Aunt Polly, as she was generally called, was a lady of more than average intelligence. Although she was not educated, yet in her use of language this was not particularly noticeable. She was never any more delighted than when surrounded by those who were anxious to know of some of her pioneer experiences, particularly those pertaining to Lincoln. She often told of being accompanied by Lincoln to spelling bees, play parties, and church, and even asserted that she was Lincoln's first sweetheart. If there be any reluctance on the part of anyone to accord this rather enviable distinction to the old lady who thus made the claim, it may be said in her behalf that her frankness in relating certain circumstances pertaining to this, and the regret occasioned by not having wisdom enough to foresee in her girlhood Lincoln's great career may to some extent plead more eloquently than any mere statement of fact by the writer. Here is Polly Richardson's story:

Yes. I was Abe's first sweetheart.

He'd take me to spelling bees and play parties and to meetin' and the like, but still I can't say that I wanted him to go with me though. Still Abe was always mighty good, and I never found any fault with him excepting he was so tall and awkward. All the young girls my age made fun of Abe. They'd laugh at him right before his face, but Abe never 'peared to care. He was so good and he'd just laugh with them. Abe tried to go with some of them, but no sir-ee, they'd give him the mitten every time, just because he was, as I say, so tall and gawky, and it was mighty awkward I can tell you trying to keep company with a fellow as tall as Abe was. But still Abe was always so good and kind I never sacked him, but bein's I didn't have no other company them days when us young folks would all start to meetin' or somewhere else that away, I'd let Abe take me. I'd sometimes get right put out the way some of the girls treated him, a-laughing and saying things, and so when we'd get off to ourselves I'd give them a piece of my mind about it. And then they'd all say that it is too bad the way we do because Abe's so good, but they'd appear to forget all about it, for the very next time they'd do the same way. Abe wanted me to marry him, but I refused. I suppose if I had known he was to be President some day, I'd a-took him.[3]

The writer was once a schoolmaster and was again and again made to think of Lincoln on daily seeing the children of the daughter of Colonel Lehmonowsky, one of Napoleon's old soldiers. The oldest son, Adam, was six feet and five inches in height; Charles, six feet and four inches; John, six feet and three inches; Anna, five feet and eleven inches; Sallie, five feet and nine inches; and Joseph, the baby, at 15 years of age was six feet and six inches! This family was not only remarkable for their great stature, but also impressive as giants mentally. The extreme stature of the youngest member, his shuffling, shambling gait, and great good nature, with some degree of humor and wit, reminded one continually of Lincoln.

Not far from where Lincoln was reared, there occurred a wedding some years since that made the story of Lincoln's first sweetheart seem all the more plausible, especially that part which relates to his great stature and awkwardness.

A veritable son of Anak, six feet and six inches in stature, married a diminutive little lady four feet and six inches tall. The nuptial bands were solemnized in a meeting house in the presence of the entire countryside. The wedding was quite simple throughout. There were no flower girls, no best man, no bridesmaids; no soloist sang "O, promise me"; nor did the bride reach the Hymeneal Altar leaning on the arm of her father, keeping step to the strains of Mendelssohn's "Wedding March." Instead, at the appointed hour, which followed the sermon, the bride and groom came down the center aisle unattended; the groom making long, ungainly strides and the bride holding onto his arm akimbo with the tip of her fingers while some wag in the choir who had a fine sense of appropriateness pitched the old-time camp-meeting hymn, "Leaning on the Everlasting Arms." And by the time the happy, but somewhat embarrassed couple reached the chancel, the choir lustily joined in the chorus.

While Lincoln was acting as ferryman at the mouth of Anderson Creek, a corn husking took place in the neighborhood which he of course attended. At such times, as at log rollings and raisings, the work was divided equally into two parts and captains elected who chose up, thus dividing the crowd preparatory to a race. On the particular occasion above referred to, Lincoln, while busily husking away, intent on making his side "beat," kept up a running fire of humorous remarks at the expense of the other side, directing his remarks toward one man. This individual, not possessing a temperamental make-up such as to endure this long, accordingly gave way to his anger and hurled an ear of corn at Lincoln across the rail that divided the pile of corn. Taking good aim he threw the hard, horny nub at Lincoln, striking him full in the breast and cutting such a gash as to leave a scar which Lincoln carried to his grave. Lincoln did not reply in kind against his assailant, but his anger arose.[4]

There were some customs more or less peculiar to this part of the State in Lincoln's day, continuing for years thereafter, and among these was the celebration of the New Year. The ceremony, while lacking the refinement and more poetic sentiments usually supposed to have attended the Yuletide in northern Europe, yet considering that it was a backwoods custom during the holiday week, the method of celebration possessed a sense of appropriateness. At the midnight hour, just as the old year was dying and the New Year about to be ushered in, large numbers of men and boys with firearms assembled before a farm residence, and without any warning a voice began reciting, rather stump fashion, a bit of crude verse which was called "the New Year's Speech." The person chosen to recite this speech was usually one possessing the gift of oratory. Knowing that Lincoln was much given to public exhibitions and disposed to make addresses on numerous occasions, it was presumed that he frequently made the New Year's Speech. This fact, however, was not certainly established. Since the custom of the pioneers has passed away, with many other things peculiar to them, the New Year's Speech brought from the South is here given:

> Awake! Awake! my neighbor dear
> And to my wish pray lend an ear.
> The New Year is now at your door,
> The Old year is past and comes no more;
> And I for you wish a Happy Year
> That you from bad luck may keep clear;
> That your family, and all the rest
> May with content be ever blest.
> That you may be free and able
> To feed the hungry at your table;
> That your barns and all your cribs
> May with much grain be stocked
> Your fields and meadows handsomely flocked
> And scarcity not be known.
> But mind there is the Blessed Hand
> Who gives and takes at His command.
> But now before I make an end,
> For too much time I cannot spend,
> Shall I salute you with my gun,
> Or would you wish the report to shun?

Just here the speaker paused and, if granted permission to fire his gun, he resumed the speech as follows:

> Now, since you gave me leave,
> I do now here declare
> The noise shall sound throughout the air,

Sausage and pudding will be right
To satisfy our appetite.
Whiskey Bounce or Apple Brandy,
Or any liquor that comes handy.
And we will receive it with thanks to thine
And this is the end and wish of mine.

Just as the speech was finished, a volley or two was fired; and when ample justice had been done to sausage and pudding, as well as satisfying the thirst, the guns were reloaded and another house sought. This was kept up throughout the remainder of the night, the speech being repeated at each place.

NOTES

1. Abraham Lincoln, "Address to the Washington Temperance Society," in Lincoln, *Speeches and Writings*, vol. 1.

2. It is not clear where Murr obtained this quotation.

3. Louis Warren addresses this incident as well (Warren, *Lincoln's Youth*, 155–156).

4. This story involves Green Taylor, known until his death as the boy who hit Lincoln with an ear of corn (Bartelt, *There I Grew Up*, 173–174).

FOURTEEN

—w—

CHURCH AND RELIGION

Nobly sustained as the government has been by all the churches,
  I would utter nothing which might in the least appear invidious
  against any. * * * God bless all the churches, and blessed be God
  who in this great trial giveth us the churches.[1]

DURING MR. LINCOLN'S EARLY LIFE, he was disposed more or
less toward fatalism, not that there was any one act of his or any
single utterance by which this fact could be established so much as
there was discerned an approach toward all undertakings in life with
this conviction dogging his footsteps. These fatalistic beliefs were
so general among the people of that day as to include practically all.

Lincoln seems to have yielded so far to the ultra-Calvinistic
teachings characterizing the pulpit efforts and emphasis of that
day as to become more or less submissive to what was conceded
to be the stern and inevitable decrees of Fate. This strange belief
must not be confounded with that bold and open opposition to
religious faith, as was the boast of some, but was in fact a religious
and Christian interpretation of the teachings of the scriptures,
especially peculiar to the primitive Baptists.

Lincoln was not a communicant of the Little Pigeon Baptist
church although his father, mother, and sister were; likewise were

the Johnstons, his step-sisters, and step-brother. His father and mother united with this church by letter, thus indicating their connection with the church in Kentucky.

While Lincoln was more or less indoctrinated with the fatalistic tendencies of a theology generally prevalent, at the same time he was not at all disposed to accept the common literal interpretation of the Scriptures and, in consequence, held aloof from formal union with the church.

That we may more fully appreciate to what extent some of these teachings influenced the parishioners, a circumstance may be detailed that transpired in this region where Lincoln reached his majority, although many years after; but it will perhaps serve quite well by way of illustration to show this same religious emphasis lingering many decades later and, for that matter, may yet be found in this region as well as elsewhere.

An aged man, just two years younger than Lincoln (well known to the writer) who was much given to theological disputation, gave as his belief that "what is to be will be, even if it never comes to pass;" that "God had decreed and foreordained certain things," and they "were bound to come to pass;" that there was no use to flee from imminent danger since each one of us was to die in a certain way, at a certain time, and no effort on our part could possibly prevent this. If we were to be drowned, or shot, or die of disease, then no matter what might befall us prior to the appointed hour, this event would eventually take place according to Divine appointment.

This particular gentleman was quite aged when the horse-powered threshing machine was succeeded by the steam thresher. A large crowd had gathered to witness the strange engine, and while many of them were gathered about it the water began foaming. This circumstance alarmed the engineer who was anything but expert, and he hurriedly indicated his fears by announcing his intention of reaching a point of safety. Acting upon his better judgment, he started at a lively pace out into an adjoining field; and without any need of further urging when the crowd witnessed his flight, they all joined in. The old brother of fatalistic beliefs brought up the rear by reason of infirmities of age and not because of any wish to be found in the extreme rear. After a safe distance had been reached and sufficient time had elapsed to allow all danger to pass, the engineer ventured back to his post again and pretty soon announced that the "Iron Horse was all right." Whereupon certain adherents of the Methodist faith, who had been again and again subjected to humiliation and defeat by the superior ability of the old Baptist brother to argue, now turned upon him mercilessly. After a good-natured laugh had been indulged in at his expense, the old gentleman remarked, "I've got as good a Baptist heart in me as any man, but I've got a cowardly pair of Methodist legs, and they run away with me."

Lincoln would have enjoyed the laugh at the old Baptist brother's expense, but the fatalistic teachings so possessed him that he would have still found a lurking belief that all such events were predetermined, and that this grip of Fate possessed us all. Later in life he threw off the major portion of these beliefs, but not all of them.

He retained the basic principle of that theology which taught the wholesome doctrine that the Almighty hath his purposes. Not only did he believe that "if we did not do right, God was going to let us go our own way to ruin," but also he expressed the belief that "the Almighty was going to compel us to do right in order that he might destroy slavery, give success to our arms, and maintain our unity as a nation." He further said:

> I do not believe that He will do these things so much because we desire them as that they accord with His plans of dealing with this nation. I think He means that we shall do more than we have yet done in furtherance of His plans, and He will open the way for our doing it. I have felt His hand upon me in great trials and submitted to His guidance, and I trust that as He shall further open the way I will be ready to walk therein, relying on His Help and trusting in His Goodness and wisdom.[2]

It is a small matter as to what particular creed or sect this theology might properly belong as compared to the greater fact that he had thrown himself fully upon the Almighty, and in so doing worthily took his place alongside Moses, Joshua, and Paul.

His early theology made the heavens brass and the unchanging decrees made God stern, exacting, and demanding justice. His later faith was so modified by sorrows and trials as to believe in the efficacy of prayer, and he came to see God's beneficence and mercy mingled with His justice. Lincoln's daily habit from early youth was to read the Scriptures and give himself to prayer. It would appear that this fact and the sentiment and spirit of some of his great State papers would be quite sufficient to have prevented Ingersoll and others possessing liberalistic views to assert, as they were accustomed to do, that he was an unbeliever.[3]

That Lincoln, after reaching Illinois, passed through a period of religious doubt, even to the extent of questioning the authenticity of the Bible and denying the divinity and sonship of Christ, is undoubtedly true. However, there was nothing ever uttered by him either in any public manner or in private conversation while a resident of Indiana that even so much as indicated any liberalistic views or tendencies. He made no pretentions, however, of being a Christian during his youth; that is, he made no public profession and was not regarded as such by his associates. Mr. Lincoln certainly was not a Christian in the orthodox sense until sometime after reaching the White House, if indeed he ever became such as measured by certain formulas. Herndon, Colonel Lamon, and Major John Hay all stoutly maintained that he never changed his religious beliefs at all.

A statement that young Lincoln was not a Christian, nor [was he] so regarded by his associates, . . . would be altogether misleading unless it be properly understood. Their standards and his for presuming upon such a claim were of course measured by the practice of the local church in demanding the observance of certain forms and subscribing to certain tenets. It was, of course, not allowed that any one could be so presumptuous as to set forth the claim that he was a Christian independent of these. Lincoln's not having done this was not considered as being a Christian.

It may be truly said, without casting any aspersion upon the character and profession of some, that there were others, indeed many, who composed the membership of Little Pigeon Baptist church in Lincoln's day who possessed doubtful morality; certainly they failed to measure up to the requirements of Christian standards of living generally in vogue today. It is not charged that gross and flagrant wrongdoing characterized any one of them, but it is claimed that delinquencies in many matters were the rule.

The ministers themselves were often indeed quite generally given to dram drinking, and certainly this was true of substantially all the parishioners—women as well as men. It will be seen, therefore, that these well-meaning pioneers hedged up the door of entrance into the kingdom by erroneous theological emphasis upon some matters by demanding of all who sought fellowship with them that they subscribe to these, but too often their own delinquencies and shortcomings were such as to be only too painfully apparent.

Lincoln, given to approaching any and all things along lines of reason, could not fail to note the inconsistencies in profession and practice. Possessing morals quite beyond most people, abstaining from the use of intoxicants and tobacco, temperate in speech, painstakingly honest and truthful, given to reading the Bible daily, and regarded as possessing such a wholesome amount of common sense and sound judgment as to be selected to adjudicate all differences arising among his fellows, it may therefore be seen that while Lincoln made no profession of religious faith in conformity to the standards of the time, yet his character was quite beyond that of others.[4]

For this youth, who if not educated in the ordinary acceptation of the term, possessed more knowledge even then perhaps than most of us are ready to allow; and being acquainted, for instance, as we know that Lincoln was, with the movement of the heavenly bodies, and then to hear in the Sunday sermon the maledictions of Heaven hurled at "eddicated" folks who presumed to think that the earth was round, that it "revolved upon its axle tree," and similar animadversions, one can deeply sympathize with a disposition to refrain from formal union with such a class.

Again, for young Lincoln to assemble with these worshippers in Little Pigeon church, for the preacher and people to engage as they often did in a give-and-take sort of fashion in the coarse, crude jokes of doubtful propriety anywhere—much less in a place of worship—hurling at one another, albeit good-naturedly, hilarious repartee and scintillating witticisms better suited to the schoolhouse debates; and for the minister to suggest that it was time for worship and for some old brother to start the hymn, "How Tedious and Tasteless the Hours," pitching it in a strange key, putting in an unconscionable number of quarter and half rests; and then for the leader, perhaps, at the close of the stanza to expectorate his ambier in a belated sort of manner, no matter where, preparatory to another effort; and when that was finished, for the sermon to be entered upon, with all of the vials of wrath poured forth and anathemas heaped upon the heads of offenders (as was often the case) in such a fashion as to indicate enjoyment in anticipation, with a great deal of sound and little sense; therefore, for a youth of Lincoln's purity of character and sense of propriety, faculty of reasoning and freedom from such habits above referred to, to refrain from formal union with the church is, after all, not a thing to excite wonder or provoke harsh criticism.

In calling attention to some of the foregoing things peculiar to the pioneer days generally prevailing, and even today found in Kentucky and Tennessee, there is no disposition to excuse Mr. Lincoln from the mistake certainly chargeable to him of refraining from formal union with the church at a later period. It is hoped that the treatment here offered concerning the crude manner of worship and erroneous emphasis of the primitive Baptists will not be taken as an intentional slight upon that branch of the church. (The writer's forebears were of that faith.) While some justification for young Lincoln's attitude toward this class is here set forth, yet it is manifestly true that this particular church so generally prevalent in large sections of the country during the formative period, furnished the sole means of worship, and so administered to the spiritual needs of the people as abundantly to justify its existence.

The question of Mr. Lincoln's religious attitude later in life has provoked considerable discussion. Substantially all creeds, like all political parties, have claimed him. Those entertaining liberalistic views have been quite as free as any in asserting the claim that Lincoln was of their number. This was the boast of Colonel Ingersoll, of agnostic fame. Mr. Herndon, his law partner, said that his religious faith was best represented by the teachings of Theodore Parker; and he and others possessing religious beliefs that classed them as deists were disposed to claim Mr. Lincoln as possessing a like faith. This class in particular has challenged those who claim Mr. Lincoln as a Christian to point out in all of his utterances at any time a sentence where the name of Jesus Christ was used. This attitude is wholly unworthy of such men as Herndon, Lamon, and others. Lincoln told his particular friend, Bishop Simpson, that he did pass through a period of doubt and distrust of the Scriptures, but that he later came to see the folly of such. It is a noteworthy fact, however, that Mr. Lincoln's language in reference to Deity was such as to give no offense to any faith or creed.

It is believed that no one today would be disposed to undertake the hopeless and thankless task of attempting to substantiate the claim that Mr. Lincoln was not a Christian in view of all the evidence at hand to the contrary. With a sincere purpose of doing the right as "God gave him to see the right," far removed as he was above the loose morality of strong partisan politics, refusing as he did repeatedly to be governed by notable examples of expediency and mere conventionalities; absolutely unmindful of probable accusations in his departure from an age-long custom of indirection in diplomacy; implicitly trusting in the plain people; relying upon the gracious favor of Almighty God, with no disposition at any time to substitute expediency for conscience; willing rather to lose popular applause or any mere temporary advantage than even to appear to take liberties with possible success by a firm adherence to the eternal principles of justice and truth; with a sublime patience and unexampled fortitude, he refused to be moved by the clamor of public opinion.

He was a statesman without craft; a politician without cunning; a great man with many virtues and no vices; a ruler without the arrogancy of pride and the bigotry of power; ambitious without mere selfish personal gratification; and successful without becoming vain-glorious. If that Hebrew lawgiver and leader Moses, in that unprecedented wilderness march with a horde of newly liberated slaves, felt that faith was depleted or courage run low, he could and did betimes climb the mountain stairway and cry to the God of battles, and Jehovah came down "in trailing clouds of Glory"; or if he were harassed by the pursuing foe or flanked by fiery serpents, he could afford to be content, for was not the Almighty himself on the picket line in a cloud by day and a pillar of fire by night? But not so this later liberator whose tall form was stooping under the terrible burdens, both North and South. What wonder that betimes we see him on his knees in the White House in prayer with Bishop Simpson, or, as when Lee flushed with victory on the gory fields of Fredericksburg and Chancellorsville turned his victorious legions north once more, Lincoln fell upon his face and cried to the God of battles, "This is your war. The North can't stand another Chancellorsville. You stand by our boys at Gettysburg, and I'll stand by you." And he did.

NOTES

1. Basler et al., *Collected Works of Abraham Lincoln*, 7:350–351. Lincoln offered these remarks in response to an address by a committee of the Methodist Episcopal Church General Conference of 1864.

2. Although not a word-for-word quotation, this originates from Lincoln's words allegedly spoken in the presence of ex-Senator J. F. Wilson with a shorter version put forth by Oliver O. Howard. Fehrenbacher and Fehrenbacher, *Recollected Words of Abraham Lincoln*, 500.

3. Robert G. Ingersoll (1833–1899), an Illinois lawyer, advances this view in his 1907 book simply titled *Abraham Lincoln*.

4. Not coincidentally, Murr lists traits and characteristics important to Methodists in the 1920s.

FIFTEEN

YOUNG LINCOLN ON THE STUMP

My opinion is that no state can, in any way lawfully, get out of the
Union, without the consent of the others; and that it is the duty
of the President, and other government functionaries to run the
machine as it is.[1]

THE BOYHOOD FRIENDS OF LINCOLN were quite pronounced
in stating that while Lincoln was ever ready to enter into all of
their boyish sports, especially to accompany them to any place
where there was a crowd, he could not be induced either to play,
fish, or accompany them on any expedition of any character if he
had in his possession a new book. Lincoln himself, in later life
said that he borrowed all the books to be found for a radius of
50 miles.[2] His habit was to commit to memory such portions as
particularly pleased him, making copious notes on paper, if he
had it, but if he did not (as was frequently the case) he made free
use of boards, the wooden fire shovel or any smooth surface presenting itself. He was an omnivorous reader, devouring anything
offered. He regularly borrowed the *Louisville Journal* from Jones,
the storekeeper, and a temperance paper and religious publication
from a neighbor by the name of Wood. Lincoln had strong convictions on the subject of temperance, and in reading the publication

borrowed from Wood was encouraged to commit some of his own thoughts to paper. He took this to his old friend and was pleased when Uncle Wood said that "for sound sense it was better than anything in the paper." Wood in turn showed the manuscript to a Baptist preacher who was so delighted with it as to believe that it was beyond anything found in the temperance journal, and proposed sending it to the editor at some point in Ohio. It is said that this article was accepted and appeared in the paper, to the great delight of Lincoln as well as of his patron and friend, Wood.[3]

Succeeding so well in this venture, he attempted a political treatment, taking as his theme, national politics. The subject doubtless suggested itself to him on reading the Louisville paper. This manuscript was submitted to his old friend Wood, as before, who showed it to Judge John Pitcher, an attorney residing at Rockport. Pitcher, on reading the article, exclaimed, "The world can't beat it." This remark greatly encouraged young Lincoln, and he journeyed to Rockport to call upon Pitcher at his office. It is said that subsequently Pitcher lent Lincoln law books and showed him considerable attention such as drawing him out in conversation on finding him a great talker and quite original in his ideas and methods of investigation.

The essay on national politics, while not preserved entirely, has been in part, and from these sentences some notion may be formed as to Lincoln's ideas at that early period: "The American government is the best form of government for an intelligent people; it ought to be kept sound and preserved forever. * * * General education should be fostered and carried all over the country; and the Constitution should be saved, the Union perpetuated, and the laws revered, respected, and enforced."[4] Lincoln's plea for educational advantages is pathetic when his own disadvantages were so marked.

Among those pioneers in this section who, after attaining old age, were rich in the remembrances of former years was Captain John LaMar. The LaMars were among the first settlers in this part of the State. Captain LaMar witnessed the killing of the last Indian by the whites in this region, there having been more or less trouble between the two races prior to the Battle of Tippecanoe as well as such minor engagements as the Pigeon Roost Massacre. However, by the time the Lincolns settled here the Indians had nearly all left this section. The writer had as a parishioner in his church Mrs. LaMar, a lady four years younger than Mr. Lincoln and being a neighbor, of course knew him quite well. Captain LaMar, on one occasion, was riding to mill with his father along the road leading past the Lincoln cabin. They observed a boy perched upon the top of a staked-and-ridered fence, reading and so intently engaged that he did not notice their approach. The elder LaMar was so impressed with this fact that he remarked to his son: "John, look at that boy yonder! You mark my words, he will make a smart man out of himself. I may not see it, but you see if my words don't come true."[5]

Captain LaMar lived to witness the fulfillment of his father's prophesy. He was present on the occasion of the unveiling of the Nancy Hanks monument in 1902.

"Nat" Grigsby said, "Lincoln was always at school quite early and attended to his studies diligently. He always stood at the head of his class and passed the rest of us rapidly in his studies. He lost no time at home, and when he was not at work he was at his books."

The schoolmates of Lincoln stated that he was never rude on the playground and was usually chosen when an arbiter was needed in adjusting difficulties between boys of his age and size. When his decision was given, it put an end to the trouble.

In an interview with Dennis Hanks by Mr. Herndon, the former said: "We learned by sight, scent, and hearing. We heard all that was said and talked over and over the questions heard, and wore them slick and greasy and threadbare. We went to hear political and other speeches, and to such gatherings as you do now. We would hear all sides and opinions and talk them over, discuss them, agreeing or disagreeing. Abe was a cheerful boy.

Sometimes he would get sad, but not very often. He was always reading, scribbling, ciphering, and writing poetry."[6]

Miss Roby, who married Allen Gentry, the young man with whom Lincoln made the celebrated flatboat trip down the Mississippi River, said that she was at Gentry's Landing while this boat was being loaded preparatory to making the southern journey. In speaking of Lincoln at this time, she said: "He was long, thin, and gawky, his skin having the appearance of being dried up and shriveled." One evening as they sat on the edge of the boat with their feet in the water, Miss Roby called attention to the sunset whereupon Lincoln explained to her that the sun did not move in fact, but only appeared to do so, that it was the earth that went around the sun. The young lady laughed at the absurdity of such notions and thought him foolish, but later came to realize that young Lincoln was not foolish, but knew much more than anyone around there supposed.

It was this same young lady who related a circumstance that took place in the schoolroom when all the scholars were engaged on a Friday afternoon spelling match. This circumstance has been related by almost all of the earlier biographers of Mr. Lincoln. The schoolmaster, Crawford, had "given out" the word *defied*, and the first one attempting it had said, *defyed*; the second, *deffyed*; and at length it came Miss Roby's turn. Not being certain she chanced to look across the room where Lincoln stood smiling. She notice him slyly placing his finger to his eye, and taking the hint she spelled the word correctly and went to the head of her class. Young Lincoln was ever regarded as a good speller and particularly so by the time he reached his 17th year. In fact, he was easily the best speller in the neighborhood and was commonly supposed to know quite as much as his teachers, and more than some of them.

As late as the year 1880, in this section, if a young man excelled in spelling so that he could "take the floor" at spelling matches and could "solve all the problems in the arithmetic," he was regarded as learned;and no one questioned his ability to teach school.

Lincoln especially liked argumentative bouts, and this caused him to be much in the company of his elders. This habit he later styled "practicing polemics."[7] His ability to argue and his particular enjoyment of it seem to have been maintained during his occupancy of the White House. His secretaries are on record as saying that he spent more time and greater pains with the famous Vallandingham letter than with any State paper.[8]

As a youth he was quite inquisitive on almost any subject, and his habit was never to leave a subject, however difficult, until he had mastered it. He was a good listener, and appeared to know when to keep silent when in company of his elders. After hearing fireside discussions, if certain phases were not clear to him, he lay awake after retiring and beginning at the first of the argument carefully reviewed it step by step until he had thoroughly satisfied his own mind of the certainty of conclusions reached. He often walked to and fro for considerable periods, repeating these arguments to himself and, after mastering them once, never forgot them. As he later put it, he "was not satisfied when on a hunt for an idea until he could bound it north and south, east and west."[9] He was slow in reaching conclusions, but when once he announced his decision in any given matter, he could not be moved by the force of argument or any other pressure brought to bear.

Many of his well-known stories, anecdotes, and yarns were of Indiana origin. He and Dennis Hanks usually spent their evenings at the Gentryville store, and on rainy days they might be found either at the store or at Baldwin's blacksmith shop. Baldwin was a great master at storytelling, and it was his yarns afterward related by Lincoln that caused members of cabinets and Congress, and even representatives of foreign countries, to smile or laugh uproariously.

It was his custom, after reading the *Louisville Journal* at Jones's store, to meditate upon what he had read; and then while at work in the fields, he would often review some of these discussions for the benefit of his associates.[10]

Lincoln has been accused of being lazy, and in support of this assertion more or less evidence has been offered. Mr. Romine, a near neighbor to the Lincolns and for whom Abraham often labored, is quoted as saying that "Lincoln was lazy." The writer did not know Mr. Romine, but Mrs. Romine was yet living when the data composing these pages were being obtained. In no single instance was this charge of laziness made against Lincoln by any of his early friends. However, it is believed that some of them would have been inclined to this belief had they been approached earlier in life when it was the fashion to make the charge against any who spent time poring over books. For any chance passerby to see a youth lying beneath the shade of a tree, busily reading, was *prima facie* evidence that he was lazy and usually occasioned, as in Lincoln's case, some such remark as, "Old Tom's Abe'd ruther fool his time away a readin' out of a book than to work any day." Indeed, this disposition to criticise those who engage in purely mental labors while others were in the fields or shops is met with frequently even today.

Not long since in this very region, an artist spent some days on an eminence sketching a landscape, and he was subjected to severe criticism by the farm laborers, remarking that "he is doubtless the son of a bloated aristocrat and was not raised to work." Thus, in Lincoln's time for one to have a day off and elect to spend it in reading was regarded as indicating a lazy disposition. Had the day off been spent along the river bank with hook and line or in the woods with the gun, it would have elicited no unfavorable comment. The major portion of Lincoln's early friends came to realize this; and where once might have been found carping criticism, at the time the writer was gathering data, he found commendation.

The fact that Lincoln frequented the Gentryville store or blacksmith shop has been cited as evidence quite sufficient to establish the charge that he was lazy. There is a rule in logic that if too much is proven, then nothing is proved. Certainly, if the mere fact that Lincoln was often found at Gentryville is deemed sufficient evidence to prove his indifference to work, then substantially all of his neighbors were lazy since Gentryville was a Saturday town or rainy-day town for the surrounding neighborhood, just as many towns are today. As congressmen and senators frequent the cloakroom, smoking and indulging themselves in the pastime of story telling, so in like manner Lincoln frequented the pioneer cloakroom—Jones's store—thus gathering that fund of stories and anecdotes which he afterward related to his associates and White House visitors. Lincoln's boyhood friends indicated that "he was ever ready to turn his hand at anything, no matter much what, and was always at work if there was any work to be had."

Joseph Gentry, a brother of Allen, told of hearing Lincoln make his first public address, apart from such efforts as the schoolhouse debates occasioned. The circumstances leading up to this were as follows: Two neighbors each owned a flock of geese, and one evening when one of these flocks returned and was being housed for the night, it was ascertained that a certain grey goose was missing. The owner, knowing that his flock occasionally mingled with that of his neighbor, and very naturally supposing that it had strayed off with these, he accordingly went to the home of the owner of the other flock. On his arrival there, he explained his mission and at once pointed to a certain goose claiming it as his, whereupon the neighbor disputed the claim, and before long this occasioned a heated argument which came little short of a personal encounter. The two disputants made sundry threats on separating, each saying in effect that the matter was not settled, and the owner of the stray goose indicated that he would bring the matter before the squire. Accordingly, attorneys were consulted and employed to prosecute and defend. The day was set for the trial, the court room being the schoolhouse about one mile east of the Lincoln cabin.

The difference between these two neighbors occasioning the litigation very naturally produced intense interest throughout the community, so much so in fact that when the day fixed for the trial came, a great crowd assembled. However, not all of these came merely to gratify curiosity, for both sides had subpoenaed a number of witnesses. Mr. Gentry stated that so far as to his having any personal interest or motive in attending, it was due solely to a boyish curiosity to witness these proceedings; and falling in with Lincoln, who was at that time in his 17th year, they walked together to the schoolhouse. Arriving early, they went well forward and sat down on a backless puncheon seat. Erelong the little house was crowded. The two litigants, together with members of their families and friends, were seated on either side of the room. There was that characteristic stillness that foreboded a storm, and presently, without any warning whatever, Lincoln arose, and advancing quickly forward, faced the assembled crowd and began making an address. Gentry maintained that Lincoln had not previously indicated his purpose to him or to others of attempting such a thing, and when he thus stood forth and began the speech he (Gentry) was greatly surprised. It was, of course, not possible for Gentry to give the exact language of Lincoln on this occasion; but since the circumstances were indelibly fixed in his memory, he found no great difficulty in setting forth the scene rather vividly, and it is believed that the following version of it is substantially what occurred:

> "Friends and neighbors, what means this great gathering of old neighbors? What is it that has called us together here?" Up to this time the speaker's face being as serious as Lincoln's face could be and then amid the painful silence his features changed, his eyebrows lifted, and irresistible humor beamed forth. "What brings us together? Why—an—old—gray—goose !" A great roar of laughter greeted this ludicrous drawl, but not being interrupted in any way and doubtless encouraged to proceed by the volley of laughter, he continued (serious again), this time stating the case. "Mr. A., here (addressing him) has lost a goose and he asserts that his neighbor, Mr. B., here (pointing) has it. Although Mr. B.

disclaims having in his possession any goose not his own, not being able or disposed to settle their difference between themselves,
they have decided to go to law, and that's why we are all here."
(Comical again.) "Mr. A. (addressing him), you say you have lost
a gray goose and that you know that Mr. B., here has it; and rather
than lose it you have resolved to bring the matter to the court.
Now you, Mr. A. (pointing and then quickly turning his face and
body half about) and you Mr. B., after you've had your trial today,
and no matter which way it goes, what have either of you gained?
W-E-L-L, Mr. A., if you win your case you'll get back your old
gray goose, and it is worth say about two bits! (great laughter).
And you, Mr. B., if you win today, you'll get to keep your old gray
goose that you claim has always been yours, and it's worth say
about two bits (laughter). Now you, Mr. A. (serious again), and
you, Mr. B., if you win today you'll get back your goose or keep
your goose as the case may be, but (very earnestly) I tell both
of you that whichever one may win, he's going to lose! And lose
what, you say? Well, you have both been neighbors, and you'll
lose your friendship for each other for one thing; and not only
that, it won't stop there. For what means this array of witnesses
here? (pointing). It means your wives and family and friends will
be at outs, and you've set up a commotion in the entire neighborhood, and what about? (Exceedingly comical). Oh, w-e-l-l, all on
account of an old gray goose! If I were in your place, men, I'd stop
all this hair-pulling and wool gathering. I'd get together here and
now and settle this thing, make up, and be friends.

The result was that just as the court and the two attorneys from
the county seat town came through the little doorway, Lincoln
had the two litigants shaking hands and smiling. Lincoln had
thus laughed the matter out of court and won his maiden case
which may not inaptly or inappropriately be called "The Gray
Goose Case."

Thoughtful consideration is invited by way of comparison of
this circumstance with Lincoln's Cincinnati speech where he
presumes to address his "friends across the river," as well as his

famous Cooper Institute address, and above all his first inaugural where he stands as the nation's peacemaker, saying, "Suppose you go to war, you cannot fight always; and when, after much loss on both sides, and no gain on either, you cease fighting, the identical old questions, as to terms of intercourse, are again upon you."

The method and manner, certainly the peculiar platform mannerisms, the skilful bringing together of humor, and the setting forth of the serious side, were pre-eminently characteristic of young Lincoln so that when he sprang into the arena of debate later, he came fully armed to meet the Little Giant Douglas, if not with a shepherd's crook and sling, with weapons more formidable—the speech and faith of the plain people, appealing as he did "to the considerate judgment of mankind and invoking the gracious favor of Almighty God" in defense of a holy cause that had been repeatedly defied.

The unrivaled genius of Lincoln whose consummate art in statement enabled him to become such a wizard with the pen and which flowered out on the prairies of Illinois, was budding forth in the morning of his life in the wilderness of Indiana, becoming, as he did in after years, the greatest leader of all with the humblest origin and scantiest scholarship, yet he "surpassed all orators in eloquence, all diplomats in wisdom, all statesmen in foresight, and the most ambitious in fame."[11]

NOTES

1. Lincoln to Hon. Thurlow Weed, 17 December 1860, Basler et al., *Collected Works of Abraham Lincoln*, vol. 4.

2. This statement is based on Lincoln allegedly telling his friend Leonard Swett that he "had got hold of and read through every book he ever heard of in that country for a circuit of about fifty miles" (Leonard Swett in *Reminiscences of Abraham Lincoln*, ed. Rice, 459). Although one neighbor called the statement hyperbole since Lincoln was selective, the story survived; many historians paid close attention to the persons, books, and information available to Lincoln within a fifty-mile radius of his home.

3. See also Warren, *Lincoln's Youth*, 169–170.

4. Lincoln's former employer, William Wood, recalled this quotation from an essay by Lincoln that Wood allegedly reviewed. Thayer, *Pioneer Boy*, 118.

5. See Tarbell, *Early Life of Abraham Lincoln*, 72.

6. Foster, *Abraham Lincoln*, 19.

7. See Holland, *Holland's Life of Abraham Lincoln*, 46.

8. Clement Vallandigham (1820–1871), a leader of the Ohio Democratic Party and a fierce critic of both Lincoln and the Civil War, was arrested for violating a Civil War order. An uproar ensued when Vallandigham was denied habeas corpus. Concerned about making Vallandigham a martyr, Lincoln ordered him sent through enemy lines to the Confederacy. In a famous "Birchard Letter" written in 1863 to several Ohio congressmen, Lincoln offered to revoke Vallandigham's deportation order in exchange for support of certain administration policies.

9. Murr's source for this quotation is unclear.

10. The *Louisville Daily Journal* began distribution in 1830. Its predecessor, *The Focus of Politics, Commerce and Literature*, was founded in 1826.

11. This quotation is attributed in other publications to John L. Ingalls.

SIXTEEN

—⚇—

LINCOLN'S AMBITION
TO BECOME A RIVER PILOT

I know there is a God and that he hates injustice and slavery. I see
the storm coming, and I know that His hand is in it. If He has
a place and work for me—and I think He has—I believe I am
ready.[1]

IT WAS GOLDWIN SMITH WHO said, "The Mississippi River was
once a mental horizon and afterward a boundary line."[2] During
Lincoln's youth this river had become the highway for the western pioneer, and what was true of the Father of Waters was true
of the Ohio river.

Lincoln came in touch with the outside world on this great
highway. Travel by boat, slow as it was, served as quite the best
means of making long journeys. Occasionally a passing steamer
landed at Anderson Creek; and since Troy was regarded as a place
of some importance most of the river crafts made port there.
Hence, young Lincoln, while acting as ferryman during his 17th
year, was privileged to see somewhat of life from without. Notable men occasionally passed, and he may have even met with
some of them.

A short distance above Troy, General Lafayette, while making
his tour of the western States by way of the Ohio River, spent a

night in a stone house on the river bank after his disabled steamer sank. Perhaps Lincoln did not see the Friend of Washington, but his passing and the circumstance of his spending the night ashore not far from where Lincoln lived furnished a theme for the pioneers for a considerable time thereafter.[3]

It was while acting as ferryman at Anderson Creek that Lincoln made his first dollar. This circumstance, which he related in later life to members of his cabinet, and to Secretary Seward in particular, was as follows:

> I was standing at the steamboat landing contemplating my new boat and wondering how I might improve it when a steamer approached coming down the river. At the same time two passengers came to the river bank and wished to be taken out to the packet with their luggage. They looked among the boats, singled out mine, and asked me to scull them to the boat. Sometime prior to this, I had constructed a small boat in which I planned to carry some produce south which had been gathered chiefly by my own exertions. We were poor, and in them days people down South who did not own slaves were reckoned as scrubs. When I was requested to scull these men out to the steamer, I gladly did so; and after seeing them and their trunks on board, and the steamer making ready to pass on, I called out to the men, "You have forgotten to pay me." They at once each threw a half dollar in the bottom of the boat in which I was standing. You gentlemen may think it was a very small matter, and in the light of things now transpiring it was, but I assure you it was one of the most important incidents in my life. I could scarcely believe my eyes. It was difficult for me to realize that I, a poor boy, had earned a dollar in less than a day. The world seemed wider and fairer before me. I was a more hopeful and confident being from that time.[4]

Young Lincoln being ambitious and desirous of bettering his condition very naturally looked to the river for employment. Possessing some skill with carpenter's tools, he had at this time constructed a boat that he deemed seaworthy enough to make the journey referred to in his conversation with Secretary Seward.

It has been asserted by some of his biographers that this journey was not made, and one writer ventures to suggest that since the Lincolns had nothing in the way of produce justifying such a trip, it was therefore merely a journey of the imagination. Such a position taken is a needless effort to establish the well-known poverty of the Lincolns; but since no such journey was undertaken by any at that time without presuming upon neighborly assistance, which proved in substantially every case to be a mutual accommodation, the proposed trip down the Ohio and Mississippi by young Lincoln might have been fully justified since it is now known that he had on his own account a crop of tobacco. The plans for the trip, as indicated in the conversation with Seward, were so changed as to cause him to leave his own boat behind and take passage upon the flatboat of Mr. Ray.

Having made this and the later trip with young Gentry down the great river, he seems to have been disposed to follow the Ohio, and a little later he went to his old friend and patron Uncle Wood, in whom he reposed great confidence, requesting that this gentleman aid him by way of a recommendation to secure a position on some steamer plying up and down this river. Mr. Wood, realizing that Lincoln was not of age, hesitated to advise the youth to leave his father and refused to give the assistance deemed by Lincoln essential to secure a position. It was quite the rule in that day for a boy to remain with his parents until reaching his majority. However, Lincoln was very insistent, and in the course of his argument remarked that "it was his best chance," and "a chance is all I want." After some persuasion on the part of Wood, he yielded and remained with his father until well into his twenty-second year.[5]

Since the river traffic along the Ohio and Mississippi at that time, and for a considerable period thereafter, was great, had young Lincoln succeeded in prevailing upon his old friend Wood to aid him in securing a position as pilot, we might have lost our great war President, but would have perhaps gained another Mark

Twain. In any case, had he been so fortunate as to find some Boswell, his fame as a humorist would have been secure.

That young Lincoln seems to have become resigned to his lot is evidenced by Mr. Wood in stating that soon after this interview relative to his becoming a river pilot, he saw Lincoln whip-sawing lumber; on asking him what he intended doing with this, Wood was told that the elder Lincoln was "planning to erect a new house in the spring." The letters of John Hanks concerning the Illinois location and the glowing accounts of Dennis Hanks on his return from that region occasioned the abandonment of the plan to erect the new home, and the lumber was disposed of to Josiah Crawford who used the major portion of it in the construction of an additional room to his house.

It was soon after young Lincoln returned to the farm from Anderson Creek ferry that he formed the habit of attending the various courts, but it was while acting as ferryman that he attended court for the first time. His presence there was not prompted by mere curiosity or due to any ambition that he possessed to take up the law as a profession, but he appeared as a prisoner at the bar, the first and only time in his life; yet, had there been debtors' prisons during a certain period of his lifetime, he might have suffered imprisonment in consequence of the overwhelming obligations that he assumed and which he failed to meet until many years after they were incurred.

The circumstance of his becoming a prisoner and his appearance in the court were as follows:

> While Lincoln acted as ferryman at Anderson creek on the Indiana side of the Ohio river, John and Benjamin Dill, two farmers residing on the Kentucky side of the river just opposite the town of Troy, had become licensed ferrymen. Occasionally, when busily engaged in agricultural pursuits, they neglected the ferry to the extent that their ferry bell would sound again and again without their hearing it; or what was more probable, on hearing it, they failed to respond to its call. On such occasions when the bell rang repeatedly, young Lincoln would push out from the

Indiana side and ferry the anxious traveler across the river; of course, he received the usual fee for such services.[6]

Whether Lincoln's ear was thought to be too attentive to the ferry bell on the Kentucky side of the river, or whether the Dill brothers wished to make him an example to any and all who were disposed to take liberties with their legal rights, we do not know. But in any case they decided to entrap Lincoln and visit him with suitable punishment. Accordingly, they requested a neighbor to sound the ferry bell; and when they did not respond as was frequently the case, Lincoln quickly oared across the river. Running his boat up to an opening in the dense willows on the river bank where the supposed anxious passenger stood in apparent readiness to step in, Lincoln was surprised to find himself seized by both the supposed passenger and the Dill brothers who had, up to his appearance been hiding in the willows. They at once announced their intention of giving their prisoner a ducking. The youthful ferryman not appearing to understand their motives became very angry, and the presumption is that he manifested this in no uncertain manner. It never appeared clear whether the original purpose of the Dill brothers was carried out or seriously attempted after the preliminary skirmish with Long Abe, but it is quite true that they at length proposed to take him before the squire where punishment could be meted out in a legal manner. Lincoln, by this time understanding his supposed offense, accompanied his captors to the local justice, one Samuel Pate, who resided one mile distant down the river. On their arrival at the farm home of Pate finding that gentleman out on the farm at work, one of their party was dispatched to inform his honor that more weighty matters needed his attention while the others stood guard over the prisoner.

More or less regularity appears to have been observed in the hearing accorded the youthful offender. At first it is said he was greatly disturbed on hearing the statements of the two Dills and about the decoy, more especially so when it appeared from some of their assertions that a jail sentence awaited him; but when the Squire proposed to him to offer his version of the affair and make any statement that he cared to, Lincoln gladly availed himself of the opportunity. In doing so, he freely and frankly confessed that on numerous occasions he had ferried passengers across the river from the Kentucky side when the travelers failed to secure a response to the repeated ringing of the bell, but he disclaimed any knowledge of the fact that in so doing he had violated any law, distinctly stating that he did not know he was thus encroaching upon the rights of the Dill brothers, that if he had known it was wrong, he would not have been guilty in any single instance. He further alleged that not only was he free from intentional wrong, but in reality he supposed he was conferring a great favor upon the owners of the ferry, who, he supposed, were at such times away from home or were otherwise engaged, as well as accommodating anxious travelers.

Without throwing himself upon the mercy of the court or pleading for leniency, he nevertheless did so all the more effectively by impressing, as he did, both his accusers and the squire with his sincerity, truthfulness and honesty, reasserting his ignorance of the law and promising that in the future he would not be found trespassing upon their rights. The appeal was effective, and the court, after listening to this recital of facts, dismissed him with some suitable words of advice. Thus, like Caesar in chains, he had talked himself free.

The squire became greatly interested in Lincoln, and finding him a great talker, inquisitive concerning court procedure especially, urged the young man to prolong his stay, which he did. On Lincoln's taking his leave the squire pressed upon him an invitation to attend a sitting of his court which Lincoln accepted; not only did he attend this particular sitting, but also he became a regular attendant so long as he remained ferryman at Anderson creek.

Squire Pate did not live to witness Lincoln's rise to fame, but many of his family did. The house is still standing in which this trial was held, and the only remaining son of Pate pointed out the room in which this memorable sitting of his father's court was held. The circumstance was known to a number of the old citizens of the neighborhood, and a full account of this incident appeared in a local newspaper in Lincoln's old home county—the *Perry County Tribune*.[7]

Young Lincoln was in the habit of attending the sessions of the circuit court as well as trials before the local justice of the peace. That he possessed an ambition at this early period to become a lawyer is certainly true.

His friend David Turnham was elected constable of the township and had in consequence gotten possession of a copy of the *Revised Statutes* of Indiana. Lincoln being especially anxious to read this volume and Turnham being loath to have it leave the house, Lincoln spent hours at Turnham's home devouring this book.

The volume contained a copy of the Declaration of Independence as well as the national and state Constitutions. These Lincoln studied, committing to memory the Declaration of Independence and large portions of the national Constitution, and for the first time in his life met with legal enactments touching upon slavery.

Aside from the flatboat trips down the Ohio and Mississippi rivers, young Lincoln saw comparatively little of the world without. As has been indicated, he frequented the sittings of the circuit courts at Boonville, in Warrick county, as well as at Rockport, the county seat of Spencer county, and was often at Troy. In addition to his visits to these comparatively small places, he had an occasion to go at least once a year, after approaching manhood, to Princeton, in Gibson county, there being a carding machine located at that place which converted the fleece into rolls ready for the spinning wheel. Hand-carding being quite tedious and slow, young Lincoln was sent with the wool to this machine. The journey was a rather long one for that time and occupied some three days. These little excursions, together with the usual trips to Gorden's or Hoffman's mills, relieved the monotony and routine of life, and it is said that these trips were gladly welcomed by the future President.

The mills for grinding corn in the early days were crude affairs. The horse-mill was the first one introduced, small mills propelled by horses hitched to a sweep. Later, and during the Indiana residence of the Lincolns, Hoffman's water mill was erected on Anderson Creek. The horse mill at Gordon's [sic] was the scene of that incident that Mr. Lincoln was accustomed to revert to again and again, professing to think that it was one of the principal incidents of his life.

The circumstance was as follows: Lincoln and young David Turnham had gone to mill, but securing a late start and having to take their turn, it was quite late in the afternoon when young Lincoln hitched his father's old flea-bitten gray mare to the sweep, and, perching himself upon the accustomed seat, began to urge the old mare to a lively pace. He was clucking and belaboring the horse with a switch, and in the midst of his urgings he started to say: "Get up here, you old hussy," when the old gray resisted the continued drubbing and lifting her hind feet kicked him full in the face. Before the sentence was finished, the young man was knocked off the sweep and lay unconscious. Young Turnham ran for help, and soon Abraham's father came with a wagon, placed the unconscious youth in it, and took him home. He lay in a stupor during the greater portion of the night, but toward morning showed signs of returning consciousness. Erelong he roused up and, opening his eyes exclaimed, "You old hussy," thus completing the exclamation attempted the evening before.

Mr. Herndon, law partner of Lincoln, said that Lincoln often called attention to this experience of his youth and entered into discussions with him as to the mystery connected with the utterance of these particular words on regaining consciousness.

Occasionally young Lincoln was privileged to get a breath of the great world from without by meeting with some chance passerby or mover to other regions in the then-far West. On one occasion a wagon of one of these emigrants broke down near the Lincoln cabin; while the damaged vehicle was undergoing repairs the wife and daughter on invitation spent the time in the Lincoln cabin. What was especially interesting to the youth was that they had a book of stories which the lady read to him. After their journey had been resumed, Lincoln, who like the great apostle to the Gentiles turned everything to his advantage, proceeded to write a story of the whole affair. But giving free play to his imagination and fancy he drew the account out at some length, describing in detail his mounting a horse, overtaking the emigrant wagon, and proposing an elopement with the young lady whose father interposed objections to their marriage. Lincoln purposed [sic] enlarging upon this story and submitting it for publication, but thought differently concerning it later. Thus the story, which was doubtless crude and altogether unworthy of a place in literature, was lost save that we have preserved the one item of value which was that he was always scribbling and writing.

It is rather remarkable that Lincoln did not appoint any of his old associates to any federal position since there were at least some three or four of them quite capable. On the score of boyhood friendship it would appear that he would under ordinary circumstances have remembered them, especially when good and efficient service would have been rendered by some of them in certain departments. So far as can be ascertained, no applications ever reached him for patronage from any of his old friends although, as has been heretofore detailed, some two or three journeyed to Washington for that purpose, but were anticipated and forestalled in such a manner as to prevent any formal request being made. This characteristic seems to have been peculiar to Lincoln, for even in the appointment of his friend Judge David Davis unusual pressure was made with some suggestion of reluctance even then. The departments were not filled with his old associates, and political loyalty was not especially rewarded by him. This practice was quite the reverse of that of President Grant.

Lincoln never forgot a kindness, as evidenced in his steadfast refusal to attack John Calhoun during the great debate with
Douglas; Calhoun had early befriended him.

Lincoln was enabled to appear before the people as a successful candidate on numerous occasions and took particular
pride in calling attention to the fact that he had never been defeated but once when the people themselves were appealed to
although his methods in some respects were anything but those
of a politician.[8]

He did not concern himself in local elections when he was not
a candidate. Being so often before the people for political prefer-
ment, there were times when others equally ambitious to serve
their party either became Lincoln's opponents or threatened to
be. At such times he would seek an interview with them, and with
an unconscious arrogancy and priority of claim he would say, "I
would rather than not that you step aside in this race and let me
have a free field so that I may show them what I can do."[9]

He was delivered from egotism only by the recognized superiority of his powers and would have been justly charged with
monumental selfishness but for his steadfast adherence to the
great basic principles of truth and justice. Meeting often with
trickery and double-dealing in politics among those high in the
councils of the party, he never lost faith in the plain people. Since
he himself never wavered in the performance of his public duties,
but administered public affairs as conscientiously as he pulled
corn blades for the Crawford damaged book, he thus more nearly
than any other before or since represented the people. It is believed that he is more highly regarded and sincerely appreciated
by the people of the South today than is Jefferson Davis, and this,
together with the fact that he preserved the unity and continuity
of our nation, is the greatest and most enduring monument to
his memory. Of all the men aspiring to the Presidency during the
campaign of 1860, Lincoln alone could have preserved the unity
and continuity of our nation.

NOTES

1. Holland, *Holland's Life of Abraham Lincoln*, 237. Some scholars doubt the validity of this quotation.

2. Goldwin Smith was a British historian and journalist, but Murr's source for this quotation is unclear.

3. In 1825, General Gilbert de Motier Marquis de Lafayette, the Frenchman who helped the United States win the Revolution, returned to America on a highly publicized victory tour. From Louisville, he crossed the Ohio River to Jeffersonville, Indiana, on 11 May 1825; we have no other written evidence he visited Lincoln's neighborhood farther downriver (Andrea Neal, "Indiana at 200 (25): Marquis de Lafayette a Big Hit in Jeffersonville," *Indiana Policy Review*, 19 May 2014, accessed 23 October 2021, https://inpolicy.org/2014/05/indiana-at-200-25-marquis-de-lafayette-a -big-hit-in-jeffersonville).

4. See Holland, *Holland's Life of Lincoln*, 33–34.

5. See William Wood interview with William Herndon, 15 September 1865, in *Herndon's Informants*, ed. Wilson and Davis, 123–124.

6. This story first appears in print nearly eighty-six years after the incident in a 1913 *Louisville Courier-Journal* article reporting everyone in the "immediate vicinity" was "thoroughly familiar with the above story, and most of the neighbors know the exact room in which the trial took place." Two other newspapers, the *Syracuse Herald* and the *Evansville Courier & Press*, ran articles about the event in 1916 and 1917, respectively. See *Syracuse Herald*, 5 March 1916, 23, and *Evansville Courier & Press*, 9 December 1917, 33. Murr offers one of the most detailed accounts of the incident, but a subsequent review of historical articles referred to Murr's work as "lore and local color, well-flavored with hero worship" ("News and Comments," *Mississippi Valley Historical Review* 4 no. 4 [March 1918]: 545).

7. Murr offers no date for the *Perry County Tribune* article. Since that newspaper ran from 1910 to 1918, it appeared in the same general era as the *Courier-Journal* piece.

8. Lincoln ran for the Illinois state legislature in 1832 and lost; in 1855, he also lost the US Senate race to Stephen Douglas. At that time, US senators were elected not by direct popular vote but by the state legislature.

9. Murr's source for this quotation is unclear.

SEVENTEEN

"NOW HE BELONGS TO THE AGES"

Broken by it I too may be; bow to it I never will. The probability
that we may fail in the struggle ought not deter us from the
support of a cause we believe to be just.[1]

AN ATTORNEY BY THE NAME of Breckenridge [*sic*] resided on a
farm not far from Boonville, the county seat of Warrick county.[2]
This town was about twenty miles from the Lincoln cabin, but the
ambitious youth frequently made pilgrimages to this gentleman's
home to borrow his law books, sometimes remaining throughout
the day and night reveling in the mysteries of the law.

Wesley Hall maintained that young Lincoln also obtained his
first opportunity of reading Shakespeare on these visits and alleged that he had heard Lincoln recite portions of some of the
great dramatist's writings.

Members of the Breckenridge family long pointed out a certain
stump in the yard of the home which they had pleased to call
"Lincoln's Stump" by reason of the fact that at certain times he
was in the habit of perching himself upon this while reading.[3]

Lincoln visited the circuit court sessions both at Rockport and
Boonville, and it was at this latter place that he heard John Breckenridge [*sic*], a member of the famous family by that name in Kentucky.

A murder had been committed, and the defendant had employed the brilliant criminal lawyer. The knowledge that "a big lawyer" from an adjoining state was to be connected with the case reached Gentryville, and a number of men journeyed to Boonville to witness this trial and particularly to hear Breckenridge. Lincoln was, of course, one of this group.[4]

Breckenridge had been greatly favored by nature, and possessing an enviable reputation as a great lawyer he had become more or less vain. Quite in keeping with the custom of the times among certain classes, his dress was particularly fastidious, and his raven black hair was made yet more glossy by a copious use of "bear's ile."

The courtroom was crowded, and Lincoln stood well to the rear throughout the whole of Breckenridge's argument. At the close of this address, a short recess was taken; and during this intermission a number of the members of the bar offered congratulations on the masterly effort of the great advocate. Young Lincoln, witnessing these expressions of appreciation and being profoundly moved by the address himself, straightway resolved to offer his congratulations also. Unmindful of the fact that he was not a member of the bar, that he was dressed in his accustomed blouse and buckskin breeches, with his coarse black hair disheveled and in wild confusion, he pressed forward, offered his hand to the great man and was on the point of expressing his pleasure at hearing the argument when Breckenridge deliberately turned his back upon the youth, not deigning to notice him.

Years went by, and when Lincoln was in the White House, this gentleman, then a resident of the State of Texas, was presented to the President, who readily recalled both the man and the circumstance at Boonville. Lincoln exclaimed as he grasped the proffered hand: "Oh, yes, I know Mr. Breckenridge. I heard you address a jury in a murder trial at Boonville, Indiana, when I was a boy. I remember that I thought at the time it was a great speech and that if I could make a speech like that I would be very happy."[5]

It will be observed throughout that Lincoln's ambition "to rise in the world" was overmastering. It was said of a great German that he was the "God-intoxicated man." So it might well have been said of young Lincoln that he was intoxicated with a consuming desire to acquire knowledge.

Very naturally one would be led to believe that had such a hungry mind been supplied with books in abundance his advancement would have been rapid. But there is even in this wasted pity and sympathy, judging by some certain things transpiring a little later.

When Lincoln entered upon the practice of his chosen profession—the law—and had more or less leisure for study, he read but few books. Associated as he was with Stuart, Logan and Herndon, and the latter possessing a rather pretentious library, yet Lincoln rarely read these books. It was his custom while out on the circuit to take on these six weeks' journeys school texts, and a great deal of his time was taken up with literature of a lighter character than one would have supposed true in his case. A great deal of his reading was desultory, and he appeared to revel in those publications of a humorous or witty character. Judging by his tastes in this regard, had he been privileged to have access to such publications as *Judge* or *Puck*, he would have been greatly delighted.

It may well be doubted therefore whether any other course than that which he did pursue would have proven any better than the self-denial which was imposed upon him and compelled his complete mastery of the few classics that fell into his possession.

Contrary to the statement of Colonel Lamon and others who alleged that Lincoln did not read the Bible during his youth, it is indisputably true that he read it again and again. Indeed, if there were no other evidence than his public addresses and State papers to verify this, that would be quite sufficient for the very spirit and sentiment of many of them are traceable to the King James version of the Bible.

But we do not need to rely upon this source altogether for information in the matter, since his associates assert that he was accustomed to read the Bible very much, and such a practice in a youth, which was not at all common then and for that matter is not so today, would well be calculated to occasion comment.

The London *Times*, in speaking of Mr. Lincoln's second Inaugural Address, likened it to the productions of one of the ancient prophets and spoke of its author as possessing such keen prophetic insight and power as to justify the appellation of a seer.

Lincoln read Bunyan's *Pilgrim's Progress* again and again, and so familiar did he become with it that he could repeat many pages from memory. He particularly admired Aesop's *Fables*, and so often did he read them that he could have said, as did Lord Macaulay of Milton's *Paradise Lost*, that if every copy had been destroyed, he could have reproduced it from memory. Dennis Hanks said that "young Lincoln would lie down on his face in front of the fire, with Aesop's *Fables* before him," and read to his stepmother and the "illiterate Denny," as Abraham called him. When some point in the story appealed to him as being funny or humorous, he would laugh and continue laughing so heartily that both Mrs. Lincoln and Dennis would be compelled to join him although Hanks asserted that "most of the time he did not know what he was laughing about, although Abe said he did."

The family Bible, *Pilgrim's Progress* and Aesop's *Fables* were the only books in the possession of the family on their arrival in Indiana. The mother of Lincoln was accustomed to read these books to both her daughter, Sarah, and little Abraham, and it is said that Aesop's *Fables* possessed a peculiar fascination and charm for him while yet a mere lad at his mother's knee.

The *Life of Washington*, which Lincoln obtained from Josiah Crawford in the manner heretofore detailed, was read many times, and if it may be charged that this volume took occasion to deify Washington and failed to meet with acceptance at a later period, it was perhaps the very best sort of publication for Lincoln and certainly better suited to him at that time than such a biography as that by Washington Irving. The *History of the United States*, as has been stated, was obtained from Jones, the storekeeper; as for *Robinson Crusoe*, and *The Life of Benjamin Franklin*, we do not know how or when they were obtained, but probably from the library of Crawford.

What marvelous transformation was thus wrought in the life of a single youth, and what potential possibilities are wrapped up in a single soul! Left, as Lincoln was, a motherless lad at the tender age of ten, living for one winter in a half-faced camp with no teachers and no schools worthy of the name, yet strange to say mastering some of the world's best classics, which fate, or chance (that Victor Hugo says is only another name for Providence) had thrown in his way, and with the Indiana wilderness as his *alma mater*, he matriculated at an early age. His curriculum was history, theology, mathematics, literature, and woodcraft. His major was history; his frat house, a half-faced camp, and his college campus, a clearing that he had made with his own hands. He left brush college during his freshman year to devote himself exclusively to athletics, in which he particularly excelled, especially with the ax and maul. After a time he took up the study of law, having found a copy of Blackstone's *Commentaries* in a barrel of plunder which, strange to say, he had purchased from one poorer than himself.[6] He later entered upon the practice of his chosen profession which he followed until he was called to be the chief executive of the nation.

Lincoln's life story surpasses anything in the pages of romance or fiction ever conceived or invented by literary genius! It is passing therefore strange that the boy Lincoln has for the most part been refused those things that in later years were so marked in his character and which were beyond question sufficiently prominent in his youth as to cause his early associates to remember him by them.

An effort has been made in the performance of this self-imposed task to show that substantially every characteristic trait so universally allowed in Mr. Lincoln as a man was also noted in him as a boy and youth.

It is believed that sufficient data have been offered to substantiate the claim made that before Mr. Lincoln reached the State of Illinois, and therefore while yet a resident of Indiana, he possessed that inimitable style in public address, his well-known sense of fairness, his strange and weird melancholy, his quaint humor and rare wit, his consuming ambition, certain weaknesses, his abiding faith in Providence, his superstitious beliefs, his Calvinistic fatalism which he usually hitched onto a sort of Arminian faith, his freedom from bad habits, his methods in original investigation, his peculiar style in controverted questions, his power with the pen, his honesty and truthfulness, and in fact every characteristic that has been noted in him again and again as a man.

It is also believed that there is sufficient data submitted to justify the claim that not only was the foundation of Mr. Lincoln's character laid in the Indiana wilderness, but also the beginning of all that afterwards made him great asserted itself during these early years.

It is of course not asserted that Mr. Lincoln's style, both in public address and in composition, was at all perfected while a mere youth, for he seems to have made steady progress in this to the very last. But it is claimed that there is sufficient evidence to warrant the belief that his peculiar style in debate, his platform mannerisms, his cool, calculating logic, and his irresistible wit and humor were quite as characteristic of his boyhood efforts as they were later noted and so generally commented upon.

It is recalled that he could set an entire neighborhood laughing and talking about his productions. He impressed himself upon Judge Pitcher and the Baptist minister so as to cause each of them to express keen appreciation of his ability with the pen when his manuscripts on national politics and temperance were submitted to them. It would seem to be only a reasonable supposition and not mere conjecture that the man who wrote the second

Inaugural Address, the Cooper Institute speech, and the Gettysburg oration in the day of his power and maturity would have manifested some intimation of this great ability and latent power earlier in life a thing which he seems to have done quite often, but more particularly in the compositions above referred to.

NOTES

1. This passage, allegedly by Lincoln in an 1839 speech, was quoted by Bishop Matthew Simpson at Lincoln's funeral at Oak Ridge Cemetery in Springfield in 1865. Miller, *Lincoln's Virtues*, 144.

2. Like many historians, Murr misspells the attorney's surname. John A. Brackenridge (1800–1862) was among the earliest and most frequent lawyers to appear at court in southwestern Indiana.

3. Years later, in 1908, when the Brackenridge homestead was demolished, Brackenridge children erected a marker saying, "Where Lincoln studied law as a boy." Unfortunately, the family left few specifics about the property on which the "Lincoln Stump" and marker sat (Sibley, *George W. Brackenridge*, 21).

4. Nearly all versions of this murder trial derive from the statement of S. T. Johnson to William Herndon or Herndon's later biography of Lincoln. Although some historians doubt Brackenridge's influence, these skeptics may have overlooked critical facts supporting it. Either way, Lincoln undoubtedly interacted with Brackenridge (Bartelt and Claybourn, *Abe's Youth*, 195–196).

5. Murr's quotation lacks precision, although it resembles that offered in S. T. Johnson's interview with Herndon, 14 September 1865, in *Herndon's Informants*, ed. Wilson and Davis, 115. Brackenridge (who died in December 1862) may never have traveled to Washington in 1862; his son George Brackenridge met with Lincoln in 1863 before George's appointment to a post in the US Treasury, and Lincoln may have actually met with the son rather than the father.

6. This detail refers to one theory, made famous in Carl Sandburg's biography, about how Lincoln first acquired the *Commentaries* in Illinois from a man driving west in a covered wagon. Yet, earlier in Indiana, Lincoln borrowed and read Blackstone's *Commentaries* from John Pitcher, another prominent Indiana attorney who influenced Lincoln (Hanby, "John Pitcher," 60–66).

EIGHTEEN

—⚭—

LEAVING THE INDIANA
WILDERNESS

The Almighty has his own purposes; . . . Fondly do we hope,
fervently do we pray, that this mighty scourge of war may
speedily pass away.[1]

THE LINCOLNS AND HANKSES LEFT Indiana in the month of
March 1830. John Hanks, after spending four years in the Indiana
home of the Lincolns, returned to Kentucky and then moved to
Illinois in the year 1828. He wrote such glowing accounts of the
new country that it caused Dennis Hanks to make a journey to
this region with a view of removing there.

The terrible blight of milk-sick which began its ravages in
Gentryville in the year 1818 continued for the next ten years.
Dennis Hanks lost all of his cattle in consequence of its ravages,
and he had been seized with the disease himself, but recovered.[2]
When Dennis Hanks decided to leave Indiana for Illinois, he
influenced his mother-in-law, Mrs. Lincoln, who did not wish to
be separated from her daughter. She seems to have been largely
responsible for the removal of the Lincolns also; accordingly
both families and that of Levi Hall, another son-in-law of Mrs.
Lincoln, began to make preparation for this change during the
winter of 1830.

The farm of Thomas Lincoln was disposed of to the elder Gentry if, indeed, it was not already his by reason of having lent the money for its purchase originally. At least, a quantity of corn and a drove of hogs were disposed of to Mr. Gentry, and such other changes were wrought as proved necessary to make this journey to begin life anew.[3] Thomas Lincoln had a chuck wagon, the woodwork being his own construction, but since it was "ironed off," it was a subject of considerable comment, for such vehicles were exceedingly rare.[4] It was necessary to have suitable teams of oxen, and accordingly there began more or less "swapping and dickering."[5] In the main this was done by Dennis Hanks, John Johnston and Abraham Lincoln. Allen Brooner stated that two of these oxen were obtained from him, Abraham Lincoln and John Johnston making this trade. There was considerable haggling over the trade on the part of Johnston, Lincoln not entering into the matter save in an incidental way. Brooner long afterward, in speaking of this circumstance, said: "If anybody had asked me that day to pick out a President, I'd a quickly made choice of Johnson."

The elder Hall sold the other yoke of cattle to Thomas Lincoln, but these were purchased by proxy, he having sent his son Abraham and Dennis Hanks to do the trading. Wesley Hall delivered the team to Hanks and young Lincoln.

Hall was present on the occasion of the beginning of the journey to Illinois. However, the Lincolns only journeyed that afternoon as far as Gentry's in Gentryville and remained overnight with that gentleman. During the night young Lincoln made a judicious selection of notions such as needles, pins, thread, knives, forks and spoons, his purchase amounting to just 30 dollars. With this "peddler's outfit" he proposed realizing a profit by disposing of it along the way at the farmhouses. This he seems to have succeeded in doing beyond his expectations, for "he wrote back after his arrival in Illinois stating that he doubled his money."

The people of Gentryville were loath to see the Lincolns leave, and it is said that on the morning of their final departure quite a crowd collected to bid them farewell. Many of them accompanied the Lincolns some distance on their journey, among them being the elder Gentry. One man in telling of seeing them begin their journey stated that "Abe drove the oxen, having a rope attached to the horn of a lead ox, and with a hickory 'gad' in his free hand."

None of the party of 13 ever returned to the scenes of their 14 years' residence in Indiana save Abraham; as has been stated, he spent three days in and about Gentryville during the political campaign of 1844 making three speeches in that county. He was the guest of the Gentrys most of the time. However, after making the speech at Carter's schoolhouse, he accepted the urgent invitation of "Blue Nose" Crawford to accompany him home. He was much the same Lincoln then that his old friends had known 14 years before. He quite readily recognized all of his old neighbors, calling them by their given names, and made inquiry as to certain things in which he had been especially interested prior to his leaving there. He expressed a desire on reaching the Crawford home to see the old whip-saw-pit where he had stood as the "under man" on many an occasion whip-sawing lumber.[6]

Sometime after Lincoln had been in the White House, 17 years having elapsed since seeing his boyhood home and meeting with his old friends, a gentleman from Gentryville visited him in Washington, his purpose in making the journey being merely to gratify his curiosity and pleasure in beholding the greatness of his old boyhood friend. On his arrival at the White House he found quite a number of people in waiting. He sent in his name, and supposed, of course, that the rule here would be something similar to what he and the then present occupant of the White House had been accustomed to in their boyhood in going to Gorden's Mill— first come, first served. But he was greatly surprised a few moments after making his presence known to hear his name called and, on entering the private office of the President, was warmly greeted with the old-time cordiality. They had conversed but a short while when Lincoln said to him, "Now, Bill, there's a whole lot of dignitaries out there (pointing) that are waiting to see me about something or other, and I'll tell you what I want you to do. This is your first visit to Washington, and I reckon you'll want to look around at the sights, so you go and do that and then come back here about supper time. After we've had something to eat, we'll go off to ourselves, and i-jings we'll have a good time talking over old times." This appealed to his old friend; and accordingly he returned from viewing the sights of the city toward night-fall and found Lincoln waiting for him. After they had dined, Lincoln said, "Now come with me" and led him to a room on the second floor. After entering, the President turned the key, pulled off his coat, and seated himself on the small of his back with his feet resting upon the table; he began asking numerous questions concerning his old neighbors. The narrator, in telling this, said, "Abe asked about everybody from the mouth of Anderson Creek to Boonville. He'd say: 'Bill, who did Sis So-and-so marry? Where does This One live? Who lives on Such-and-such farm?' By and by, closing his eyes and drawing a long breath, he said, 'Bill, how did the Gentry boys vote in the last election?' I hesitated to tell him, for I know'd ever one of 'em voted for Douglas and were agin him. But finally I out with it, and Abe opened his eyes slow like, and looking straight at me for a little bit he sorter sighed."

The statement made by some of the biographers that Allen Gentry voted for his old flat-boat partner, in spite of the fact that he was a Democrat, is incorrect. The writer, in an interview with James Gentry [Jr.], referred to this Gentryville neighbor's visit to Lincoln, and Mr. Gentry exclaimed with a laugh,

> Yes, Bill told me all about it when he got back from seeing Abe, and he said Abe 'peared to ask about everybody from Anderson clean down to Boonville, but he left us boys to the last. Never even mentioned our names till he asked how we all voted, and when Bill told him we all went agin him, by gum, it mighty nigh broke old Abe's heart. Course, fellows like us goin' agin him would hurt, I reckon, but them was purty stormy times, and we

know'd it would take a smart man to run things, and we'd all grow'd up with Abe; and while we liked him, and we know'd that Abe could hold his own in a tussle, we didn't think he was big enough to wrastle with such questions that was up then. Besides, by gum, we was all Democrats and believed Judge Douglas could take matters in hand.

When it was suggested that Lincoln managed to keep house pretty well after all, Gentry laughed heartily and said,

> O, Abe always tracked the Constitution, and as long as he done that he had 'em. Then he followed Henry Clay in lots of things such as his African Colonization scheme and gradual emancipation and the like, and you know old Henry was purty tolerable hard to head off. So Abe just stood there between all of them fellers and made 'em take their medicine. Abe come out all right in the end, but if he hadn't a stood by the Constitution, and if he'd got off on something else like a whole lot of the rest of 'em did, he'd a never a made it. It was stickin' to the Constitution that done it.

When Wesley Hall was asked as to whether he at any time during his youth was inclined to the belief that Lincoln would some day become famous, he straightway replied, "Abe would have been one of the last ones of our crowd that I'd a ever dreamed about becoming President. I would have picked out one or two of the boys that was a heap more likely than him. Not but what Abe was smart and all that, but he was so tall, lean, lank, and ugly, and went lumbering around so and was always a jokin' and cuttin' up, and I couldn't see anything in him then that looked like my notion of what a President ort to be."

When it was suggested to Hall, by way of provoking further comment, that Lincoln certainly was one of our great men, he exclaimed,

> Yes, he is and the greatest too, but what made him so great? I'll tell you, it wasn't because he was educated, for he had no chance down here them days, but Abe just acted up there at Washington like he would anywheres else, and whenever anything comes up he just done what wuz right, that's all. It was nothing but Abe's

honesty that made him great, and when you come to think about it, that oughn't to be so strange. That's what all of us boys was taught them days, and I think I've been honest myself all of my life, just as honest as Abe ever was fer that matter.

When it was further suggested that Lincoln managed things pretty well and overcame great obstacles, Hall observed, "Yes, that's so, but after all when all is said and done, it always comes back to what I say. Abe always just done what was right about everything, that's all. If somebody else'd been in his place that'd a been as honest as he was and a allus done about what's right, everything'd a come out all right."

The simplicity of Lincoln's life, his democratic spirit, his approachableness, living the life of a commoner while the executive head of the nation, are quite in keeping with his oft expressed partiality for and faith in the common people. He was the very embodiment of the homelier virtues of truth, sincerity, and honesty. The temptations ordinarily would have been strong upon one like Lincoln in the heyday of his power either to attempt to conceal his humble beginnings, his poverty, and lack of schooling, or on the other hand, to have referred boastfully to them. Not the least mark of his greatness is the fact that he did neither. What modesty forbade in this, as in other things, his honesty and good sense approved, so that the democracy of manhood in him shines like a beacon light, dimming the glare of burnished and furbished greatness in the many so-called great men.

NOTES

1. This quotation is found in Lincoln's second inaugural address. Lincoln derives the text from Matt. 18:7: "Woe unto the world because of offences! for it must needs be that offences come; but woe to that man by whom the offence cometh!"

2. Although Dennis Hanks undoubtedly lost cattle to the illness, no reliable records indicate that he lost all of them. In his 7 March 1866 letter

to Herndon, Hanks indicates he lost "4 Good Milch Cows . . . in one week
and Leve young Calfs." Wilson and Davis, *Herndon's Informants*, 226. That
may have been the extent of Hanks's losses. Herndon does not record
Hanks getting sick himself.

3. Murr confuses some of the land exchanges here. For a more accurate
account, see Warren, *Lincoln's Youth*, 205.

4. *Ironing off* the wagon means binding the edges with iron, often securing the axles and other parts with iron to make them sturdier.

5. *Swapping and dickering* is a slang term meaning "bartering."

6. For a full account of Lincoln's return trip in 1844, see Bartelt, "Aiding
Mr. Clay," 29–39.

NINETEEN

—w—

DEATH AND BURIAL OF
NANCY HANKS LINCOLN

All that I am or ever hope to be I owe to my angel of a mother.[1]
I feel how weak and fruitless must be any words of mine that would
attempt to beguile you from a grief of a loss so overwhelming.[2]

IN THE YEAR 1818 ABRAHAM Lincoln experienced a great misfortune in the death of his mother. The many exacting duties
incident to pioneer life doubtless constituted a factor in producing that strange melancholy that ever [after] possessed him, but
to be bereft of his mother at the age of ten was perhaps in the
main responsible for this.[3] At least it justifies the belief that such
a sad misfortune at this period of his life, together with some of
the attending circumstances, readily took advantage of a latent
predisposition so characteristic of his mother.

Comparatively little is known concerning Nancy Hanks, and
there is small wonder, since nothing eventful happened in her life
beyond those things common to the pioneer. Allusion has already
been made to the early belief of her neighbors and her more immediate relatives as to her obscure origin. She certainly did not
attempt to correct this belief and doubtless was possessed with
the same idea as were others. That there has been a more or less
labored effort on the part of certain biographers of Mr. Lincoln to

account for his exceptional ability by professing a marked partiality for his maternal ancestry is known to all.

Dennis Hanks, as reported by Elinor Adkinson in *The Boy Lincoln*, said,

> We wus all pore them days, but the Lincolns was poorer than anybody. Choppin' trees an' grubbin' roots an' trappin' didn't leave Tom no time. It wus all he could do to git his family enough to eat an' to kiver 'em. Nancy was terribly ashamed of the way they lived, but she knowed Tom wus doin' his best an' she wusn't the pesterin' kind. She wus purty as a pictur an' smart as you'd find 'em anywhere. She could read and write. The Hankses wus some smarter 'n the Lincolns. Tom thought a heap of Nancy, an' he wus as good to her as he knowd how. He didn't drink or swear or play cards or fight; an' them wus drinkin,' cussin', quarrelsome days. Tom wus popyler an' he could lick a bully if he had to. He just couldn't get ahead some how.

Mr. Herndon, the friend and law partner of Mr. Lincoln, and later his biographer, in speaking of Lincoln's mother, said,

> At the time of her marriage to Thomas Lincoln, Nancy was in her twenty-third year. She was above the ordinary height in stature, weighed about one hundred and thirty pounds; was slenderly built and had much the appearance of one inclined to consumption. Her skin was dark; her hair dark brown, eyes grey and small; forehead prominent, face sharp and angular with an expression of melancholy which fixed itself in the memory of anyone who ever saw or knew her. Though her life was seemingly clouded by a spirit of sadness, she was in disposition amiable and generally cheerful. Mr. Lincoln said to me in 1851, on receiving the news of his father's death, that whatever might be said of his parents and however unpromising the early surroundings of his mother may have been, she was highly intellectual by nature and had a strong memory, acute judgment, and was cool and heroic. From a mental standpoint she no doubt rose above her surroundings, and had she lived, the stimulus of her nature would have accelerated her son's success. She would have been a much more ambitious prompter than his father ever was.[4]

That Mr. Lincoln possessed the melancholy self-control, cool and calculating judgment and natural goodness of his mother is apparent, and even marks of facial resemblance are conceded. Some certain and important traits of character are also traceable to the father, and taking it all in all these latter qualities are quite as important as were the others. That faculty and habit of storytelling so natural to the President, his peculiar and quaint method of relating them and their apparently inexhaustible supply were characteristic of not only his father, but also his uncles, Mordecai and Josiah, as well as of many of his Lincoln cousins.

Without suggesting any lack in the family of his mother of that greatest of all traits which he possessed—that of honesty—and for which he is so justly famed, it must be said in all fairness that whatever by nature, example, and precept he received from the mother that caused a nation to call her son "Honest Abe," certainly honesty was a dominant trait of the father and the one characteristic that stands out so prominently in the life of practically every Lincoln. Dennis Hanks confessed that Lincoln was indebted to his father for his uncompromising honesty rather than to the Hankses.

Judging by the data in hand, therefore, it may be said that the Lincolns were the equal of the Hankses in social standing and ancestry; and in fact, there is discerned a favorable comparison in substantially all other things ordinarily considered in such matters.

It should particularly be said that the meagerness of knowledge concerning Nancy Hanks, and more especially her early death, furnished a large field for conjecture and the freest possible play of the imagination. Since Thomas Lincoln lived until the year 1851, having ever remained a simpleminded, illiterate pioneer, never at any time distinguishing himself, it became the fashion to speak lightly and even disparagingly of him as compared to his wife, Nancy Hanks who, dying while quite young, became a subject for adulation and eulogy. Whatever was deemed wanting in the father and husband was readily supposed to have been possessed by the mother and wife.

That Nancy Hanks was somewhat exceptional and in every way worthy of such an illustrious son appears to be abundantly evident in spite of the meagerness of data at hand. That she must have wielded a strong influence upon him is equally true, and perhaps even greater than we can possibly know. Yet, in all fairness it must be said that Mr. Lincoln seldom mentioned his mother in later life, but again and again paid great tribute to his stepmother and it was the stepmother, not Nancy Hanks, of whom he spoke when he used these oft-quoted lines (usually misquoted): "All that I am and ever hope to be I owe to my angel of a mother."[5]

Any attempt to account for the remarkable career of Abraham Lincoln must give a large place to the plans and purposes of the Almighty. The Jewish nation spent four centuries in a strange land before it produced its great prophet, military leader, and law-giver, Moses. We do not ordinarily attempt to account for the career of Moses by emphasizing his lineage and learning so much as we do the fact that God was with him from the time he was placed in the little pitch basket among the bulrushes of the Nile until the day when he climbed the mount to die.

Bishop Charles Fowler, in his lecture on Abraham Lincoln, related the following incident in the life of the President which happened when Lincoln was 28 years of age. A short distance from Springfield, Illinois, an old-fashioned camp-meeting was in progress in a grove. A party of seven men, composed of physicians, lawyers, and ministers, had decided to attend these services one night.

On this particular occasion Lincoln was in a hilarious mood, joking with the lawyers, preachers, and doctors in succession, and even thrusting humorous remarks upon the horses drawing the vehicle in which they were riding. He kept everyone laughing by his stories and yarns, until the grove was reached.

That evening a pioneer minister preached a sermon of unusual power, occasioning considerable religious excitement. While the discourse throughout was stirring and thoughtful, the peroration was particularly so. In this he referred to Moses leading the children of Israel out of Egyptian bondage and laid stress upon the fact that God had called him for such a purpose in the fullness of time. Then, as was frequently the case in pulpits of that day, he pronounced a curse upon African slavery in America, prophesying that "the Almighty would raise up a leader to smite this curse." As he closed his remarks he lifted his hands beseechingly, and in a burst of prophetic fervor he exclaimed, "Who knows but that the man destined to liberate the slaves in our land is here tonight?"

On the return journey of the group, for whom Lincoln had furnished so much amusement and fun, he was strangely silent, so much so as to speak only occasionally when addressed by some member of the party. This silence was noted by all and elicited more or less comment on the following day. Sometime during the day after the journey taken, one member of the camp-meeting visitors had occasion to call on Lincoln and found him still gloomy and depressed. Thinking to rally him by some reference to the occurrences of the evening before, he proceeded to do so, and thereupon Lincoln remarked as follows: "You remember, of course, what the preacher said about slavery and in his peroration that 'God would raise up a man to smite slavery,' and closed by saying: 'Who knows but that he is here tonight?' Well, you and others may think me foolish, but I had the conviction then and still have it that I am that man."[6]

At the time of the death of Lincoln's mother there was mourning in practically every home of the entire neighborhood, for that dread disease peculiar to the pioneer days, known as milk-sick, had appeared in epidemic form and attacked beasts as well as men. Thomas and Betsy Sparrow, who had in part reared Nancy Hanks, and who had followed the Lincolns to Indiana, living in the abandoned, half-faced camp, were both stricken with this scourge and died about the same time Mrs. Lincoln did. In fact, of the 25 families in this settlement, many of whom were former Kentucky neighbors of the Lincolns, more than half were claimed by this strange malady.

Medical assistance was not to be had nearer than 30 miles; and even had there been sufficient attention, it is altogether doubtful whether the ravages of this destroyer of the pioneers could have been arrested.

One may form some idea of the extent to which the pioneers were governed by stern necessity when it is recalled that Thomas Lincoln, the husband, on the death of his wife was forced to perform a part of the offices of an undertaker. There being no one save himself in that community sufficiently skilled with tools to construct a coffin, he did this, and at the same time made coffins in which to bury Thomas and Betsy Sparrow. He was not a stranger to this kind of work since he was in the habit of doing it for the entire community. The lumber with which the coffin for Nancy Hanks Lincoln was made was whipsawed out of a log unused in the building of the wilderness cabin. Dennis Hanks and Thomas Lincoln sawed the planks, and while they were thus engaged, Abraham whittled out the wooden pins which the elder Lincoln used to fasten the planks together, there being no nails in this part of the world at that time.

The writer knew two persons who were present at the funeral of Nancy Hanks Lincoln. Her burial, which took place a few hundred yards to the south of the cabin home, was denied even the usual committal services, there being no officiating minister present. Indeed, at this time there was no church or minister nearer than thirty miles.

The writer on one occasion had pointed out to him the spot near the foot of the grave where little Abraham stood weeping while the rude casket was being lowered. The Reverend Allen Brooner, then a mere lad, was present on this occasion. He lost his own mother a few days after the burial of Mrs. Lincoln, and she was buried by the side of Lincoln's mother; consequently the circumstances became indelibly fixed in his memory. No stone marked these graves for years; and when it was proposed to erect a small monument to the memory of Nancy Hanks Lincoln, there was some difference of opinion as to which of the two graves was hers, but the statement of Brooner was final.

Although Abraham was but ten years of age at this time, yet impressed with the fact that his mother's memory was entitled to the usual funeral services that he had been accustomed to witness, he wrote a letter requesting the services of Parson Elkins, an itinerant Baptist minister who resided in Kentucky, and who had visited the home of the Lincolns in that State, frequently conducting services there and doubtless officiated at the burial of his baby brother. At any rate, Elkins had impressed himself upon the mind and heart of the lad so that he did not hesitate to presume upon his good offices by asking that he travel a hundred miles through this wilderness.

The boy's confidence in thus presuming upon the willingness of the pioneer preacher to come to him in his need was not misplaced, for although he made this journey and preached the funeral discourse at the graveside without remuneration, yet, like Mary in breaking the alabaster box of precious ointment, Parson Elkins's offices on this occasion have enshrined his memory in the hearts of Christendom and his name by this one deed alone has been redeemed from that oblivion to which it would have otherwise been consigned.

One may stand at the graveside of the mother of Lincoln to-day, look through the woods to the north, and see the little knoll on which then stood the cabin where now looms up with comparatively large dimensions a high school building immediately in front of the cabin site—an institution that would have been regarded by Lincoln in his youth as Heaven-sent.

Marked changes have been wrought since that mournful pioneer funeral procession took its sad way down the slope and through the wood to the elevated spot where his mother sleeps.

In making this little journey now, one crosses the steam-railroad track, passes beneath the telephone and telegraph wires, and walks by the mouth of a coal mine—all telling of another civilization and another age, for they all came after Lincoln's removal to Illinois.

It is asserted, and not without sufficient grounds, that the place where the future President spent his youth and reached his majority, and where he formed and matured his character, possessing as he did, while yet a youth, substantially all of those eminent traits that we are accustomed to note in him as a man, that place where his mother now sleeps and where his only sister lies buried, is of the greatest possible interest; and in view of such world-wide admiration of Lincoln, it is deserving of suitable recognition by our general government.

The State of Indiana some years since, aided by individuals, erected a modest monument to the memory of Nancy Hanks Lincoln, the mother of the President, and made purchase of the grounds adjoining her burial place which now constitute what is known as Lincoln Park.

As commendable as was this belated tribute, unfortunately the site of the cabin home of Lincoln was not included in this purchase, and this place yet remains in the hands of private individuals. Should there come a time (and it will) when this spot will have been appropriately honored beyond that hitherto attempted, and some President of the United States in official capacity will journey thither and deliver an address, if perchance in the course of his remarks he should give utterance to some such sentiment as the following, he would only be speaking true to history:

> Here on this spot in the year 1816, Thomas Lincoln erected a log cabin in which was reared his son, Abraham, our first typical American, who in temperamental make up, in certain marked characteristics, in the simplicity of his life and character, was the embodiment of those traits of honesty and truthfulness which pre-eminently characterized the pioneer Hoosier citizen. Three States of our Union had to do in shaping his destiny and

fashioning his great career. Kentucky gave him birth; in the day
of his power Illinois offered him to the country in the hour of
the Nation's crisis; but it was here in Indiana that these enduring
traits of character found their setting, without which he would
have failed in his gigantic task. And possessing them as he did,
they later fashioned him into a mighty leader destined under God
to give this nation a new birth of freedom, that "the government
of the people for the people and by the people might not perish
from the earth."[7]

In a year after the death of Mrs. Lincoln, Thomas Lincoln
made a visit to his old home in Kentucky, leaving Dennis Hanks,
Abraham, and his sister, Sarah, in the wilderness. The motive in
making this visit became apparent to those remaining behind
when on his return he brought with him a bride and her three
children, Matilda, Sarah, and John D. Johnson, children by a
former marriage. The second Mrs. Lincoln, who was destined
to wield a remarkable influence over the future President, was
a woman somewhat above the average pioneer. Her coming to
this destitute home was timely since Abraham had now reached
that age when he stood in need of just such encouragement and
sympathy as she was eminently capable of giving and which she
freely bestowed upon him.

In an interview with Mr. Herndon she said, in speaking of this
period and of Abraham in particular: "I induced my husband to
permit Abe to read and study at home as well as at school. At first
he was not easily reconciled to it, but finally he seemed willing
to encourage him to a certain extent. Abe was a dutiful son to
me always. We took particular care when he was reading not to
disturb him, and we let him read on and on until he quit of his
own accord."[8]

Notwithstanding the fact that Mrs. Lincoln had been left a
widow and at the time of her marriage to Thomas Lincoln was
living "on an alley of the town in a log cabin," she was highly
regarded by her neighbors and possessed a pride and bearing

quite beyond that which her condition would ordinarily appear to warrant. The proud spirit that characterized her then was never broken by any of the vicissitudes of her later years. She was quite superior in many ways to her husband. Her gifts and graces were so pronounced as to call forth in later years splendid tributes of praise from both her own children and her stepson. The changes wrought in the wilderness-cabin home soon after her coming occasioned neighborhood comment and made such an impression upon Dennis Hanks, an inmate of the home and later her son-in-law, as to cause that gentleman to pay her grateful praise.

Aside from the refinement and culture which she possessed, tending to inspire her household to emulate her, she caused her husband to make certain needful changes in the cabin by hanging a door, laying a floor, and cutting a window. She brought with her certain household effects such as beds, bedding, bureau, many cooking utensils, knives and forks—in all a four-horse wagon load, so that there is small wonder the cheerless cabin took on new life and caused Abraham in later life, when recalling these scenes, to say, "She made me feel like I was human."

It is asserted that at this time young Abraham was a good boy, affectionate, loving his parents well, and obedient to their every wish. Although anything but impudent or rude, he was sometimes uncomfortably inquisitive when strangers would ride along or pass by his father's fence; and he always, either through boyish pride or through teasing his father, would be sure to ask the first question. For this his father would sometimes knock him over; but when thus punished he never "bellowed, but would drop a kind of silent unwelcome tear as evidence of his sensitiveness or other feelings."

So inquisitive and eager for news was he that on one occasion when a stranger rode up to the Lincoln home to make inquiries as to the road, Abraham straightway asked, "What's the news, stranger?" Before any reply could be made, the father, who was attempting to give proper directions of the way, turned and rebuked his son for his interruption. In a moment or two young Abraham again asked, "Stranger, what's the news where you come from?" This time the indignant father, desiring to silence the inquisitive son, quickly swung his arm, struck the boy full in the mouth with the back of the hand, knocking him down. Young Lincoln, on regaining his feet and perching himself at a safe distance on the fence, as the stranger was drawing rein preparatory to ride on his way, once more eagerly asked: "I say, stranger, what is the news?"

During his Indiana residence up to the time of his mother's death, Abraham Lincoln had not been privileged to attend school. Soon after the coming of his stepmother to the home he was sent to school, his first teacher being Mr. Dorsey who kept school not far from the Little Pigeon church. In all he attended three different sessions or terms during his Indiana residence, one at ten years of age, another at 14 and a very brief term during his 17th year. The entire time thus spent in the schoolroom was less than one year during his life, and he was indebted to his stepmother for the privilege of attending school at all after reaching an age when such an opportunity might reasonably promise profit. Such privilege was accompanied by a keen appreciation and gratitude that enabled him richly to repay her in later years for her kindness and partiality. The debt that mankind owes this elect lady can never now be paid save in grateful remembrance of her timely foresight and thankfulness for wisdom and direction perhaps not altogether of Earth. From the first Lincoln and his stepmother became great friends. In her old age she expressed a decided partiality for him, even indicating a love beyond that for her own son.

Lincoln's great stature and lumbering gait were a subject of neighborhood comment, and Mrs. Lincoln and his father often joked with him concerning them also. The elder Lincoln was in the habit of remarking that "Abe looked like he had been chopped out with an ax and needed the jack plane to smooth him down." Mrs. Lincoln said to him on one occasion when she saw him bump his head as he came through the cabin door, "Abe, I don't care much about the mud you carry in on the floor, for that can be scrubbed, but you must be careful with my whitewashed ceiling and not damage it." The next day, young Lincoln hunted up a crowd of youngsters and, after causing them to wade through a pond of muddy water, marched them to the Lincoln cabin, picked them up one by one, and made them walk across the ceiling with their muddy feet. When Mrs. Lincoln came home and noted the condition of the ceiling, she laughed right heartily. Abraham then walked a long distance after lime, prepared whitewash, and once more made the cabin ceiling immaculate.

NOTES

1. Herndon to Ward Hill Lamon, 6 March 1870, Lamon Papers, Huntington Library, San Marino, CA.

2. Basler et al., *Collected Works of Abraham Lincoln*, 8:116–17.

3. Abraham Lincoln was born on 12 February 1809, and Nancy Hanks Lincoln died on 5 October 1818: Abraham was nine years old when his mother died.

4. Herndon and Weik, *Herndon's Lincoln*, 13–14.

5. Herndon and Weik, *Herndon's Lincoln*, 3. Many scholars believe Lincoln was thinking of admirable genetic traits he believed came from Nancy and her "well-bred" father, including his ambition and intelligence (qualities not necessarily prevalent in the Hanks family). Other Lincoln historians assert Lincoln referred to his stepmother, Sarah.

6. This instance appears to be the only documented evidence of this quotation, calling into question its validity.

7. In 1927, the Indiana Lincoln Union formed to support a memorial recognizing Lincoln's years in Indiana. In 1932, the state established Lincoln State Park near his boyhood home to protect the area and preserve the homestead site. In 1962, the Indiana legislature donated substantial acreage to create Lincoln Boyhood National Memorial. That same year, the National Park Service began administering the site.

8. Herndon and Weik, *Herndon's Lincoln*, 33.

PART III

ALBERT BEVERIDGE
CORRESPONDENCE

ALBERT J. BEVERIDGE (1862–1927), A US senator from Indiana, achieved an acclaimed career outside elected office by writing popular history. He published a four-volume *Life of John Marshall* (1916–1919), which won a Pulitzer Prize in 1920, and then undertook a similar four-volume biography of Abraham Lincoln. Unfortunately, Beveridge died in 1927 with only two volumes completed, both published posthumously in 1928 as *Abraham Lincoln, 1809–1858*. Murr served as an important consultant to Beveridge on those two volumes, frequently offering ideas and suggesting changes that Beveridge often adopted. Some of their more substantive correspondence, housed in the Library of Congress (MSS12591), appears here in part 3.

Beveridge to Murr
16 August 1924
Beverly Farms, Massachusetts

Rev. J. Edward Murr
Princeton, Indiana

Dear Dr. Murr:

I have read with keenest interest your valuable articles in the *Indiana Magazine of History* on "Lincoln in Indiana" and am so much impressed by your statements of facts, which constitute an original source, that I am making several footnote citations from them in my *Life of Lincoln* on which I am now engaged. Of course, in each citation I give you credit by name.

I am wondering if you will do me the favor of reading over the first rough draft of my chapter on Lincoln's life in Indiana. I would take it as a favor if you would.

I am leaving today on a very short vacation, for I have been working rather hard this summer; and on my return I hope to have a letter from you telling me that you will be willing to look over my MSS.

Let me congratulate you, dear Dr. Murr, on your admirable articles. When I return to Indiana, I am going to give myself the happiness of coming down to see you, if you can spare me a little time.

With every good wish,

Faithfully,
Sen. Albert J. Beveridge

Murr to Beveridge
29 August 1924
Princeton, Indiana

Senator Albert J. Beveridge
Beverly Farms, Mass.

My dear Senator:
I have your letter in which you speak of your forthcoming treatment of Lincoln, of which I had knowledge, and also the request
that I make some examination of certain portions of the MSS. I
thank you for your words of partiality evidenced in the reference
to my own attempt on the Life and Character of that—to me—
greatest of Americans. My own contribution doubtless possesses
some historical value, but of course it does not belong to the pretentious treatments. Mr. Moores of Indianapolis—whom of course
you know so much better than myself—is on record as saying that,
in his judgment, I know Lincoln better than anyone in our State.[1]
Doctor Esarey of Bloomington, I believe, has said substantially the
same thing.[2] Of course I greatly appreciate such an utterance by
these men, but I need not say to you that I make no such exalted
claim as that at all. But I do claim to know some things at least and if
I can be of some little service to you in this matter in any way, I shall
count it a privilege to do so. I shall be at our Annual Conference in
Indianapolis from Sep., 9 to 15; and should it be changed, as might
be true, I would in that case be quite busy for a few days beyond the
15th.[3] In any case I shall be pleased to do my best in the matter.

                                                 With best wishes,
Princeton, Aug., 29/24   I remain yours cordially,
                                                 J. Edward Murr

Beveridge to Murr
21 October 1924
Beverly Farms, Massachusetts

Dr. J. Edward Murr
Princeton, Indiana

Dear Edward:

Under separate cover I am sending you the Indiana chapter which you so kindly agreed to read. It is, of course, very rough, imperfect and unfinished. But, perhaps, you can get the picture I am trying to draw.

Please do not hesitate to correct any errors or make any suggestions that may occur to you.

Oh, by the way, it just occurs to me that in order to get the swing of the thing, you may possibly want to see the Kentucky and Illinois–New Salem chapter—so I am sending them too.

I have purposely over-annotated for two reasons: first, because this is the controverted period which the remaining Mid-Victorians have tried to Tarbellize and, second, because I want, at the very beginning, to inspire the reader with confidence in the more important chapters that follow.[4]

Also, I have tried to state a multitude of facts so as to reveal the development of Lincoln's mind and character.

With every good wish, always,

Faithfully,

P.S. Of course, since this is a very rough draft and subject to change, please regard everything said in it as confidential.

Dictated but not signed by Senator Beveridge.

Murr to Beveridge
21 November 1924
New Albany, Indiana

My dear Senator:

I have gone over all three chapters of your Lincoln. I have ventured to make a number of annotations and herewith offer some observations upon certain matters.

First, permit [me] to make a general observation or two. Herndon had the best chance of all the old biographers and, to a very great extent, missed his opportunity. He was at Gentryville five days in all. He made Joseph Gentry's home his headquarters. This was a very wise choice as Jo Gentry and Lincoln were just exactly of the same age—same year. Jim (James) was some two years younger. Allen, with whom Lincoln made the celebrated flatboat trip down the Mississippi, was two years older than Lincoln. Allen Gentry was lost in the Mississippi while yet a young man aged 25. Mrs. Romine was living—another Gentry—at the time I made my Lincoln inquiry.

In all, I knew eleven of his boyhood and girlhood associates. Now I very well know that they were of necessity quite along in years, but I must say that none, save perhaps "Red" Grigsby, was in his dotage. Certainly the Gentry Brothers were clear as a bell mentally. And Wesley Hall was more than an ordinary citizen. He was looked up to by people generally—a well-to-do man. His character was of the best, and his life was above reproach in every way.

I made my investigation at the same time or about the same time that Ida Tarbell made hers. She remained overnight in Spencer County just one and only one night! She interviewed just *one* person who knew Lincoln while a resident of Spencer County—James Gentry. Mr. Gentry informed me with some considerable heat seasoned with a blanky blank or two, that he "sent that Tarbell woman away as mad as a hornet."[5] Of course, the whole of the Tarbell *Life of Abraham Lincoln*, so far as his adolescent period is concerned, was borrowed from the older writers. I believe that she was misled by the Hanks group on the Kentucky Trail also. You of course, know that the Hanks crowd have (see Mrs. Hitchcock's treatment of Lincoln) tried to prove that all of Lincoln's greatness came from Hanks blood.

Nicolay and Hay missed their opportunity since they, in point of fact, write a history of the Civil War and miss the real objective of an opportunity to give somewhat of an interpretation of Lincoln. John Hay was in Spencer County three days.[6] Lamon of course failed us considering his opportunity and was not at all a historian in the first place.[7] What little contribution I have ventured to make is somewhat negligible, save that I have gone on the theory that some of my gleanings might serve someone in sending forth the *real* Lincoln.

Perhaps I am not capable of passing critically upon the treatment as a whole but I venture to make some references to certain statements made as well as call attention to some matters that appeal to me which are not especially stressed by you.

Page 3 you say: "Thos Lincoln arrived at Posey's mid-Autumn." Are you sure of that? As I was told the Lincoln's Larder was helped somewhat by small patches of corn, beans, etc., I was informed that they came late Summer and came in time to plant some grain. Perhaps Thos Lincoln did clear up small patches with fire and Ax on those high places and did in fact plant some grain and when they came over. Later they found that they had a little help in this matter.

Page 3 you say, "Lincoln reached the vicinity of a scattered cluster of other dwellings etc." I was informed that he had an objective when he left Posey's down on the River. There was a man by the name of Carter out in the Brush whom Lincoln knew and he made him, hence this location. You, of course, know that this became Carter Township. Maybe after all there was some sort of orderly procedure on the part of Thomas Lincoln in this Indiana Hunt for a Home.

Page 4 you give it as your judgment that perhaps the Wagon was a sled etc. and drawn by oxen. You may be quite correct as oxen, of course, could get through the undergrowth much better than horses. But I wonder where he would get oxen, and did he not have at least two horses with him?

Milk Sickness. Dr. A. H. Rhodes, formerly a physician located at Milltown, Crawford County, but now and for many years has been at Princeton, Indiana, informed me that some 35 years ago, he had a pronounced case of this pioneer disease. It was real interesting to me to hear him give his experience and the treatment.

Death of Nancy Hanks. You mention the death of Mrs. Brooner. A son was yet living when I made my investigation. He stated that his mother died within a day or two of Nancy Hanks. That they were buried side by side. Certain it is that when Clem Studebaker decided to place the Nancy Hanks Monument, no one could point out her grave save this Brooner or Bruner.[8] He even pointed out to me the exact spot (east end of the Nancy Hanks grave) where little Abraham stood when his Mother's rude casket or coffin was lowered. I suppose things like that would be somewhat reliable since the impressions were vivid upon the boy's mind.

Food. You quite properly go into the matter of the food in these pioneer homes, etc. Mostly flesh. I wondered in reading it that you do not venture to suggest that Lincoln's extreme melancholy following almost throughout life might not have been to some certain extent attributable to this very sort of food.

The Hoosier Schoolmaster's Portrayal, Top Page 19 and elsewhere.[9] Judge J. E. Iglehart of Evansville, whom you no doubt know very well, I fear would be aggrieved at the treatment here given.[10] Certainly the Judge allows quite readily that some such portrayal as you here give is altogether correct insofar as it has to do with a certain class; but the Judge insists and that quite strongly, that we also had quite another class here at that time and that Lincoln came in touch with that class also. If indeed the

Judge is correct in the matter and Lincoln did, in fact, meet up with more or less refinement and culture, it would be a real discovery indeed. The Judge has gone into that matter pretty largely; and if you have not discussed this with him, I suggest that you do so. The Judge is exceedingly tedious, but a great fellow; and I am bound to say, Senator, I am more than half persuaded in the belief that he has a trail that would pay to follow up somewhat. For instance, he has followed up the Brackenridge matter. Better get in touch with him.

Top of page 20, "Loud School." Now most of the old pioneers in talking with me about such schools persisted in speaking of them as BLAB Schools.[11]

Carpentering. Wesley Hall's father was well to do. A large farmer, riverman, and tanner, the elder Hall often employed both the Lincolns to do more or less carpenter work as well and also to labor in the tan-bark mill and cut the bark.[12] Wesley was two years younger than Lincoln. They were chums. Hall was such a level-headed fellow I found myself greatly taken with him. He merely related to me what he had been talking about all his life. He did not enlarge upon his stories as years came on. In fact, I was brought in touch with him for that very reason in part. The older men informing me of him and what he had been saying all through the years. He insisted that Lincoln did not drink at all. He asserted that he even refused to eat at the table out in the grove near the tan-bark mill for the very reason that the black bottle was passed, and [he] took this method to escape the jeers, etc., that would have been visited upon him. When Lincoln made his journey down by way of the sea from Washington to the celebrated war conference do you not recall that he refused liquor and accompanied the act by saying that he never at any time drank etc.? Then the cold-water story must be true at Springfield when notified of his Chicago nomination.[13] I very well understand that you make it clear that he was not given to drink later in life, etc. Now I am rather fully persuaded that he never at any time drank, even while in Spencer County. If really true of him it was almost unbelievable since even preachers and other splendid men were much given to drinking their drams. The same thing holds good as to Lincoln in the matter of oaths. You, of course, doubtless recall that Marse Henry Watterson in his great lecture on Abraham Lincoln actually made the bold statement in endeavoring to account for such an unbelievable character that "Abraham Lincoln was DIVINE!" Bishop Mat Hughes—brother of our own Ed Hughes, formerly president of DePauw and now a bishop—had a lecture titled "An Interpretation of Lincoln."[14] He tried to interpret him but always failed to do so. Watterson in attempting it—an impossible task—merely slipped out with the above assertion. You can't account for Shakespeare, Caesar, Hannibal, Gladstone, or Napoleon. They were all impossible men. Lincoln is one of them. I wonder sometimes just how much of the old Calvinistic theology may have been true in such a life as was Lincoln's.

Lincoln Songs. You mention "Barbara Allen." It is interesting to note that this particular song came from North England or North Europe and was much used throughout the South as it is today all through the Great Smokies. My blood is all from the South. I am a great-grandson of General John Sevier, six times governor of Tennessee. He resided at Jonesboro, Tenn., as did my immediate family or forbears. I have heard them tell of this song in that period in the south.

Lincoln Speeches. You touch up[on] this phase of Lincoln's youth very well. You may recall that in my treatment of this peculiar habit of his, I take occasion to relate the circumstance of his first speech as told by Jo Gentry. Dr. Buckley, the old editor of Our Advocate in N.Y.

for 34 years, who had a standing offer from White-Law Reid to edit the New York Tribune for $25,000 a year, took this story of Lincoln's first speech and made considerable out of it. I observe that you make no reference to it in your treatment here. Your judgment of its worth would of course, be quite beyond my own; but

I am much taken with that story as it appears to indicate almost the exact method of Lincoln somewhat later in life. You may have entertained some doubt of its occurrence, etc. Now on that score, surely there can be no good reason to doubt this particular story any more than any other story related by Mr. Gentry. And to him, in the main, Herndon was indebted for his discoveries of incidents and men.

<u>Aesop's Fables</u>. As I have it, this book was brought to Indiana by Nancy Hanks. This was certainly one of the very first books read by Lincoln.

<u>Lincoln's Religion</u>. You quite properly enlarge upon Lincoln's great kindness of heart. His freedom in the main from bad and vicious habits, etc. Making him rather exceptional in his moral standards and this compels me to see a manifest inconsistency in such allegations and assertions as "Abe had no particular religion, etc."; "Didn't think about such things and didn't read the Bible much etc." I may be pardoned, I am sure, when I venture here to say that, after a careful look into that very mooted question, that my chapter on this subject appeals to me as substantially correct in portraying the religious life of his day. It is my conviction that Lincoln was prevented from formal entrance into the Church by reason of the crude and ignorant sort of preachers characterizing his day and time. On the other hand, Lincoln certainly did become skeptical in the matter of revealed religion after a stay at New Salem.

<u>Abe Didn't Go Much with the Girls</u>. Aunt Polly Agnew, his first "girl," was a sister of old Bill Henderson to whom we are indebted for numerous stories concerning Lincoln.[15] Aunt Polly was a woman of unusual native ability. You doubtless well know the Masons at Rockport. The Attorney Chris Mason as well as the other Chris, the insurance man. They are grandsons of this lady. She belonged to the better-class folk. She stated that Lincoln did not go much with the girls for the reason that the girls "sacked" him or "gave him the mitten." And this was due to the fact that

he was so unmercifully tall; and in going out to the spelling bees, etc., with the girls, it was exceedingly embarrassing for them to walk with him, etc. She alleged that Lincoln very much wished to accompany the girls just as did other young men, but they vetoed the matter on the above basis. I am inclined to think this correct, too.

Flatboat Trips. In my treatment of this period, I make mention of an earlier, southern, river trip than any other biographer mentions.[16] I must believe that I am altogether correct in this since I had it so immediate and direct. It was while Lincoln was at the mouth of Anderson Creek as ferryman. I had it from William Forsythe whom, of course, you knew quite well and with whose son, Samuel, you perhaps roomed while a student at DePauw. Forsythe informed me that he was a lad himself at Troy, Indiana, and used to go down to the Creek and listen to Abe spin yarns. More than once Forsythe was "set across Anderson by Lincoln." He knew the circumstance of Jefferson Ray building the flatboat farther up Anderson and of the visit of Lincoln to Ray and the bargain to go with Ray on this southern journey, etc. To me it is worth just this much that Lincoln thus had an earlier look at slavery with whatever impression it may have made upon him.

You do not mention the fact that Lincoln failed to reward a single old-time Hoosier chum with office. Perhaps you mean to do so somewhat later. He was, as you of course know, exceedingly wily and appeared to avoid studiously the appointment of mere friends to official position.

Bill Grigsby Fight with John Johnston. Lamon is the chap who has Lincoln waving the bottle of whiskey and exclaiming, "I am the biggest buck of the lick," etc.[17]

Kentucky Period. On page 33, footnote 1, you are surely in error here. Harrison County was of course then doing business right along since the Capital of the new state was within its borders.

Slavery. I note what you say relative to the matter of Thomas Lincoln and slavery, etc. You feel convinced that slavery did not enter into the equation at all as a reason for his leaving Kentucky. You very largely base this upon the fact that there were comparatively few slaves in that county or part of the state at that time, etc., as well as the fact that there is no evidence as such that he did in fact quit Kentucky for any such reason. And yet you clearly indicate that this very controverted subject, even in a slave state, was [so] pronounced as to occasion a schism in a Baptist church of which Thomas Lincoln, at least a little later, joined and that during the very time (year) that Abraham was born. My people owned slaves, and I feel that I know through their discussions of such matters about how this question was hotly debated rather far South. My people voluntarily manumitted a number of their slaves. I am persuaded to believe that the very fact that there were few slaves in that portion of Kentucky at that time may have been a much better reason for heated debates, etc.

Frankly, my dear Senator, I can't see how you are to undo the unquestioned statement of President Lincoln himself upon this very point when he distinctly asserts that one of the reasons for his people leaving Kentucky was on account of slavery. Lincoln would either have to be mistaken in his interpretation of their purpose or else made use of this for political purposes—and I scarcely think that we would venture to allege the latter.

Lincoln and Jo Holt. Those old pioneers clearly stated that Abraham himself was a half-brother to Judge Joseph Holt.[18] I am mentioning this fact merely. I have no proof at all there could be more. I submit, however, that it is a very singular thing indeed that this sort of notion was so general and so persistent. [Because] all of my library is in storage just now, I can't look up the matter, but suppose you look up the old residence of Judge Holt's father, say in 1808. It was not far from Thomas Lincoln. It won't harm anyone at least to satisfy conjecture or curiosity, should you have any.

Mordecai Lincoln. You speak of the "Provident" elder brother, etc. Perhaps all that you say of him at this time was true, but you must not forget that this same "Mord," as Abraham always called him, later in life also quit Kentucky, removing to Hancock County, Illinois, and was not any better off in the world than were his brothers.[19]

Josiah Lincoln. Undoubtedly Thomas Lincoln visited his brother Josiah in Harrison County, Indiana, sometime prior to his (Thomas's) removal to Indiana.[20] I grew up in the general neighborhood of Josiah Lincoln. I have interviewed the old pioneers concerning him. It was this visit to Josiah that determined the coming to Indiana of Thomas. Waldo Lincoln is, of course, in error when he says that Josiah came to Perry County—Harrison County was doing business right along when Josiah came in 1812. Josiah was a fairly well-to-do pioneer. He stood up about on a level with his neighbors, no more, no less. Thomas Lincoln always has suffered greatly by way of unfair comparisons with the already rather well-to-do Gentry Hall and others in his immediate locality. They all had money when they came to Spencer County.

Lincoln's Visit to Spencer County in 1844. I observe that you go to some considerable extent to show how well Lincoln remembered the Knob Creek Farm and people, etc., in Kentucky. I wonder that you did not also call attention to his visit to his old Indiana home during the campaign when stumping for his beau-ideal, Henry Clay.[21] You will recall that he made three speeches in Spencer County. While there he went about looking up everything, even the whip-saw pit etc. It is worth just this much that he wished to come back home once again; and then it evidences interest and impressions formed concerning his boyhood and young manhood. He wrote no poetry as was his wont on occasions concerning his Knob Creek home, but he did concerning his Hoosier home.

Linkhorn. No one now or scarcely anyone in our general neighborhood in Harrison County ever speaks of the Lincolns—it is always the Linkhorns. Merely the pioneer method of pronunciation, still in vogue.

Kentucky a Virginia Colony. Colonel Henry Watterson was much accustomed to make the narrow claim that Lincoln was a Kentuckian—reared by Kentuckians, etc.; and to justify this claim in view of Lincoln's absence from the state of his birth after the age of 7, Marse Henry would say, "What was Illinois, but a Kentucky Colony?" Of course, all of that was quite narrow since we may well ask, "What was Kentucky but a Virginia Colony?" All southern Indiana, as you of course well know, was, with very few exceptions, from the South—and largely citizens from the Carolinas, Tenn., and Virginia, and of course from Kentucky, but in the main those from Kentucky originally came from farther South. Do you not recall what Grant said when asked on one occasion why Southern Indiana was filled with Knights of the Golden Circle, etc., and Southern Illinois was not? He struck deep when he made the laconic reply—"LOGAN."[22] I mention all of this to say that most of the men who wore the blue from these sections were former slave owners or sons of slave owners. But notwithstanding that fact the influence of such men as Dennis Pennington and Hugh Cull made Indiana free. Strong convictions were registered by these former slave owners against slavery. Where did Lincoln get his strong and early convictions against slavery? Certainly I can anticipate you in the main, but did he not come to this to some extent by way of his forebears—the elder Abraham—his grandfather as well as his more immediate forebears who perhaps in no single instance ever owned slaves? It must have been easily possible at least for his rather well-to-do grandfather to have owned slaves. I wonder if we do not find here at least some family or tribal opposition to this regime? Anything just here would be informing and help out immensely. How much of the Quaker blood and thought gets into the equation for Lincoln? May it not have been latent and only had need of a Clay or Douglass with his strange ideas—the Dred Scott matter and such other things to bring it to the fore?[23]

Old Jim Gentry discussed this with me at length. I questioned him carefully and found that he was a Democrat in politics and voted for Douglas against Lincoln, a thing that grieved Lincoln greatly. Uncle Jim insisted strongly that Henry Clay was responsible almost entirely for Lincoln's slavery notions. He said that

Lincoln was ever and always talking about Clay, etc. As I view it, Lincoln was immensely more in favor of the perpetuity of the Union than he ever was against slavery. His Dr. [Jekyll] and Mr. Hyde make up was much in evidence in that he personally stood squarely against the human traffic in the black man, but his paramount impulse was the preservation of the Union. I have ventured this comment in order to have you see Gentry and Lincoln back there.

Legitimacy of Nancy Hanks and Her Son Abraham. I have been delivering addresses on Lincoln for a number of years. On one occasion I made a little speaking tour right through Spencer County speaking at Grandview—where resided Mrs. Lamar, a friend of Lincoln, a pioneer lady whom I later buried. Also the home of Forsythe, who personally knew Lincoln, and the home of Jefferson Ray, with whom Lincoln made the hitherto unmentioned flatboat trip south. Also a Mrs. Laymon, whose age was not far from that of Lincoln and whose people resided neighbors to the Lincolns in Kentucky and who removed to Spencer County sometime after the Lincolns came here and then resided neighbors to them here. Mrs. Layman told me after sending the house girl from the room, "I am a cripple as you see, and yet I had them take me to hear you lecture on Lincoln. Now I hear you say last night that you had read all of the Lincoln biographies. I want to ask you what they say about Nancy Hanks, her birth, etc." I reviewed this for her. She then said, "I am old enough to be your grandmother, and I may speak plainly to you. My mother was present when Abraham Lincoln was born. I have often heard her relate the circumstances, etc. My mother was a neighbor to the Lincolns, and she liked them, but she always said that not only was Nancy Hanks an illegitimate child herself, but that Nancy was not what she ought to have been herself. Loose, etc." She made no mention of the Holt matter.

My Father-in-Law, John Tipton Conner. Mr. Conner was a son of General Samuel Conner of Tippecanoe and one of the builders of the state.[24] He was, in turn, a son of Terrence Conner, playmate of Washington who served with him throughout the Revolutionary War. My father-in-law was born in Troy in 1824.

Certainly altogether too late to have any remembrance of Lincoln, yet he came in just right to catch all the talk such as would pass about concerning Lincoln later. Mr. Connor was a very dignified Southern gentleman of the Old School although Northern-born of course. I hesitated to ask him about the Judge Holt matter, knowing very well he was an old-time Republican in politics and, of course, a great admirer of Lincoln. We were seated on a large veranda engaged in conversation as we faced Kentucky, and Judge Holt's home was in plain view. It was my opportunity and I put the question squarely to him: "Father Connor what is there in this insistent talk that I hear making Lincoln a half-brother of Judge Holt?" He turned to me and said in a very dignified way, "J. Ed., I never heard anything else all my life," etc.

That Thomas Lincoln was a better workman than is evidenced in statements usually made of him is my judgment. This Holt matter came to the fore in that very matter. That Thomas Lincoln possessed a tolerable kit of tools—carpenter tools—is beyond dispute. He was the carpenter in all that Spencer County community. There is no sort of doubt about that. Certainly that may not have meant a skilled workman, but good for that day. He certainly made cupboards and tables, etc. I have seen some of these. Someone made them in that far-off day, and they claim Lincoln as the maker, and I am inclined to the belief that he did. It was insisted that he got his chest of carpenter tools by way of the Holt affair! They spoke much concerning these tools, and I submit that a man who possessed such a superior kit of tools must have possessed some skill at least in the use of them; but why this persistent assertion that the tools came by way of the Holt affair? I am merely giving you coloring without the dye pot. I have no proof at all. That is manifestly impossible now. There may be nothing to this at all, but I give what I found.

Beveridge to Murr
26 November 1924
Beverly Farms, Massachusetts

Dr. J. Edward Murr
254 Spring Street
New Albany, Indiana

Dear Dr. Murr:

Thank you for your good letter of November 21, and thank you particularly for the sixteen pages of notes on my MSS. They are helpful and of value. I shall observe most of them. It would take too much time to discuss them in a letter; you really must give me a whole evening, and I will come down to New Albany for that purpose sometime during the winter. Or, still better, if you happen to be in Indianapolis at any time, please let me know, and come out to my house, and lunch or dine with me, and then we can talk to our hearts' content.

I may say just now, however, that I have written and shall write only from original sources—the MSS. letters of those who were actually on the ground and personally saw and heard everything they related; or MSS. narratives written at the time of the interviews with men and women who were eyewitnesses. When I refer in my footnotes to the "Weik MSS," I mean the great Herndon collection, the like of which never before was assembled and never will be again. For example, I do not rely on Lamon, but on the source material mentioned.

Lincoln rose to spiritual heights and to heights of statesman-like vision that no other mere mortal man ever attained. The Second Inaugural approaches the Sermon on the Mount. But I agree with Professor Channing (I mean the great Channing) that all this came in his last two years—Channing sees no sign of it in his entire previous life.[25]

I am not willing yet to go that far—indeed I am not willing to give any opinion whatever on any phase of Lincoln's life and shall not be willing to do so until I have gathered *all* the evidence, sifted, weighed, and studied it. But, so far as I have gone, I must say that I cannot explain the last amazing phase of Lincoln's life except on the ground of inspiration; and, of course, science rejects inspiration. Nevertheless I cannot, as yet, account for those last two marvelous years by any other reason except on this very ground of inspiration.

Of course, as you say, it was what he said and did during that time for which the whole world now worships him and will increasingly worship him. But that does not mean that we must try to change, modify, or suppress—or all of these processes—the actual facts of his life before that time in order to make them fit this sublime period. With your scholar's mind—for, dear Dr. Murr, you have a scholar's mind as distinguished from the clergyman's—you will see that.

So you are the great-grandson of General Sevier! That is good news; and it accounts for a lot about you that has caused me to wonder. Sevier was one of the most extraordinary men in our history. I consider him to have been a *great* man in the big sense of that misused word.

Thank you, dear friend, for your kindness in having gone over my MSS. with such meticulous care. As I have written you, I intend to lean very heavily upon you because it is clear to me that you have done more original research concerning Lincoln in Indiana than anybody else, and have done it with the scholar's spirit and well-nigh with the scholars method, extravagant as that statement is. Perhaps I ought to except Herndon: All of us must take our hats off to the painstaking and exhaustive investigation which that wonderful man did. What a shame and an outrage that he was assailed by the Mid-Victorians and by a class of preachers which now, happily, is extinct, just because he repeated what Lincoln said about his mother's origin and other things they did not like about Lincoln's religion. As Dr. Morse, editor of the *American Statesmen* series, wrote me after having gone over my MSS.: Herndon, after all is said and done, has been a great source of all our knowledge concerning Lincoln's early and personal life—Morse referred to Herndon's book, but I am going to the sources from which that book was written—the astonishing Herndon collection which, I repeat, has been unequalled and never again will be repeated.

I shall arrive at Indianapolis on December 5 and will be there all winter and until next summer; and before I come East again, I repeat, I want to be sure to see you for a good, long conference. Also you may expect me to bore you by frequent letters of inquiry. I shall have to spend a great deal of time in Springfield going over the *Sangamon Journal* and other papers at that place, and I shall also have to come down to Kentucky again two or three times.

But let me say again what a happiness it will be to me and Mrs. Beveridge if, when you are in Indianapolis, you will favor us by coming out to our house.

Thank you again, dear Dr. Murr, and believe me, with every good wish, always,

Faithfully.

[Sen. Albert J. Beveridge]

NOTES

1. Charles W. Moores (1862–1923) was a prominent attorney in Indianapolis, Indiana. In addition to his legal practice and several other civic board positions, Moores served as a member and vice president of the Indiana Historical Commission and trustee of the Indiana Lincoln Memorial Association.

2. Logan Esarey (1873–1942) was superintendent of the Perry County school system and was principal of Vincennes High School before becoming dean of Winona College. After earning a PhD in 1913, he joined the

faculty at Indiana University as professor of history and was regarded as an authority on Indiana history. His published works include *History of Indiana, Courts and Lawyers of Indiana, Letters and Papers of William Henry Harrison, Messages of Indiana Governors*, and *The Indiana Home*.

3. Each district of the Methodist Church hosts an annual conference. Most pastors at the time attended.

4. *Tarbellize* refers to Ida Tarbell (1857–1944), a popular Lincoln author at the time, who some believed overly romanticized Abraham Lincoln.

5. Tarbell told the *Evansville Courier* that although she did not visit Lincoln City, she did stay for "several days" in Rockport interviewing locals. Wick, "He Was a Friend of Us Poor Men," *Indiana Magazine of History*, 273, citing Tarbell, memorandum: *In the Footsteps of Lincoln*, Tarbell Collection, Pelletier Library, Allegheny College, Meadville, PA.

6. John G. Nicolay and John Hay, Lincoln's personal secretary and assistant secretary, respectively, set out to write Lincoln's definitive biography. Their work appeared serially in *The Century Magazine* from 1886 to 1890 and then in book form as the ten-volume *Abraham Lincoln: A History* (1890). Nicolay and Hay did not focus on Lincoln's youth and did not interview his boyhood associates.

7. Ward Hill Lamon (1828–1893), Lincoln's bodyguard, published two books about Lincoln, one of which was ghostwritten by Chauncey Black.

8. In 1879, wealthy Hoosier businessman Peter E. Studebaker paid to erect a marble stone on Nancy's presumed gravesite; the monument still stands today.

9. Edward Eggleston's popular 1871 novel, *The Hoosier Schoolmaster: A Story of Backwoods Life in Indiana*, associated the state with ignorance, poverty, hardships, and an odd dialect.

10. John E. Iglehart, a railroad lawyer who read voraciously and studied history, founded the Southwestern Indiana Historical Society (SWIHS) in 1920. Although he was not a judge, many referred to Iglehart with that title out of respect. SWIHS sought to examine all history of the region, but Lincoln's Hoosier roots formed the focal point of their efforts. SWIHS hoped their work would improve the state's image by refuting myths and errors and reveal a more balanced account of Lincoln's life on the Indiana frontier. See Bartelt and Claybourn, *Abe's Youth*.

11. In a *blab* school, children repeat their teacher's lesson at the top of their voices, often in harmonized unison.

12. A tan-bark mill extracts tannic acid from the bark of chestnut and oak trees, acid then used in tanning animal skins for making leather.

13. Upon winning the Republican nomination for president, Lincoln allegedly used cold water for a celebratory toast.

14. Henry Watterson, nicknamed "Marse," served as part owner and editor in chief of Louisville's *Courier-Journal*. A prominent Democrat, he also served as a representative in Congress from 1876 to 1877.

15. As Murr explains in chapter 13 and in the appendix of this book, Polly Agnew (maiden surname Richardson) was born to a pioneer family arriving in Spencer County, Indiana, in 1817, about a year after the Lincolns.

16. Lincoln never mentions this additional flatboat trip in any recollections or accounts of his time in Indiana, a fact that undercuts its believability. Indeed, Lincoln stated his first trip of this nature occurred when he was nineteen. Lincoln's two flatboat trips to New Orleans, the first in 1828 with Allen Gentry and the second in 1831 with John Johnston and John Hanks, formed the longest journeys of Lincoln's life up to that point and were his only visits to the Deep South.

17. Ward Hill Lamon does cite this incident, but the quotations do not sync with Lamon's account. Perhaps Murr is quoting a different biographer. See Lamon, *Life of Abraham Lincoln*, 65–66.

18. Joseph Holt (1807–1894)—a native of Breckinridge County, Kentucky, about fifty miles from the Lincoln homestead—was the judge-advocate general for the US Army and later served as chief prosecutor in the Lincoln assassination trial.

19. Mordecai Lincoln lived from 1771 to 1830.

20. Josiah Lincoln lived from 1773 to 1835. Aside from Murr's assertions, there is no historical evidence that Thomas Lincoln visited Harrison County, Indiana, before the family's move from Kentucky to Indiana.

21. For a full account of Lincoln's return trip in 1844, see Bartelt, "Aiding Mr. Clay," 29–39.

22. This refers to John A. Logan (1826–1886), a prominent Democratic politician and general in the Union Army whose allegiance to the Union helped ensure northern Democratic support for the war effort.

23. The *Clay* refers to Henry Clay, and the other reference may be to abolitionist Frederick Douglass.

24. John Tipton (1786–1839) served in the Battle of Tippecanoe, eventually achieving the rank of brigadier general of the Indiana Militia. He was twice elected sheriff of Harrison County, Indiana, and served as a state representative from 1820 to 1823, during which time he helped select a site for the new state capital and establish the border between Indiana

and Illinois. In 1831, Tipton was elected to the US Senate; he retired in 1839.

25. Murr refers to Edward Channing (1856–1931), professor of ancient and modern history at Harvard University. He was well known for his six-volume *History of the United States*, which won the Pulitzer Prize for history in 1925.

APPENDIX: MURR'S INFORMANTS

Editor's Note: In the papers he left at DePauw University, Edward Murr identified the primary informants used in constructing his Lincoln history. Murr's informants include Rev. Mr. Allen Brooner, John Brooner, Joseph and James Gentry, Wesley and Porter Hall, Polly Agnew, Professor J. M. Johnson, Jacob Summers, Jefferson Ray, Dr. Loren Gage (a descendant of the Hanks family), Dr. John White, William Herron, Redmond Grigsby, Mrs. John Romine, Mr. and Mrs. John W. Lamar, William Forsythe, Charles Painter, many of their children, and the children of others who knew Lincoln.[1] Eleven of these persons were Lincoln's boyhood companions.[2] This appendix presents—without corrections—some of Murr's informants as he knew and summarized them.

WESLEY HALL

Born Kentucky 1815. Came to Indiana, Spencer County, when a mere babe in his mother's arms. Was of a large family. I knew his brothers and sisters and buried some of them. His father was a tanner, farmer, and flatboat-man. He often employed Thomas Lincoln and his son, Abraham. They worked in the Bark mill, etc., and did some building for him. The two families, Lincolns and

Halls, were neighbors, and neighbored much. Wesley Hall was a typical pioneer in the highest and best sense of that time. He possessed such schooling as the pioneer usually had. He was a Methodist class leader for 50 years. He resided in Union County, Kentucky, later in life, died there, and was buried there.

Hall was level-headed, well-informed, modest, and truthful. He was in my home. I met him a number of times elsewhere also. He informed me that he had never been so much as interviewed by a newspaper reporter concerning Lincoln. My interviews with Hall were during the years 1898, 1899, 1900, and 1901. His father sold the oxen to John Johnson and Abraham Lincoln that were destined to carry the Lincolns and Hankses to Illinois. Hall delivered the ox team to the Lincolns at the cabin, was there to bid them goodbye as they started on their journey. He recalled Abraham's dress, etc. He strongly asserted that Lincoln never touched liquor at any time in his youth.

Hall stated to me that when he and Abe were running about together, it never occurred to him that Lincoln would be great. He never so impressed Hall, although he stressed the fact that Lincoln read much, etc., particularly dwelling upon the fact that Lincoln frequently made journeys to the Brackenridge home near Boonville and spent days, and even remained overnight often in the Brackenridge home, at which time he pored over the Brackenridge library, not only law books, but literary volumes, and among these a copy of Shakespeare. He often heard him refer to Shakespeare, quoting certain passages, etc.; and once when reading for Granny Hanks (who could not read) from [Isaiah], he ran in portions of Shakespeare as one of his (Lincoln's) practical jokes.

He remembered (often) being in the Lincoln cabin and heard Lincoln read from those now celebrated books—*Pilgrim's Progress*, *Life of Ben Franklin*, Weems's *Life of Washington*, etc.

Hall stated that old Tom Lincoln could not read much and was quite proud of Abe's ability to read these books, etc.; he would often say as they sat about the back log blaze: "Now Abe, bring out one of your books and read for us." Hall added, "At such times Abe would read for us until bed time." He told of the Brackenridge trial, etc., the lawyer from Kentucky, etc. He spoke of the Lincoln poverty as a mere matter of course since all the pioneers were comparatively poor.

Hall was present at the celebrated "Johnson-Bill Grigsby" fist fight, which took place on the exact site of the present Lincoln City Depot. James Gentry, as well as Redmond Grigsby, stated they were there, and all gave same story of the affair, which was not as Lamon gives it. There was no cursing by Lincoln and no whiskey bottle in evidence.

Wesley Hall was a Republican in politics, was proud of his boyhood chum. He was passing well-to-do, indeed quite so. He was a man held in the highest esteem. While not schooled, his mentality was in evidence constantly. He was such a man as would have graced a seat in a legislative assembly. His habits, ideals, and morals were of the best.

WILLIAM FORSYTHE

Born and reared in Troy, Indiana. Was down at the Anderson Ferry when Lincoln was ferryman there. Often the boys would congregate at the Ferry to hear Abe talk. He crossed in Lincoln's boat, met him, often, etc.

Forsythe well knew the incident of Jefferson Bay, flatboatman, building a boat up Anderson Creek while Lincoln was ferryman, and he (Lincoln) having cultivated a tobacco patch of some size, went to Ray and proposed going as a hand at the oar down to Memphis, proposing to work his passage, and thus market his tobacco. Thus Lincoln saw slavery some years earlier than the world has been led to believe.

Forsythe was a businessman later in life at Grandview. He was very well schooled, easily above the average. Held in high favor by all. Was 27 years superintendent of Methodist Episcopal

Sunday School, a leading man in the community life. His son Samuel made it possible for Albert J. Beveridge to go through DePauw University, by the loan of books, etc. They were roommates. Samuel became an attorney and died at Cincinnati while in the practice of law.

Jefferson Ray was a Grandview man, and Forsythe came to know him exceedingly well. They frequently discussed the flatboat trip referred to above. Ray did make the Memphis trip, taking Lincoln along as a hand at the oar.

I talked with at least a score of citizens at Grandview who often heard Ray relate the circumstance of Lincoln's journey with him. I was pastor of Forsythe as well as Jefferson Ray Jr., son of the elder Ray, this in 1900, 1901 and 1902.

Forsythe was a Republican in politics.

Forsythe was a portly gentleman, commanding in air and bearing. He was easily one of the first citizens of that classic little town where we have had through the years some quite pretentious citizens.

JAMES GENTRY

It must be remembered that there were three Gentry brothers— Allen, two years Lincoln's senior, with whom he made the celebrated flatboat journey down the Ohio and Mississippi; Joseph, just the age of Lincoln; and James, some 3 years younger than Lincoln.

In the years 1900, 1901, 1902, I interviewed James Gentry personally and verified all in other ways.

He was well-preserved physically and keen as a brier mentally. I found him out on his large farm, a mile perhaps from the house, and superintending some ditching. He employed many men. He was bluff, hearty, and hale, and refused to talk about Lincoln until we got to the house. He walked all the way to the house like a youth.

Gentry was a Democrat. He and his brother Joseph both voted against Lincoln.

The elder Gentry—father of James, Allen, and Joseph—came to Spencer County in 1818, two years after the Lincolns. He was passing well-to-do on his arrival there. He was engaged in farming, river traffic, and merchandise. Allen Gentry was drowned in the Mississippi when yet young. Lincoln remained overnight with the Gentrys the last night spent in Spencer County. He [went] there from the Gentry General Store at Gentryville, "outfitted" for his part of the Illinois journey, stocked up on needles, pins, buttons, etc., etc., notions, and sold these as he trekked to Illinois. Lincoln paid Gentry cash $30 for his outfit and wrote back to Gentry subsequently from Illinois that he just exactly doubled his money on the venture. Lincoln was not altogether penniless.

James Gentry said that Lincoln was often in their home. They were much together, coon hunted, wrestled, etc., went to school together, etc.

He allowed that everybody liked Abe, with the exception of some of the Grigsbys. He referred to the "Chronicles of Reuben," quoted some of these rhymes, etc., and said, "I met old Red (Redmond Grigsby) the other day, and told him to let the Chronicles come out now as nearly everybody was dead but me and him, etc." Gentry maintained that Red Grigsby yet had the original "Chronicles of Reuben." I tried to get these from Grigsby, but failed; I never saw them.

Gentry greatly admired Lincoln, and yet he said, "We were Democrats and we voted against him." He said a neighbor man visited Lincoln in the White House and talked with him "until the wee small hours of the morning about everybody and everything from Boonville up to the mouth of Anderson." He was hurt to know that the Gentrys voted against him.

He maintained that Abe always was opposed to slavery when a youth. He insisted that even before Lincoln quit Gentryville he was reading Henry Clay and believed in gradual emancipation. He spoke of Lincoln's speeches (as a boy), his reading of books, etc., etc., etc., and ended by remarking: "Abe turned out right because he followed the Constitution—although he was always following Henry Clay around."

JOSEPH GENTRY

Born same year as Lincoln. I looked him up as early as 1892 (33 years since). I wanted that story concerning the "old Gray Goose." Herndon came to Spencer County first, of all the biographers. He stopped with Uncle Jo Gentry three nights. Herndon's Spencer County notice of Lincoln is in the main due to what he got from Joseph Gentry.

REV. ALLEN BROONER

United Brethren preacher. Looked him up 1892. He was the man who pointed out the grave of Nancy Hanks when Clem Studebaker wanted to put the marker up. He and he alone knew her burial place, and it appears that he was correct in this since the circumstantial evidence is of the best. His own mother was buried at about exactly the same time as was Nancy Hanks, and they were buried side by side. Brooner was present at both funerals. Lincoln stood on the east end of his mother's grave crying as they lowered the rude box containing Nancy Hanks (statement, made by Brooner who witnessed this). It was Rev. Brooner who related the story of the "shoes," and Jones refusing Lincoln credit, etc.

Brooner was a man of intelligence and fine character, a minister of the Gospel standing high in the community, as did Mr. Jim Gentry who served in the Lower House of one General Assembly. There is no sort of doubt about the high standing of these men.

MRS. ROMINE

I merely saw and met her briefly. Lincoln was a farmhand on their farm. They regarded him as "lazy," not "work brittle," etc. This was their reason: "He read too much!" He had a habit of carrying a book in his blouse. Wesley Hall maintained that Lincoln always carried some book with him. I met Mrs. Romine August 1902.

MRS. POLLY AGNEW

Mrs. Agnew's maiden name was Richardson, brother of "Old Bill," to whom the older biographers are indebted for the story of Lincoln carrying squared timbers such as three men could not carry as well as lifting bodily a chicken house on one occasion.

The Richardsons came to Grandview in 1817. They tied up there and the elder Richardson went out in quest of a cabin site. This was near the Lincoln cabin. They were neighbors. Lincoln courted Aunt Polly. She was a remarkable woman, typical pioneer. She often related the circumstance of killing a panther in her room.

She was the mother of Chris Mason, the lawyer of Rockport. She was married three times. She alleged that Lincoln was "smarter" than any youth she knew. He would accompany her to spelling bees, church, etc.

I got these things in 1900. Mrs. Agnew was not particularly schooled, of course, but intelligent, vivacious, alert, chatty, and well-informed.

THE LAMARS

I buried Mrs. Lamar in 1900. She and her husband were both associates of Lincoln. Her husband and Captain Lamar were cousins. Captain Lamar was present at the dedication of the present monument of Nancy Hanks. I saw him 1902. He it was who, in company with his father, was passing by the Lincoln cabin and seeing Abe seated on top of the woodpile (wagon length) reading a book, heard his father, say, "Lincoln will some day be President," etc. He related that incident all his life. It was one of the Lamar girls who told of the Brag Horse of a braggart neighbor, who could outstrip all competitors and "never draw a long breath," and Lincoln who was courting Miss Lamar, on hearing this, slyly observed, "Yes, but I suppose he drew some short breaths," etc. Mrs. Lamar and Captain Lamar both verified all of the stories current concerning Lincoln.

OTHER SOURCES

I got some of my very best material from sons of men and women who were Lincoln's boyhood and girlhood associates. This was but natural and quite as reliable as things more immediate and direct.

I interviewed men and women who had him in the double log house of the Grigsbys, where Sarah Lincoln and Amos Grigsby were married. The double wedding you will recall which occasioned Lincoln's "Chronicles." I was fortunate to find a Mr. Painter, a very intelligent gentleman, a blacksmith (yet living), who had lived in the Grigsby home. Mr. Painter, as well as scores of others, personally knew "Blue Nosed" Crawford and other characters such as Nat Grigsby.

I thus visualized scenes and substantiated stories concerning Lincoln's youth as well as manners, customs, etc., generally prevailing.

I found one man who underwent the ordeal of having "Cy" Crawford introduce a Twister pair of forceps in his mouth and twist out a molar for him!

NOTES

1. Murr, "Wilderness Years of Lincoln," 267, 342.
2. Murr, "Some Pertinent Observations," 2.

BIBLIOGRAPHY

BOOKS

Bartelt, William E. *"There I Grew Up": Remembering Abraham Lincoln's Indiana Youth*. Indianapolis: Indiana Historical Society, 2008.

Bartelt, William E., and Joshua A. Claybourn. *Abe's Youth: Shaping the Future President*. Bloomington: Indiana University Press, 2019.

Barton, William E. *The Paternity of Abraham Lincoln: Was He the Son of Thomas Lincoln? An Essay on the Chastity of Nancy Hanks*. New York: George H. Doran, 1920.

Basler, Roy P., ed., Marion Dolores Pratt and Lloyd A. Dunlap, asst. eds. *The Collected Works of Abraham Lincoln*. 9 vols. New Brunswick, NJ: Rutgers University Press, 1953.

Beveridge, Albert J. *Abraham Lincoln, 1809–1858*. 2 vols. Boston: Houghton Mifflin, 1928.

Burlingame, Michael. *Abraham Lincoln: A Life*. 2 vols. Baltimore: Johns Hopkins University Press, 2008.

Carpenter, Francis Bicknell. *Six Months at the White House*. New York: Hurd and Houghton, 2016. First published in 1866.

Eckley, Robert S. *Lincoln's Forgotten Friend, Leonard Swett*. Carbondale: Southern Illinois University Press, 2012.

Eggleston, Edward. *The Hoosier Schoolmaster: A Story of Backwoods Life in Indiana*. New York: Grosset & Dunlap, 1871.

Ehrmann, Bess V. *The Missing Chapter in the Life of Abraham Lincoln: A Number of Articles, Episodes, Photographs, Pen and Ink Sketches*

Concerning the Life of Abraham Lincoln in Spencer County, Indiana, between 1816–1830 and 1844. Chicago: Walter M. Hill, 1938.

Fehrenbacher, Don, and Virginia Fehrenbacher. *Recollected Words of Abraham Lincoln.* Stanford, CA: Stanford University Press, 1996.

Foster, Ernest. *Abraham Lincoln.* London: Cassell, 1893.

Herndon, William H., and Jesse Weik. *Abraham Lincoln: The True Story of a Great Life, Vol. 2.* New York: D. Appleton, 1920.

———. *Herndon's Lincoln: The True Story of a Great Life.* Cleveland: World Publishing, 1949.

Holland, J. G. *Holland's Life of Abraham Lincoln.* Lincoln: University of Nebraska Press, 1998.

———. *Holland's Life of Abraham Lincoln.* Springfield, MA: Gurdon Hill, 1866.

Lamon, Ward. *The Life of Abraham Lincoln.* Carlisle, MA: Applewood Books, 1872.

Lincoln, Abraham. *Speeches and Writings, 1832–1858.* New York: Library of America, 1989.

May, Ruby Murr, ed. *The Murr Family.* Jonesborough, TN: Ruby Murr, May 1996. Held in the DePauw University Archives and Special Collections. Box DC 1568.

Miller, William L. *Lincoln's Virtues: An Ethical Biography.* New York: Vintage Books, 2003.

Monroe, Paul, and Irving E. Miller, eds. *The American Spirit: A Basis for World Democracy.* Yonkers, NY: World Book, 1918.

Murr, J. Edward. *Glimpses of an Itinerant.* Typescript of an autobiography, 1952. John Edward Murr Papers. DePauw University Archives and Special Collections. Box DC 1568.

Peterson, Merrill D. *Lincoln in American Memory.* New York: Oxford University Press, 1994.

Pratt, Silas G. *Lincoln in Story: The Life of the Martyr-President Told in Authenticated Anecdotes.* New York: D. Appleton, 1901.

Rice, Allen Thorndike, ed. *Reminiscences of Abraham Lincoln by Distinguished Men of His Time.* New York: Harper & Brothers, 1886.

Rothschild, Alonzo. *Lincoln, Master of Men: A Study in Character.* Boston: Houghton Mifflin, 1906.

Sibley, Marilyn McAdams. *George W. Brackenridge: Maverick Philanthropist.* Austin: University of Texas Press, 1973.

Speed, Joshua F. *Reminiscences of Lincoln and Notes of a Visit to California.* Louisville, KY: John P. Morton, 1884.

Tarbell, Ida M. *The Early Life of Abraham Lincoln: Containing Many Un-published Documents and Unpublished Reminiscences of Lincoln's Early Friends.* New York: S. S. McClure, 1896.

———. *In the Footsteps of the Lincolns.* New York: Harper & Brothers, 1924.

———. *Life of Abraham Lincoln: Drawn from Original Sources and Contain-ing Many Speeches, Letters and Telegraphs Hitherto Unpublished.* 2 vols. New York: Doubleday & McClure, 1900.

Thayer, William Makepeace. *The Pioneer Boy and How He Became Presi-dent: The Story of the Life of Abraham Lincoln.* London: Hodder and Stoughton, 1882.

Whipple, Wayne. *The Story-Life of Lincoln: A Biography Composed of Five Hundred True Stories Told by Abraham Lincoln and His Friends.* Philadel-phia: John C. Winston, 1908.

Wilson, Douglas L., and Rodney O. Davis, eds. *Herndon's Informants: Let-ters, Interviews, and Statements about Abraham Lincoln.* Urbana: Univer-sity of Illinois Press, 1998.

———. *Herndon's Lincoln.* Urbana: University of Illinois Press, 2006.

Warren, Louis. *Lincoln's Youth: Indiana Years 1816–1830.* Indianapolis: Indi-ana Historical Society, 1959.

JOURNALS, MAGAZINES, AND NEWS

"American Men of 1776 Said to Have Stood Tall." *New York Times*, 15 April 1982, 7.

Anderson, Christopher W. "Native Americans and the Origin of Abraham Lincoln's Views on Race." *Journal of the Abraham Lincoln Association* 37, no. 1 (Winter 2016): 11–29.

Bartelt, William E. "Aiding Mr. Clay: Abraham Lincoln's 1844 Visit to In-diana." *Traces* 32, no. 1 (Winter 2020): 29–39.

———. "Pebbles or Diamonds: How Do We Know What We Know about Lincoln in Indiana?" Historic Southern Indiana, Lincoln Institute, 2004. https://setv.usi.edu/media/2939283/Pebbles-or-Diamonds.pdf.

Chandler, Albert B. *Harper's Monthly* 32 (February 1866): 405.

Hanby, Alice Harper. "John Pitcher." *Indiana Historical Commission Bul-letin*, no. 16, *Proceedings of the Southwestern Indiana Historical Society* (October 1922): 60–66.

Kniffen, Fred, and Henry Glassie. "Building in Wood in the Eastern United States: A Time-Place Perspective." *Geographical Review* 56, no. 1 (1966): 40–66.

Komlos, John. "On the Biological Standard of Living of Eighteenth-
    Century Americans: Taller, Richer, Healthier." *Munich Economics*
    (Discussion paper 2003–July 9, 2003). http://citeseerx.ist.psu.edu
    /viewdoc/download?doi=10.1.1.197.6596&rep=rep1&type=pdf.
Murr, J. Edward. "Lincoln in Indiana." *Indiana Magazine of History* 13, no.
    4 (December 1917): 307–348.
———. "Lincoln in Indiana." *Indiana Magazine of History* 14, no. 1 (March
    1918): 13–75.
———. "Lincoln in Indiana." *Indiana Magazine of History* 14, no. 2 (June
    1918): 148–182.
Rice, Judith A. "Ida M. Tarbell: A Progressive Look at Lincoln." *Journal of
    the Abraham Lincoln Association* 19, no. 1 (Winter 1998): 57–72.
Robinson, Cliff. "The Truth about Lincoln." *Courier-Journal* (Louisville,
    KY) 8 (February 1959): 115–117.
Sellars, Richard West. "Lincoln's Logs." *Opinionator* (blog). *New York
    Times*, 12 February 2013. opinionator.blogs.nytimes.com.
Shuda, Nathaniel. "DNA Study Helps Solve Lincoln Lineage Debate."
    USA Today, 3 November 2016. www.usatoday.com
    /story/news/nation-now/2015/11/03/dna-study-helps
    -solve-lincoln-lineage-debate/75078140.
Wick, Robert G. "'He Was a Friend of Us Poor Men': Ida M. Tarbell and
    Abraham Lincoln's View of Democracy." *Indiana Magazine of History*
    114, no. 4 (December 2018): 255–282.

CORRESPONDENCE AND UNPUBLISHED TYPESCRIPTS

Beveridge, Albert J. Papers, 1788–1943 (MSS12591). Library of Congress,
    Washington, DC. Ward Hill Lamon Papers. Huntington Library, San
    Marino, CA.
Mather Papers (Folder 97). Filson Club Lectures, 1887–1992. Filson Soci-
    ety. Louisville, KY.
Murr, J. Edward. Collection (S3096). Indiana State Library, Indianapolis.
———. "Some Pertinent Observations Concerning 'Abe Lincoln the
    Hoosier.'" Unpublished typescript. John Edward Murr papers, MSD.
    1901.019. DePauw University Archives and Special Collections. Box DC
    1568.
———. *The Wilderness Years*. Unpublished manuscript. John Edward Murr
    Papers. DePauw University Archives and Special Collections. Box DC
    1568.

Pitcaithley, Dwight. "A Splendid Hoax: The Strange Case of Lincoln's Birthplace Cabin." Washington, DC: National Museum of American History Colloquium, 30 April 1991. irma.nps.gov/datastore /downloadfile/474735.

Tarbell Collection. Pelletier Library. Allegheny College, Meadville, PA.

INDEX

Note: Family named in subheadings are referred to by their first and last initials only, for example, Nancy Hanks Lincoln (mother), becomes "N. L." States are referred to by their common abbreviations in the subheads: IL, IN, and KY, for Illinois, Indiana, and Kentucky.

blab schools, 164, 259n11

Black, Chauncey, *Life of Abraham Lincoln*, 54n16, 259n7

books and reading habits: book catches fire, night reading, 161; books brought from KY to IN, 215; books obtained from friends, 215–16; Brackenridge's library, 212; childhood favorites, 63; Crawford's library, 160–61; favorite books, 164, 215; favorite poets and authors, 146; as law student, 159, 214; laziness, viewed by neighbors as, 195; N. L. teaches A. L. to read, 63, 137; reading aloud to family and friends, 92–93, 194–95, 215; Scripture, 184, 214–15; tannery lunch hour, 171, 172; thirst for knowledge, 114, 134, 190, 199n2

Brackenridge, John A. (friend, attorney): A. L. borrows law books and literature, 212, 218nn1–2; influence on A. L., 212–13, 218n4; son meets with A. L. in Washington, 218n5

Bunyan, Paul, *Pilgrim's Progress*, 63, 145, 215

Bush, Sarah. *See* Lincoln, Sarah Bush (stepmother)

Calhoun, John, offers assistant surveyor job to A. L., 159

Calvinistic fatalism, 181–83, 217

camp meetings: A. L. religious experience in IL, 229–30; Cane Ridge, KY, 34–36, 52nn2–3

career and jobs; assistant surveyor in IL, 159; blacksmith trade, 50, 51; carpentry work for Mr. Hall, 171, 247; ferryman, 128–29, 202–6; presidential ambitions, 143–44; saw pit work, 27–28; tannery work, 171–72; tobacco cultivation, 129, 202, 203

Carter (acquaintance), 86, 87, 245

Carter's schoolhouse, A. L. speech at, 165–66, 221

Chandler, Albert P., story of Chicago photo, 54n19

Channing, Edward, *History of the United States*, 256, 261n25

character traits. *See* Lincoln, Abraham, character traits and personality

Chronicles of Reuben (Lincoln), 154–55, 165, 267

Civil War: A. L. family participation and attitudes, 74–75, 77; attitudes of Atlantic toward western US, 126–27; Gettysburg prayer, 188

Clay, Henry: comparison with A. L., 124–25; influence on A. L., 130–31, 223, 253, 260n23

Commentaries (Blackstone), A.L. obtains a copy of, 216, 218n6

comments by Lincoln. *See* stories, comments, and quotations

correspondence, Beveridge and Murr, 239–61; B. requests M. to review draft biography, 241; M. agrees to review B.'s draft, 242; B. provides IN portion of biography to M., 243; M. responds to B. with observations on biography, 244–55; B. discusses M.'s comments and information sources, 256–58. *See also* Beveridge, Albert J. (1862-1927); Murr, J. Edward (1868-1960)

Crawford, Josiah "Cy" (neighbor): personal library of, 160, 161; pioneer doctor and dentist, 110, 111

culture. *See* Hoosier manners and customs; pioneer lifestyle, manners, and customs

Culver, J.S., monument to Nancy Hanks Lincoln, 80n9

Lincoln (*Cont.*)
201–2, 208–9; court attendance and
prisoner experience, 204–6, 211n6;
diet, 88, 246; emigration from KY,
reasons for, 1, 85, 250–51; emigration
to IL, 39, 219–21; first sweetheart,
176–77; girls and, 149–50, 249–50;
historians' dismissal of, 95–97, 132,
136–40; home, description of, 87–88,
94n6; home, land selection and
clearance, 86, 245; home, location of,
78, 86–87; home life and poverty, 89,
90–93, 202–3; horse mill incident,
208; influence on career, 125, 127–28,
141–42; influence on character, 120,
123–25, 132–33, 136, 216–18; kicked
by horse, 208; milk sickness, 22; as
"mother's boy," 52; murder trial,
212–13; neighbors' impressions,
220, 221–24; not invited to sister's
wedding, 154–55; quarrel with
Grigsby over pup ownership, 152–53;
response bragging neighbor, 150–51;
schooling and education, 185–86,
192, 193, 235, 236; sports and games,
144; youth's impact on adulthood,
60–61, 157–58, 216–18. *See also*
Anderson Creek, Troy, Indiana;
Hoosier manners and customs;
Little Pigeon Church (Indiana);
trials and court procedure
Lincoln, Abraham, Kentucky years,
62–70; chores, 62–63; church
attendance, 67, 68; dog called Joe,
63, 70n1; education, 63–64, 70n3;
encounter with soldier, 64–65;
family life, 62–63; games and
sports, 63; historians' emphasis
on, 136–39; Murr's comment on,
250; neighborliness, 65; reasons for
removal to IN, 1, 250–51; slavery,
beginnings of hatred for, 65–66. *See
also* Knob Creek farm (Kentucky);

Little Mount Baptist Church at
Knob Creek (Kentucky)
Lincoln, Abraham, physical traits and
appearances: awkwardness, 148–49;
big feet, 164, 171; dress, 151–52; height
and girls' reaction to, 177; Indiana
years, 114; resemblance to mother,
47–48, 49, 50; scar on breast from
ear of corn, 178, 180n4; stature, gait,
height, 172; strength, 148, 149, 175–76;
tallness, 17, 236–37; unruly hair,
47–48, 54n19
Lincoln, Abraham, presidential years:
as commoner president, 120–21,
223–24; diplomacy in difficult
situations, 166–68, 169n11; friends
and political appointments, 166–68,
209; public admiration, 120–21
Lincoln, Josiah (uncle), 24, 73–76, 78,
80n2, 252, 260n20
Lincoln, Mordecai "Mord" (uncle), 82,
251–52
Lincoln, Nancy Hanks (mother),
34–54; burial site, 38, 231–33, 246;
character traits and disposition,
36, 50–51, 227; death, 226, 230–32;
impact on A. L. character, 51; lack of
knowledge about, 42–43, 45–46, 228;
legitimacy question, 52nn5–6, 53n8,
106n4; lineage and origins of, 12n21,
37–39, 103–6, 226–27; marriage to
T. L., 34, 42; melancholy, 44, 50, 227;
monuments and memorials to, 78,
80n9, 233–34, 246, 259n8; mysticism,
51; physical appearance, Murr's
estimate, 45–50; physical traits and
appearances, 54n18, 54n20; religion
and church membership, 19, 20; as
teacher, 26, 63, 137; T. L. courtship,
34–36, 42n2
Lincoln, Sarah (sister): marriage to
Amos Grigsby, 154–55, 270; physical
appearances, 51

11n11, 12nn14–17; personal ties to
A. L. and IN, 102–3, 128; preferred
biographers, 6–7; research and
criticism of historians, 4, 6–9;
research biases and errors, 10;
testimonials and reliability, 103,
104–5; *The Wilderness Years*, 8, 15. *See
also* correspondence, Beveridge and
Murr

Nancy Hanks (book, Hitchcock), 52n5
neighbors from IN visit White House,
165-66, 221–22
Nicolay, John G. (personal secretary),
Abraham Lincoln: A History, 259n6

O'Flynn, Anna (teacher), 3–4
Ohio River, Lincoln family travel via,
10, 93. *See also* Anderson Creek,
Troy, Indiana

Pate, Samuel (judge), trial of A. L.,
205–7, 211n6
Pilgrim's Progress (Bunyan), 215
pioneer manners and customs:
annoyances of settler life, 146–47;
beliefs and superstitions, 107–8,
109–10, 121–122nn3–5; Calvinistic
fatalism, 181–83; church pastors, 67,
114–15; church style and music, 67,
69, 112, 122n7; dress, 112; education,
67–68; Hoosiers, 97–101; morality,
185; neighborliness, 111–12; physical
prowess, esteem for, 17; physicians
and faith doctors, 110–11; poverty,
89–90; pronunciation of "Lincoln,"
252; social activities and sports, 113;
songs, Murr discusses, 248; T. L. as
product of, 30–31. *See also* Hoosier
manners and customs
poetry and essays: always writing,
193, 209; *Chronicles of Reuben*,
154–55, 165, 267; lost story about

visitors with broken wagon, 209; on
national politics (IN years), 191; on
temperance, 190–91
Posey, Francis: Lincolns' arrival to
IN, 86, 87, 245; T. L. borrows wagon
from, 33n24
poverty, Lincoln family, 81–93; L. birth
scene as evidence of, 58; hospitality
and poverty, 90–93; influence
on character development, 216;
mother's views on, 227; pioneer life
and, 89–90; Wesley Hall's account
of, 90–93

Quakers, question of Lincoln family
connections to, 24–25
quotations. *See* stories, comments, and
quotations

Ray, Mr. (neighbor), 128–129
religion and church membership:
affiliations of extended family,
24–25; A. L. attitude toward, 25, 118;
A. L. moral standards and conduct,
249; Murr's comments on, 249. *See
also* beliefs and faith
Richardson, Polly (neighbor):
A. L.'s first sweetheart, 176–77;
birth and settlement in IN, 260n15;
neighborliness of A. L., 172–75
Riney, Zachariah (first teacher), 64,
70n3

Simpson, Matthew (friend and
adviser), 108, 121n2, 187, 188
slavery: faith in destruction of, 183, 201;
first views of, 65–66; flatboat trip
and A. L. first look at, 128, 130, 250;
as one reason for Lincolns' move to
IN, 1, 85, 250–51; prophecy about end
of, 230
Society of Friends, question of Lincoln
family connections to, 24–25

Southwestern Indiana Historical
Society (SWIHS), 259n10
Sparrow, Betsy "Granny" Hanks (aunt
of Nancy Hanks Lincoln): A. L.
birth, 58–59; milk sickness, 32n14;
relation to N. L. and A. L., 38–39,
53n9
Sparrow, Lucey Hanks. *See* Hanks,
Lucey (mother of Nancy Hanks
Lincoln)
Sparrow, Thomas (uncle of Nancy
Hanks Lincoln), 32n14, 38, 39
speeches: debate skills and style, 113,
116, 194; *Emancipation Proclamation*,
55, 128, 131, 145; Gentryville 1844
campaign speech, 165–66; Gray
Goose Case trial, 196–98, 248–49;
method and manner, 134–35, 199;
oratory skills and style, 113; as
politician, 198–99; practicing on the
stump, 134, 150, 192; to IN regiment,
141. *See also* Inaugural Addresses;
poetry and essays
stories, comments, and quotations:
on childhood, performing chores
in KY, 62; on education in IN, 11n2;
Gettysburg prayer, 188; on origins
of his mother, 105–6; on politics,
80n8, 87, 135–36, 150; of preacher
undressing to find lizard, 116–17; on
reasons for immigration, to IN then
IL, 22; regarding father's education,
32nn18; regarding mother, 44, 50–51,
226, 229, 237n5; on slavery, 65–66,
70n4, 70n6, 201; story of travelling
pastors, 116–17; on terrapin and
cruelty to animals, 115; on youth, 1,
106n2, 120–21
Studebaker, Peter E., monument to
NHL, 80n9, 246, 259n8
SWIHS (Southwestern Indiana
Historical Society), 9, 259n10

Tarbell, Ida: *Life of Abraham Lincoln*,
4, 244–45, 259nn4–5; Murr
criticism of, 6; research, 3–4, 11n8,
12nn19–20
Taylor, Green (boy who hit A. L. with
an ear of corn), 178, 180n4
Taylor, James (employer, ferryman), 29
temperance: A. L. writes article on,
190–91; friends' recollections,
170–72, 190–92, 247–48; toast at
presidential nomination, 260n13. *See
also* Lincoln, Abraham, character
traits and personality
The Hoosier Schoolmaster (Eggleston),
140, 259n9
trials and court procedure, A. L.
interest in law, 206–7, 212–13
Troy, Indiana, 87
Turnham, David (friend): A. L. reads
Revised Statutes at home of, 207;
present when A. L. kicked by horse,
208

Vallandigham, Clement, A. L. letter
regarding, 194, 200n8
Virginia: KY as colony of, 252–53;
Lincoln family emigration to KY, 24

Walters, Margaret LaRue "Peggy"
(neighbor), on birth of A. L., 58, 61n3
War of 1812, soldier encounter, 64
Weems, Mason L., *Life of Washington*,
160
Wilderness Years, The (Murr), 8, 15
Wood, "Uncle" (neighbor): advises
A. L. about river pilot aspirations,
203; encourages A. L. to write essays,
190–91

youth, A. L. statements on, 1, 106n2,
120–21. *See also* stories, comments,
and quotations

THE REV. J. EDWARD MURR (1868–1960) was an early researcher and writer of Abraham Lincoln's youth. Born in Corydon, Indiana, Murr grew up with Lincoln's cousins there. He spent two years studying law but ultimately entered DePauw University in 1897 to study theology. Murr served various churches in and around Lincoln's boyhood home in Spencer County, Indiana, and later became superintendent of the Methodist Church district in that region. He became intimately acquainted with many who had been neighbors and boyhood associates of the future president.

JOSHUA CLAYBOURN is an attorney and author or editor of several books, including *Abe's Youth* and *Our American Story*. He serves on the board of directors of both the Abraham Lincoln Association and Abraham Lincoln Institute and is host of the *Lincoln Log* podcast. Claybourn frequently serves as a featured speaker on Abraham Lincoln and the American Civil War. He lives in Evansville, Indiana.